D1200606

COMPILER DESIGN AND CONSTRUCTION

COMPILER DESIGN AND CONSTRUCTION

Tools and Techniques

(With C and Pascal)

Second Edition

Arthur B. Pyster

BISHOP MUELLER LIBRARY
Briar Cliff College
SIOUX CITY, IA 51104

VNR VAN NOSTRAND REINHOLD COMPANY
NEW YORK

Copyright © 1988 by Van Nostrand Reinhold Company Inc.

Library of Congress Catalog Card Number: 87-8190
ISBN 0-442-27536-6

All rights reserved. Certain portions of this work © 1980 by Van Nostrand Reinhold Company Inc.
No part of this work covered by the copyright hereon may be reproduced or used in any
form or by any means—graphic, electronic, or mechanical, including photocopying, recording,
taping, or information storage and retrieval systems—without permission of the publisher.

Manufactured in the United States of America

Published by Van Nostrand Reinhold Company Inc.
115 Fifth Avenue
New York, New York 10003

Van Nostrand Reinhold Company Limited
Molly Millars Lane
Wokingham, Berkshire RG11 2PY, England

Van Nostrand Reinhold
480 La Trobe Street
Melbourne, Victoria 3000, Australia

Macmillan of Canada
Division of Canada Publishing Corporation
164 Commander Boulevard
Agincourt, Ontario M1S 3C7, Canada

15 14 13 12 11 10 9 8 7 6 5 4 3 2 1

QA
76.6
.P9
1988

Library of Congress Cataloging-in-Publication Data

Pyster, Arthur B.
  Compiler design and construction.
  Bibliography: p.
  Includes index.
  1. Compiling (Electronic computers) I. Title.
II. Series.
QA76.6.P9 1988   005.4'53   87-8190
  ISBN 0-442-27536-6

15518277

To my parents and to Tony Peluso,
who introduced me to FORTRAN II so long ago.

15518277

Keep a fire burning in your eyes . . . Jackson Browne

PREFACE

This book explores translator writing, focusing in particular on compilers. The compiler is among the most fundamental tools of the software developer, and understanding its construction is a basic part of any computer scientist's education. *Compiler Design and Construction: Tools and Techniques* offers a highly focused and structured framework in which to explore compiler writing by presenting the design of specific tools and by revealing the design and partial implementation of many pieceparts of compilers for *C* and Pascal. The scope of the material has been limited to the fundamentals of design and some compromises between breadth and depth have been made. For example, the material on syntax-directed translation covers the fundamental principles and illustrates them well by example, but does not go into the numerous variations on evaluating attributes that have appeared in the literature. The primary sources of code optimization are covered in Chapter 11, leaving the reader with a clear understanding of several key strategies for both local and global optimization, but that topic deserves a lengthy volume by itself. The book provides a solid foundation for the practitioner with an immediate need to apply compiler writing techniques or can be used in a one semester course on compiling.

The style of the book is based on three pedagogical principles which I wholeheartedly embrace:

1. People learn best from examples.
2. The hardest part of any job is integration.
3. Build complex things from simple pieces.

This text steps through the general principles of compiler design, illustrating those design principles with many partial and complete examples. Many of the examples focus on how to build compilers for *C* and Pascal; e.g., there are complete lexical analyzers for both languages and a parser for Pascal.

Comparing this book with the earlier volume (published in 1980), the reader will find little in common except the basic theme of focusing compiler construction through illustrative examples. The material has been totally rewritten and updated reflecting the changes in compiler technology over the last decade. The earlier book centered around the skeletal design of a compiler which mapped Pascal to IBM mainframe assembly language. The design itself was also written in Pascal. This new volume instead provides several smaller but more complete examples to illustrate the same concepts, but always keeping the ultimate goal of designing a complete compiler in mind.

C has replaced Pascal as the primary implementation language and as the primary vehicle for illustrating compiler concepts because of the burgeoning influence and popularity of *C* (with the corresponding decline of Pascal). Abandoning the IBM mainframe family as the sole vehicle for exploring code generation was an easier choice because of its relatively old architecture and the exploding growth of microcomputers in the 1980 s. Chapter 12 explores the code generation problem in a more abstract setting with relevance to many modern machines such as the Motorola 68000, VAX * , and Intel 8086 families.

Also new in this edition is the heavy influence of Unix ** throughout the book. Such standard Unix utilities as *make, cc,* and *cpp,* as well as the translator-writing tools *lex* and *yacc* play a central role in

---

* VAX is a trademark of Digital Equipment Corporation.
** Unix is a trademark of AT&T Bell Laboratories.

the presentation. The almost universally accepted suitability of *C* as a systems programming language and Unix as a software development environment motivated these changes. However, even if Unix is not accessible to the reader, the material should still be quite tractable. The variant of *C* and Unix used in the book is that found in 4.2BSD Unix distributed by the University of California at Berkeley (since that was the variant most readily available to me), but I have not intentionally used any features of 4.2BSD that are not available in most other Unixes including System V. Many but not all of the examples have also been run on System V Unix.

The book includes the design and complete code for several interesting examples. Chapter 2 shows the implementation of a subset of the *C* preprocessor, while Chapter 3 shows a compiler for arithmetic expressions. The first example reveals the basic structure of a translator including the most important "front-end" subsystems—lexical analyzer, parser, and symbol table routines. The second example focuses on code generation and has a more sophisticated parser. The examples in later chapters become gradually less detailed, concentrating more on algorithms and design principles as the implementation of those designs becomes lengthier and as the reader becomes more comfortable with compiler design techniques. However, even later chapters occasionally include complete implementations to illustrate some concept. For example, Chapter 8 offers a complete parser for Pascal written using *yacc.*

In the Unix tradition much of the text is devoted to exploring, specifying, and implementing tools to support translator writing. This text shies away from theory except to support tools and tool building. For example, when lexical analysis is studied in Chapter 4, a simple working lexical analyzer generator, *gioconda,* is designed. Such a generator relieves much of the tedium of building lexical analyzers by automating much of the process of writing one. However, the theory of finite-state machines on which lexical analysis is based is not explicitly studied. *Lex,* the standard lexical analyzer generator found on Unix, is also studied and well-illustrated in this chapter. *Lex* is a full-feature generator suitable as a building block for a complete compiler. Its design cannot be studied in the same depth since the code is proprietary, but the external properties and interface of *lex* are explained in some detail and used in subsequent chapters. Complete lexical analyzers for both *C* and Pascal are presented.

To get the most out of the book I recommend reading the material and developing a working compiler and translator-writing tools from the algorithms, exercises, and designs presented.

ACKNOWLEDGMENTS

I am grateful to Digital Sound Corporation for their support in preparing this text, to Bob Frankel for his interesting telephony example, and to Isaac Asimov for a wonderful talk I once heard him give on how he writes so prolifically. It embarrassed me into finishing this book sooner than I otherwise would have.

CONTENTS

COMPILER
DESIGN AND
CONSTRUCTION

Chapter 1
COMPILER OVERVIEW

. . . successful compilers have pervasive elements of both Science and Sorcery.

foreword from "Proceedings of the
SIGPLAN Symposium on Compiler
Construction," 1979

1.1. INTRODUCTION

The single most important advance in programming productivity occurred when the first FORTRAN compiler was built by IBM for their 704 computer [ACM 78]. By freeing developers from the drudgery of assembly language programming, that compiler increased programming productivity sixfold. A *compiler*, of course, maps a higher-order language, such as FORTRAN, Pascal, or Ada* into an assembly or machine language. A higher-order language program must be translated into machine language before it can be executed.

The very first FORTRAN compiler took 18 staff-years to write, using technology that is unbelievably primitive and ad hoc by today's standards. The field of compiler writing has advanced so far that today during a semester course on compiler writing an undergraduate student can produce a FORTRAN compiler with most of the same functionality and many times the elegance of that first effort.

There has been a virtual explosion of new languages over the more than thirty years since FORTRAN was first implemented. In many cases a new language has been introduced to address a specific application area. For example, SNOBOL4 was designed at Bell Labs for string processing [Griswold and Griswold 73, et al.]. Ada was originally designed for complex embedded systems such as missile guidance and satellite communications, although it is now viewed as having much wider application [ANSI 83]. COBOL has been the mainstay of the business data processing world for over 25 years [ANSI 85]. The fundamental design goal of BASIC [ANSI 78] was that it be easily learned, a goal achieved at the expense of elegance and power.

Today there are dozens of higher-order languages in active use, although most of the activity centers around a mere handful of languages, especially COBOL, FORTRAN, *C*, and BASIC. More recently data base management system languages and fourth generation languages such as dBase III and expert system oriented languages such as Prolog [Clocksin and Mellish 81] have become more prominent, but still account for only a small percentage of overall code. Yet despite the disparity of form and function in these languages, they can nearly all be implemented using the same basic techniques that are studied in this text.

Relatively few people ever write commerical compilers, but the study of compiler design and construction is very important because:

1. A good "liberal" computer science education should include some study of every major field of computer science.

---

* Ada is a registered trademark of the U.S. Government, Ada Joint Program Office.

1

2. Some people, in fact, do write and maintain compilers.
3. The techniques used in compiler design are widely applicable, such as in writing a command language interpreter or language processor.

Depending on how liberal a view of education the reader holds, the first reason might provoke a chuckle, and the second might be dismissed as improbable, but the third reason is important from a practical view. Translators are far more common than is often understood; for example, an early version of this text was prepared using *nroff*, the text formatter on Unix, which maps formatting commands and text into prettyprinted documents. Complementing *nroff* on Unix are at least three more processors: *pic* (pictures), *eqn* (equations), and *tbl* (tables). In any software development project, it is not unusual to spend 10–15% of the effort writing support tools, many of which rely on the techniques discussed here, for example, test harnesses, syntax-directed editors, complexity analyzers, and debuggers. Taking a larger perspective, areas such as computer-aidcd design and computer-aided engineering, robotics, and process control all rely heavily on translators.

Command	Action
delay \<n\>	delay n seconds
goOffHook	go off hook; i.e., pick up the phone
hangup	hang up the phone
outdial \<a\>	outdial number \<a\>
play \<n\>	play voice message \<n\>, if no \<n\> is given, then play appended messages
seize	seize a phone line
: \<n\> ...	restrict subsequent commands to port \<n\>
:	remove any port restrictions
#	print current status
$\<l\>	define label \<l\>, where \<l\> is in 'a'..'z'
!\<l\>	goto \<l\> or top of script if \<l\> is empty
?\<l\>	perform !\<l\> if previous command failed
@ \<n\>	accept DTMF digits 0–9 followed by #

Command Set

```
         seize; ?a              ¦ call voice messaging machine
         outdial 601a; ?a       ¦ goto $a if failure
    :1
         outdial 11#11#         ¦ simulate login port 1
    :2
         outdial 22#22#         ¦ simulate login port 2
    :
         outdial 3              ¦ record message on all ports
         delay 15
         play 1

         outdial #33###         ¦ send message to subscriber 33

         outdial 5#             ¦ terminate session

         hangup
         delay 5

         #                      ¦ display status
         !                      ¦ proceed with next pass

  $a
         #                      ¦ display failure status
         hangup
         delay 30
```

Script

Figure 1-1. *loadbox* Script to Drive a Voice Messaging Application.

An example of a simple but more unusual application of compiler writing techniques is a tool for controlling phone traffic on a voice application processor (VAP) built by Digital Sound Corporation. The VAP is a Unix based microcomputer system which supports a host of voice operations including voice messaging and speech recognition. *loadbox* is a VAP program that interprets a *loadbox script*. This script can tell a VAP to perform such telephone operations as seize a line, outdial digits, play a voice message, and hang up. The primary use of *loadbox* is to test voice applications developed on a VAP by simulating real telephone traffic. An application can be subjected to thousands of simulated calls in a controlled lab setting.

The script language is relatively simple, but has a lexical analyzer, parser, and symbol table manager used to map the raw input into an internal format more suitable for interpretation. Figure 1-1 shows the permissible *loadbox* commands and a sample *loadbox* script for one VAP to call a second that is running a voice messaging application. The implementation of *loadbox* is about 600 lines of *C* code, making extensive calls to voice processing libraries developed separately.

1.2 LOOKING OUTWARD

A compiler is only one of several tools in a chain necessary to produce executable programs under Unix. In the Unix tradition, each tool runs as a separate process, producing a temporary file that is read by the next tool in the chain. Figure 1-2 shows the components and the flow of information through this chain. The first standard tool in the chain is the *C* preprocessor, *cpp*, whose input is a file containing a *C*

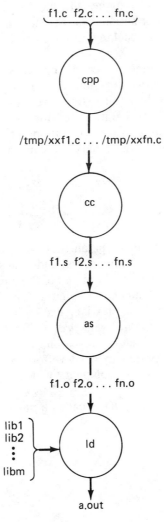

Figure 1-2. Steps to Produce an Executable Program.

program (ending with a *.c* or *.h* extension) complete with special statements understood by the preprocessor. The preprocessor executes these statements producing a temporary file containing a new program that has only *C* statements in it. In Chapter 2 a minipreprocessor for *C* is studied since that is an interesting translator in its own right.

Preprocessor statements are generally used to aid in program construction and portability, for example, there is a `#include` statement of the form:

```
#include  "file"
```

which causes *file* to be read and inserted into the program at that point as if it were originally part of the program text. `#include` is typically used to allow different programs to share the same header files of declarations. Each such program can include the one copy of the headers found in *file* so that any updates to the declarations can be made in one place.

The *C* compiler, *cc*, translates the temporary file produced by *cpp* into assembly language (*.s* extension). The compiler could have produced object code directly, but to do so would violate the spirit of Unix tool development [Kernighan and Pike 84]. There already is an assembler, so why duplicate it?

The Unix assembler, *as*, produces linkable object code modules (*.o* extension). *cc* and virtually all other language implementations on Unix allow programs to be constructed from separately compiled files. This permits a large program to be organized into several logically related pieces, each of manageable size. Code in an object file can either refer to identifiers in the same file or in other object files. A reference to an identifier that is declared in the same file is said to be *local* to the file and to be *resolved* at assembly time because all of the information necessary to map a reference to the declaration is available then. A reference to an identifier not declared in the same file is said to be *external* and *unresolved* at assembly time.

as operates on just one file at a time and cannot correlate a declaration in one file with a reference in another file. The linking loader, *ld*, does just that. It takes a collection of object files and builds one executable binary file by resolving all external references. It scans all of the object files being linked for the declaration of an as yet unresolved identifier. *ld* can be told to search through any number of previously developed libraries for declarations as well. Failure to resolve all references during linking is fatal. A successfully linked binary file can be loaded into memory by the Unix kernel and executed.

1.3 LOOKING INWARD

A compiler supports the *analysis–synthesis* paradigm in which the source language is first analyzed into its lexical, grammatical, and semantic components, and then synthesized into equivalent constructs in the target language. Analysis is done in the *front-end* of the compiler, and has become relatively routine over the last twenty years for most "standard" languages using the techiques described in Chapters 4–8. Challenges remain in newer more complex languages such as Ada and in languages adopting novel development paradigms such as *smalltalk* and *prolog*. Synthesis, done in the *back-end*, studied in Chapters 9–12, has been the focus of intense research over the last decade especially in systematizing code optimization and generation. Despite extensive efforts by industry, at the time of this writing, there are only a handful of Ada and smalltalk compilers which are generally accepted as producing truly efficient code.

Each of the major activities of a compiler is called a *phase* as shown in Fig. 1-3:

1. Lexical analysis
2. Parsing
3. Semantic analysis
4. Intermediate code generation
5. Optimization
6. Code generation

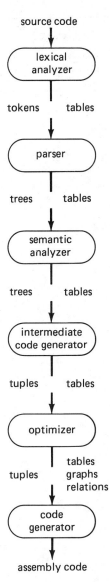

source code

lexical
analyzer

tokens   tables

parser

trees   tables

semantic
analyzer

trees   tables

intermediate
code generator

tuples   tables

optimizer

tables
graphs
relations

tuples

code
generator

assembly code

Figure 1-3. Typical Compiler Structure.

Each of these major phases may in turn have minor subphases; for example, it is not unusual in an optimizing compiler to divide the many optimization strategies into separate modules.

Some phases may be physically integrated into other phases. For most languages the functions of semantic analysis are typically dispersed into the lexical analyzer, parser, and intermediate code generator, although for languages as complex as Ada semantic analysis is quite hard and usually performed separately. The front-end of one commercial Ada compiler is approximately 100,000 lines of Ada, most of which is devoted to semantic analysis. Figure 1-4 shows the translation of an assignment statement through these various phases.

[Anklam et al. 82] report on the relative time spent in the various phases of one version of the DEC VAX PL/I and *C* compilers, both of which perform extensive optimization. The *C* compiler spends almost 60% of its time in the front-end doing lexical analysis, parsing, and semantic analysis, 25% performing optimization, and the remaining 15% generating code. This compares rather closely to the PL/I compiler which spends 54% of its time on front-end activities, about 28% performing optimization, and 18% generating code. The relatively equal amount of time spent on these activities in the two compilers is somewhat surprising because PL/I is a much harder language than *C* on which to perform lexical, syntactic, and semantic analysis. The *C* compiler is written using *yacc*, while the PL/I compiler

| source code | ```
x := (y+z)*(y+z)/2.0
``` |
| lexical analysis | ```
IDENT   ASSIGN   '('   IDENT   '+'   IDENT   ')'
270      256      40    271     43    272     41
 x        :=             y            z


'*'   '('   IDENT   '+'   IDENT   ')'   '/'   REAL
42    40    271     43    272     41    47    273
             y            z                   2.0
``` |
| parsing | |

| semantic analysis/ intermediate code generation | ```
t1 := y + z
t2 := y + z
t3 := t1 * t2
t4 := inttoreal t3
t5 := t4 /f 2.0
t6 := realtoint t5
x  := t6
``` |
| optimization | ```
t1 := y + z
t3 := t1 * t1
t4 := inttotreal t3
t5 := t4 /f 2.0
t6 := realtoint t5
x  := t6
``` |
| code generation | ```
LD     R3,y
A      R3,z
MR     R3,R3
LD     R1,R3
CALL   INTTOREAL
DIVRL  R0,#2.0
LR     R1,R0
CALL   REALTOINT
ST     R0,x
``` |

Figure 1-4. Steps in Translating an Assignment Statement.

uses a hand-crafted recursive descent parser. The authors attribute the high overhead of front-end effort to *yacc*, which at the time they used it was not nearly as flexible and efficient as it is today.

Optimization of a compiler phase can have a dramatic impact on overall compiler performance without a fundamental change in compiler organization or technology. [Pennello 86] reports that by tweeking the implementation of standard LR parsers to use assembly language in key modules a speedup of 10 times in parsing performance was obtained; for example, a speed of 240,000 lines per
```

minute on an Intel 80286 was achieved with a tuned LR parser compared to 37,000 lines per minute using a standard parser.

Lexical Analysis

The *lexical analyzer* or *scanner*, as it is sometimes called, reads the input stream and maps it into an internal format more suited for further manipulation by the remainder of the translator. The lexical analyzer performs four major tasks:

1. Identifies the basic lexical units of the program, which are called *lexemes* or *tokens*.
2. Removes extraneous blanks, carriage returns, newlines, and other symbols characteristic of the input medium.
3. Removes comments.
4. Handles errors it discovers.

There are two common relationships between scanner and parser. In the first relationship, the scanner works in tandem with the parser, passing off tokens to the parser as it assembles them. In the second, the scanner finishes all of its work before the parser is ever invoked. In the latter case, it typically produces a file plus several primary memory data structures which represent the results of scanning the entire program. The parser references this file and data structures after the scanner has completed execution. This text only studies parsers and scanners that work in tandem.

A lexical analyzer is typically constructed as a finite-state transformer, perhaps extended in some way for convenience. Finite-state techniques are moderately powerful, allowing the scanner to uniquely identify the beginning and end of each token and to classify it as a literal, keyword, nonkeyword identifier, string, or other symbol. However, this approach is limited. For example, no finite-state analyzer can properly identify which parentheses in an arithmetic expression in *C* match up. This more sophisticated analysis is performed by the parser.

Example 1-1. Figure 1-5 contains a small sample Pascal program. The lexical analyzer breaks the program into lexemes shown in Fig. 1-6. There are several interesting things to note about this token stream. First, extraneous whitespace and the comment on line 3 of the source code are gone. Second, the scanner correctly notes that "0.1e-4" is an atomic unit, not four tokens as in "0.1", "e", "-", and "4". This means the scanner must be clever enough to recognize that the "-" sign used in the real constant is different than the "-" used in line 8 to denote subtraction. Third, it correctly bundles character strings in lines 9 and 11, including the period on both lines as part of the string, unlike the period on line 12.

The scanner would probably not emit a token sequence in quite the format just shown. Rather than just passing on character strings to the parser, it would likely categorize each token with an identifying integer value and pass on to the parser both the actual string plus that integer. This is how *lex* works. The integer representing a single character token such as " (" would likely be its ascii representation 40. Keywords would be distinguished from ordinary identifiers by returning a unique code for each keyword

```
1    program sample (input,output);
2    const
3        eps = 0.1e-4;   {a small positive number}
4    var
5        x: real; y: integer;
6    begin
7        readln (x,y);
8        if x-y>eps*2 then
9            writeln('Big enough.')
10       else
11           writeln('Too small.')
12   end.
```

Figure 1-5. Sample Pascal Program.

```
"program"  "sample"  "("  "input"  ","  "output"  ")"  ";"
"const"  "eps"  "="  "0.1e-4"  ";"  "var"  "x"  ":"  "real"
";"  "y"  ":"  "integer"  ";"  "begin"  "readln"  "("  "x"
","  "y"  ")"  ";"  "if"  "x"  "-"  "y"  ">"  "eps"  "*"  "2"
"then"  "writeln"  "("  "'Big enough.'"  ")"  "else"  "writeln"
"("  "'Too small.'"  ")"  "end"  "."
```

Figure 1-6. Output of Lexical Analyzer on Sample Program.

and another code for all other identifiers; for example, ordinary identifiers might map onto 256, while "const" maps onto 257, "program" onto 258, and so on.

◆

Parsing

Each programming language has its own set of grammar rules characterizing the correct form of programs in that language. The *parser* or *syntactic analyzer* accepts the output of the scanner, that is, tokens, and verifies that the source program satisfies the grammatical rules of the language being compiled. English grammar rules are normally not stated with great precision. Each person's view of what constitutes correct English seems highly colored by the quirks of his or her school English teachers. However, the syntax of each programming language is simple enough to be written in a precise mathematical notation called a *context-free grammar*. Using such grammars, a program can be mechanically classified as belonging to the programming language or not. Actually, things are not quite that simple. A number of programs that should not belong to the language on *semantic* grounds will be syntactically valid. The grammar of a real programming language typically describes a superset of the intended language, for example, an assignment statement in *C* in which the left-hand side identifier is not a declared variable is meaningless, but has the correct form for an assignment statement.

Example 1-2. When the lexemes of the sample Pascal program are parsed, they produce what is called a *parse tree* representing the grammatical analysis. This is shown in Fig. 1-7. The leaves of the tree are the tokens. The interior nodes are grammatical categories such as *block* and *prog_stmt*. The groupings under each node reflect the logical structure of the source code. Chapters 5, 6, and 7 are all devoted to studying parsing techniques in detail.

◆

Intermediate Language

The output by the parser is transformed into a program of sorts written in an *intermediate language* which is closer in form to assembly language than to the source text, and yet is in a notation that makes further manipulation easier than if actual assembly or machine code were emitted.

Example 1-3. Intermediate code produced from the sample parse tree might look like:

```
1              prolog
2              param x
3              param y
4              call readln
5              t0 := inttoreal y
6              t1 := x-t0
7              t2 := inttoreal 2
8              t3 := eps*t2
9              if t1≤t3 goto L0
10             param 'Big enough.'
11             call writeln
12             goto L1
13      L0:
14             param 'Too small.'
15             call writeln
16      L1:
17             epilog
```

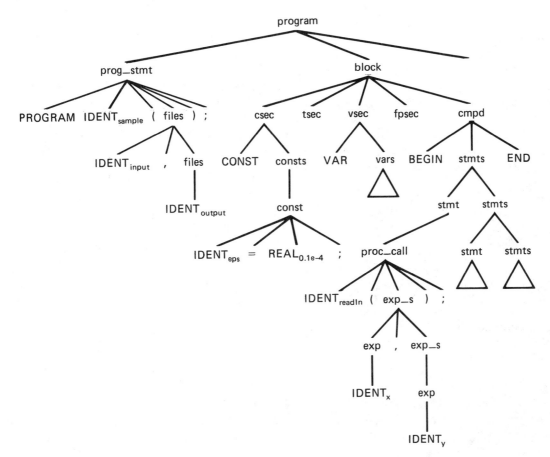

Figure 1-7. Partial Parse Tree for Sample Program.

The intermediate code does not allow mixed mode arithmetic expressions and only allows a single operator on the right-hand side of an assignment statement, so that computing the operands of "x-y>eps*2" had to be done in lines 5–8, creating four temporary variables to hold the results. Each parameter of a procedure call is listed as a separate statement.

♦

Semantic Analysis

The primary purpose of the semantic analyzer is to supplement the parser by using ad hoc means to insert additional information into the symbol table and to guide the generation of intermediate code based on special understanding of how data types affect code generation. For example, in C and Pascal which have both a real and an integer numeric data type, intermediate code might use two different operators for real and integer addition, and might include an explicit conversion operation when an integer and real variable are added. By the time the semantic analyzer is finished, the data type of each identifier will be known and the intermediate code will reflect the implications of that analysis. For the sample program, it is actually the semantic analyzer integrated with the intermediate code generator which caused lines 5 and 7 to be emitted casting integer valued y and 2 as reals.

Example 1-4. A few languages such as PL/I have a large number of type attributes with very complex rules governing implicit data type conversions. This makes semantic analysis much more difficult than for relatively simple languages like Pascal. Consider the PL/I statement:

```
PUT LIST (25+1/3);
```

which requests that the result of computing `25+1/3` be written to the printer. This rather innocuous statement causes a `FIXEDOVERFLOW` condition to be raised! Numbers can either be represented in `DECIMAL` or `BINARY` number bases, and can be `FIXED` or `FLOATING`. `FIXED` numbers can have fractional parts. In addition, each number has a precision. The precision of a `FIXED DECIMAL` number with i total digits and j digits to the right of a decimal point is expressed by (i, j). Constants `25`, `1`, and `3` have attributes `FIXED DECIMAL (2,0)`, `FIXED DECIMAL (1,0)`, and `FIXED DECIMAL (1,0)`, respectively.

The first operation performed is the evaluation of "`1/3`". The precision of the result is `FIXED DECIMAL (15,14)` because the largest possible result has one digit to the left of the decimal point. The result precision does not depend on the actual value—only on the precision of the operands. Next `25` is added:

```
FIXED DECIMAL (2,0) + FIXED DECIMAL (15,14)
```

causing the following:

```
    2 5
+   0 . 3 3 3 3 3 3 3 3 3 3 3 3 3 3
    ? 5 . 3 3 3 3 3 3 3 3 3 3 3 3 3 3
```

There is no room for the `2` in the result because one of the operands does not have room for a digit in that position. `FIXEDOVERFLOW` occurs. The seemingly identical:

```
PUT LIST (25+01/3);
```

does not cause overflow because the result of `01/3` has type `FIXED DECIMAL (2,0)`. The leading zero affects the precision of the result! Now the result is `FIXED DECIMAL (15,13)`. When the addition is performed, there is room for the leading `2` of `25.33...`. No overflow occurs (groan).

◆

Optimizer

Intermediate code can be converted directly into the object language by the code generator. However, it is common to insert another phase between the semantic analyzer and the code generator; namely, the *optimizer*. If the code generator transforms intermediate level text into assembly language in a straightforward manner, the generated object code is probably not as efficient with respect to execution time and storage space as it might be. If a compiler is more than superficially concerned with producing efficient code, it will include a module specifically designed to improve some combination of time and space characteristics of the code. The optimizer transforms the code given to it into a more efficient version. The Portable *C* Compiler [Johnson 79] performs rather limited optimizations. The *-O* optimizer flag Unix programmers are familiar with invokes a *peephole* optimizer which operates on actual assembly code produced by the first two passes of the compiler. It is highly machine specific and is not actually part of the Portable *C* Compiler. A peephole optimizer peers into small windows in the assembly code (hence the name) searching for redundant operations or other small patterns that can be replaced by more efficient machine instructions. For example, it is not unusual for optimizations in the first two passes of the compiler to force the emission of code segments such as

```
load  reg,X
store reg,X
```

A peephole optimizer would remove the redundant `store`, improving both speed and space requirements.

Some optimization strategies depend on the particular target language; for example, *register allocation* is the assignment of a computer's registers to the operands of the object code. Since most operations in a computer are more efficient when one or more operands is in a register, dramatic differences in

```
1    for (i=0; i<10; i++) {
2        if (x[j] == i)
3            x[j]++;
4        else
5            x[j]--;
6    }
```

Figure 1-8. Optimizable Loop.

time and space performance are possible depending on which register allocation strategy is used. Recognizing this, the C language itself supports the **register** attribute in declarations:

```
register int  x
```

which advises *cc* to put variable x into a register instead of main memory if possible, presumably because x will be frequently referenced. The particulars of register allocation clearly depend on the architecture of the target machine although there are broad general strategies which can be particularized for each specific machine. Register allocation is performed by the code generator, independent of the optimizer component of the compiler.

Most optimization strategies are relatively independent of the target machine; these are performed by the *optimizer*. For example, some computations can be moved from inside the scope of a loop to outside that scope.

Example 1-5. Figure 1-8 contains an optimizable loop. Translating this code in a straightforward way causes the address of array element x[j] to be calculated twice for every traversal of the loop. In fact, this code is equivalent to the much more efficient code in Fig. 1-9. Now the address is computed just once for all 10 times through the loop! A compiler can automatically detect such potential optimizations so the programmer can write code in a readable fashion.

◆

Another optimization is *constant folding*. If the value of each operand of an operation is known at compile-time, and these values cannot change at execution-time, then the compiler itself can execute the operation and substitute the computed result for the original expression; for example, in the C assignment statement:

```
x = y+3*6-z;
```

the subexpression "3*6" can be replaced by "18" without changing the value assigned to x

```
x = y+18-z;
```

The compiler can effectively substitute "18" for "3*6" rather than produce object code that performs the multiplication. This substitution has the effect of adding to the compiler's work and increasing compilation time with a corresponding reduction in the execution time of the generated object code.

In the intermediate code produced for the sample Pascal program in Example 1-3, the computation of eps*2 in line 8 can be done by the compiler, eliminating a run-time conversion of an integer to a real and a multiplication.

```
1    p = &(x[j]);
2    for (i=0; i<10; i++) {
3        if (*p == i)
4            (*p)++;
5        else
6            (*p)--;
7    }
```

Figure 1-9. Optimized Loop.

A more subtle and more interesting situation arises when the compiler applies the *commutative law of addition*:

```
x = 3+y-z+8;
```

is equivalent to:

```
x = 3+8+y-z;
```

which in turn is equivalent to:

```
x = 11+y-z;
```

A compiler can be made arbitrarily smart in looking for such optimizations. However, as the complexity of the search for optimizable code increases, the compiler itself becomes more complex and compilation time increases. It has been shown in several studies that programmers rarely write sophisticated arithmetic expressions, discouraging the compiler designer from focusing much attention on fancy arithmetic optimizations. Improvements in speed from loop optimization have a much higher payoff. Languages such as *C* allow the programmer to advise the compiler about simple optimization opportunities with operations such as self-increment, "++" and add to oneself, "+=".

Because of numeric underflow and overflow, reordering expression evaluation and then performing the evaluation at compile-time can change a program's behavior. If *maxint* stands for the largest legal integer value a machine can hold, then the two expressions *maxint-1+1* and *maxint+1-1* evaluated left to right yield quite different results. The former evaluates to *maxint*, while the latter is erroneous.

The fact that optimization can dramatically change the order of expression evaluation can be disconcerting to a programmer who is doing assembly level debugging of source code (still occasionally done). It is common under these circumstances to disable compiler optimization so that when stepping through the assembly code the correlation to the original code is more transparent.

Code Generator

The *code generator* takes the intermediate code it receives from the optimizer and produces assembly or machine language code; obviously code generation is the most machine dependent part of the translation process. When the object machine is altered, the code generator must be revised. In recent years great advances in producing table driven code generators have substantially reduced the level of effort to change the back-end of compilers where code generation is done. However, no compiler phase is, in general, totally immune to a change in the target machine. For example, *C* implemented on an IBM mainframe will use the EBCDIC character set, while a *C* compiler for a Digital Equipment VAX will use ASCII. Differences between the character sets would affect the scanner considerably.

During code generation additional optimization relies on an intimate knowledge of the machine's architecture. Intelligent assignment of operands to registers is probably the greatest single optimization opportunity since operations on registers are typically 50% or more faster than those requiring fetches from primary memory. *C* compilers are notorious for poor register optimization in part because the language itself allows the programmer to advise the compiler which variables to place in registers.

Example 1-6. The program in Fig. 1-10 took 5.6 seconds to run on an unloaded VAX 11/750 running 4.2BSD Unix. When the declaration of variable i in line 3 was changed to

```
register int i;
```

the overall run time was reduced to 3.6 seconds. The assembly code produced by *cc* with the *-O* optimization flag for the two versions is shown in Fig. 1-11. Nearly all of the execution time in both programs is in lines 11-16. In the first program, variable i is offset 4 from the primary memory top of stack pointed to by fp. In the second program, variable i is in register r11.

◆

```
1    main ()
2    {
3        int i;
4
5        for (i=0; i<1000000; i++);
6    }
```

Figure 1-10. Impact of Register Allocation.

1.4 DIAGNOSTIC TOOLS

No commerical translator is marketable unless it generates informative commentary about each program that it processes. A compiler which generates correct object code but does nothing more is unusable and unsellable; at a bare minimum, the compiler must give some indication when it encounters an error in a program. Any reasonable compiler also makes extensive checks for errors so it has something to report. If the error occurs at execution-time, it might be trapped by the operating system, detected by run-time support within the object code, or even go undetected. All errors detected during compilation should be reported by the compiler itself. The compiler should identify the nature and location of the error in some detail.

Besides reporting errors, a compiler may also generate other informative commentary to aid a programmer in documenting and debugging a program; for example, three common aids are a cross-reference map, set-use analysis which reveals such logical problems as when a variable is referenced without ever having been assigned a value, and an execution profile which permits a programmer to see how many times each statement of the program was executed on a particular run. The profile option permits a programmer to quickly identify potential bottlenecks in the program, as well as detect code that is executed a suspiciously high or low number of times. The latter may be symptomatic of a logical error. Dozens of other tools are found in the literally thousands of commercially available language implementations. They range from the relatively trivial indication of how much time the compiler took to compile a program, to an elaborate analysis of the flow of control of a particular program run. On some systems, such as Unix, tools that produce additional information, such as cross-reference maps, are often separate programs; for example, *cxref* on System V. Many companies also offer tools to supplement a compiler when it fails to offer valuable diagnostic services. There are several offerings on the

```
          Without Register Declaration              With Register Declaration

1     LL0:                                      LL0:
2             .data                                     .data
3             .text                                     .text
4             .align    1                               .align    1
5             .globl    _main                           .globl    _main
6     _main:                                    _main:
7             .word     L12                             .word     L12
8             jbr       L14                             jbr       L14
9     L15:                                      L15:
10            clrl      -4(fp)                          clrl      r11
11    L18:                                      L18:
12            cmpl      -4(fp),$1000000                 cmpl      r11,$1000000
13            jgeq      L17                             jgeq      L17
14    L16:                                      L16:
15            incl      -4(fp)                          incl      r11
16            jbr       L18                             jbr       L18
17    L17:                                      L17:
18            ret                                       ret
19            .set      L12,0x0                         .set      L12,0x800
20    L14:                                      L14:
21            subl2     $4,sp                           jbr       L15
22            jbr       L15                             .data
23            .data
```

Figure 1-11. VAX Assembly Code Showing Register Optimization.

market which will profile a FORTRAN program. Interestingly enough, many of the techniques described in this text for writing compilers are also used to implement these separate tools.

The difference in the quality of error detection in commericial compilers is far greater than might be expected. Although somewhat dated now, [Softool 77] compares the ability of eight commerical FORTRAN 66 compilers to detect errors. Many went undetected by the compilers. The compilers were especially spotty in reporting language extensions as violations of the standard. Of course, vendors rarely implement any *standard* language; instead supporting extensions to differentiate their product from others, helping to defeat the purpose of the standard. Ada is one of the notable exceptions with a standard that mandates no subsetting or supersetting. The Ada Joint Program Office enforces this uniformity.

Example 1-7. [Pyster and Dutta 78] showed that the lack of error detection can have severe consequences when porting code from one machine to another or across compilers for the same machine. For example, the code segment:

```
     DO 20 I = 1,10
        ...
 20   CONTINUE
     J = I
```

is illegal ANSI FORTRAN. The value of the index variable is undefined after loop termination. Neither the IBM FORTRAN G (debugging version) nor IBM FORTRAN H (optimizing version) compilers reported this error, even though it is straightforward to detect such a language violation using standard techniques. What is most damaging about this particular error is that the code generated by the two compilers produced different results! The FORTRAN G compiler assigned J the value 10, while the H compiler assigned it 11. There is no reason to expect identical behavior on programs that violate language standards, and strong reason to expect subtle differences.
♦

1.5 MULTI-PASS COMPILERS

A compiler can be organized so that all transformations from source to object code are performed in a single pass over the original program text. Such compilers are called naturally enough *single-pass compilers*. Problems arise when there is a reference to a name whose value is not known at the time code is emitted, e.g., when the statement

```
goto  L
```

has to be compiled, but the address of label L is not known. Such *forward references* are resolved by leaving holes in the code where the address needs to appear and noting that hole in a separate list. When L is finally encountered, the compiler can go back and fill in the hole by consulting the list. This process is called *backpatching*. Since the compiler really has to revisit some small percentage of the code, it really takes 1+ passes to complete.

It is quite easy to imagine a strategy in which the compiler is broken into several modules, each representing one or more sequentially invoked phases. The input of the nth pass is the output of the $(n-1)$th pass. Such compilers are called *multi-pass compilers*. Normally the module that performs a pass reads its input from a combination of files kept on secondary storage and data structures resident in primary memory. The files and structures were built by the previous pass. For example, the first pass of a five pass compiler might scan the program, the second parse the output of the scanner, the third perform semantic analysis, the fourth optimize the code, and the fifth generate object code.

The chief advantages of a multi-pass compiler over a single-pass compiler are:

1. Increased modularity achieved by the division of the compiler into passes; each pass can be a separate process under Unix.

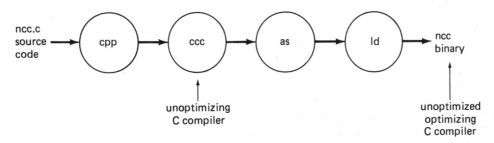

Figure 1-12. Construction of *ncc*.

2. Improved ability to perform global analysis of the program, since the *n*th pass has the complete output of the $(n-1)$th pass available to it. This is especially important for optimization since some information needed for optimizing will be scattered throughout the program.

3. Decreased space requirements, since the code for each pass need only be present during the execution of that pass. Each pass can be run as a separate process, overlaying the next pass on the old one when the latter's job is finished.

The third reason is especially important in computers with small address spaces or small physical memories. Although it is less true today than it was a few years ago, many microcomputer systems suffer from this limitation.

The chief disadvantage of a multi-pass compiler relative to a single-pass compiler is that if secondary storage is used to hold most of the output of each pass, a considerable amount of time may be spent on the overhead of reading and writing. Of course, a multi-pass compiler can keep the output of each pass resident in primary memory if that much memory is available.

1.6 BOOTSTRAPPING

Suppose a development group decides to build a new pristine *C* compiler, *ncc*, which is to run under Unix. It should produce very good code using all of the latest optimization techniques. *ncc* is to replace the current *C* compiler (*ccc*) which is based on a hacked up, badly documented, poorly structured compiler written over the last 10 years by programmers who have long since disappeared. The tools available to support this effort include *yacc*, *lex*, and all of the other standard tools available under Unix—plus *ccc*. After several months of diligent effort, the development team constructs *ncc* as shown in Fig. 1-12. *ncc* is an operational unoptimized optimizing compiler. The next step is to produce an optimized optimizing compiler as shown in Fig. 1-13. The optimized version of *ncc* is constructed by recompiling it using the unoptimized *ncc* instead of *ccc*. Building a compiler (or any tool) in this manner is called *bootstrapping*, based on the old adage about pulling oneself up by the bootstraps. It is a very powerful paradigm that applies wherever a tool could be used profitably in its own construction if only it were available. One can certainly imagine using *yacc* to build *yacc*, *lex* to build *lex*, and so on.

Much of the work in the last several years in producing portable Ada compilers has focused on creating simple, ineffient, but correct compilers for a subset of Ada which could eventually be bootstrapped into fast optimizing compilers for the complete language written in Ada. This is shown in Fig. 1-14. The first compiler for subset Ada/0 of Ada might be written in *C* since there already is a working version of *C* available. Ada/0 is carefully chosen so that it is complete enough to write a compiler for Ada/0 in Ada/0. The Ada/0 compiler is now rewritten in the Ada/0 language. Next a compiler for a more complete subset, Ada/1, is implemented in Ada/0. Depending on the granularity of the steps taken by the

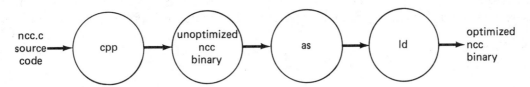

Figure 1-13. Bootstrapping Optimized *ncc* from Optimizing *ncc*.

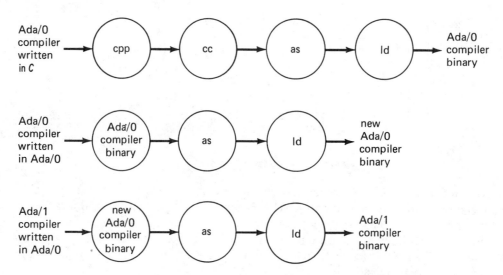

Figure 1-14. Bootstrapping an Ada Compiler from a C Implementation.

developers, several intermediate subsets of Ada might be implemented before the first full Ada compiler written in Ada appears. Finally, an optimizing version could be produced using the bootstrapping technique described earlier.

EXERCISES

1. If you have two implementations of the *same* language for which a standard exists such as Pascal or FORTRAN, compare the two implementations for conformance to the standard. Find features of each implementation which are extensions of the standard. Find other features mentioned in the standard which are not inplemented. Does the official documentation for these implementations point out such discrepencies? Does the compiler itself contain an *extension* flag which will warn the user when he or she is using nonstandard features?

2. Programming languages often use a symbol in many different contexts. This makes parsing and error recovery more difficult. Take any language you know well and determine in how many different ways parentheses are used; the word `end` is used; the comma is used.

3. Language definition is much more difficult than it first appears; for example, integer division is surprisingly ill-defined. Does the remainder have the same sign as the quotient? For example, is $3/(-2)$ equal to -1 with a remainder of $-\frac{1}{2}$ or -2 with a remainder of $+\frac{1}{2}$? Languages that specify the former are said to truncate *toward* zero. Devise a rigorous definition of integer division which (a) truncates toward zero; (b) truncates away from zero. Choose three compilers available to you and verify which definition of integer division they use.

4. Run the Pascal program in Fig. 1-5 through your Pascal compiler with and without the optimizer flag. Compare the assembly code produced in each case, making sure you understand what optimizations have been performed.

5. Test whether your C compiler has problems correctly performing compile time arithmetic on the expressions:

    `maxint+1-1     minint-1+1`

where `maxint` and `minint` are the largest and smallest integers representable on your machine.

Chapter 2
GINEVRA: A C MINI-PREPROCESSOR

2.1. A MINI-PREPROCESSOR LANGUAGE

This chapter reveals some of the principles of translator writing by building a simple preprocessor for *C* which supports the #define statement of the standard *C* preprocessor, *cpp. ginevra* deviates from *cpp* in several places to simplify the example and also to present some interesting exercises for the reader. Differences are pointed out in the text.

As discussed in the last chapter, the *C* preprocessor extends *C* to support flexible program construction and to improve portability. There are several statements in *cpp*, but to keep the example manageable, only one is handled here:

```
#define   identifier   expression?
```

The expression is optional, indicated by the trailing question mark. *ginevra* is invoked by

```
ginevra   filename.[ch]
```

writing its output to stdout and errors to stderr.

Each preprocessor statement begins with a "#" in column 1 of a line, consuming the whole line. It can be continued onto the next line by using a backslash " \ " immediately preceding the newline or by beginning a comment on one line but not terminating it until a subsequent line. Comments begin with "/*" and terminate with "*/" in the style of *C*. Lines which do not begin with "#" and are not part of a preprocessor comment are presumed to be part of a *C* program. Statements beginning with "#" that are not recognized by *ginevra* are passed unchanged to stdout with the warning

```
line %d: warning: # in column 1, but not a #define
```

where "%d" is replaced by the number of the offending line.

Example 2-1. The program in Fig. 2-1 illustrates the features of *ginevra*. Figure 2-2 shows the output of *ginevra* on this program with stderr mixed with stdout. Comments except in unrecognized prepro-

```
1     /*   The classic "hello world" with a slight twist. */
2
3     #include <stdio.h>      /* passed unchanged */
4
5     #define  MACH  "vax"  /* assume I am
6                             on a VAX computer */
7     #define  WORDSIZE 32  /* 32 bit machine */
8
9     main ()
10    {
11        printf ("Hello world from a %s with %d wordsize.\n",
12            MACH, WORDSIZE);
13    }
```

Figure 2-1. *hello:* **Demonstrating** *ginevra*.

```
1        line 3: warning: # in column 1, but not a #define
2
3
4        #include <stdio.h>      /* passed unchanged */
5
6
7         main ()
8         {
9         printf ("Hello world from a %s with %d wordsize.\n",
10        "vax" , 32 );
11        }
```

Figure 2-2. *hello* **Run Through** *ginevra***.**

cessor statements have been removed. The warning that a #include appeared has been written to stderr. Spacing between tokens is occasionally altered in a nonharmful way; for example, if the first word of a line is an identifier, a space is padded in front of it. Since *ginevra* assumes it is actually processing source rather than arbitrary text, this change is innocuous. The defined constants VAX and WORDSIZE have been replaced by their values.

◆

ginevra has just one keyword, "define". Many languages and language implementations forbid the use of keywords outside their special context. In such cases, the keywords are said to be *reserved*. *ginevra* reserves the word "define"; for example, the statement

```
#define define
```

will generate the message

```
"identifier expected after #define"
```

Identifiers may be as long as an input line, with upper- and lowercase letters distinct, following *C* tradition.

A language implementation imposes restrictions based on the computing environment in which the translator itself runs and also on the environment in which programs produced by the translator run. Such restrictions are called *pragmatics*. For example, a preprocessor implementation could restrict the permissible length of identifier names because of limited physical memory in which the preprocessor will execute (common on most personal computers that do not support virtual memory architectures). If space for the symbol table that holds information about defined names is statically allocated, there will be a maximum number of symbols the preprocessor can handle. All *C* compilers have a maximum and minimum int value and a limited float precision determined by the architecture of the machine for which they generate code. Pragmatics in *C* programs are usually referenced through the preprocessor rather than in *C* directly; for example, full *cpp* has the machine type as a predefined symbol. This allows code segments such as that in Fig. 2-3. Using #ifdef statements to customize code for a particular machine is a popular programming technique in commerically marketed Unix programs since Unix is available on such a wide range of processors.

```
1    #ifdef vax
2        ... vax specific code
3    #endif
4    #ifdef m68000
5        ... motorola 68000 specific code
6    #endif
```

Figure 2-3. Using #ifdef Statements to Customize Code.

2.2 STRUCTURE OF *GINEVRA*

The implementation of *ginevra* is about 375 lines of code including comments, broken into five files:

File	Purpose
main.c	main program and define processor
table.c	symbol table
error.c	error handling
lex.c	lexical analyzer
global.h	global declarations

A simple *makefile* for *ginevra* together with its output is in Fig. 2-4.

```
1      ginevra: error.o lex.o table.o main.o
2              cc -O -o ginevra error.o lex.o table.o main.o
3
4      main.o: global.h
5              cc -c -O main.c
6
7      error.o: global.h
8              cc -c -O error.c
9
10     lex.o: global.h
11             cc -c -O lex.c
12
13     table.o: global.h
14             cc -c -O table.c
```

Makefile for *ginevra*

```
1    % make
2    cc -c -O error.c
3    cc -c -O lex.c
4    cc -c -O table.c
5    cc -c -O main.c
6    cc -O -o ginevra error.o lex.o table.o main.o
```

Output of *make* on *ginevra*

Figure 2-4. *makefile* and Output of *make*.

2.3 PARSING AND MAIN PROGRAM

The parsing effort for *ginevra* is relatively simple, but for sophisticated languages such as *C* or Pascal, the analysis becomes quite involved. Chapters 5, 6, and 7 are all devoted to the study of parsing. The parser for *ginevra* appears in the main program. It looks for lines beginning with "#define", handling them specially. Otherwise, it looks for identifiers, replacing any identifier that has been previously defined. The parser does not really care whether the program is legal *C*; for example, *ginevra* is indifferent to whether the parentheses in an arithmetic expression match. It will pass on such badly formed expressions to the *C* compiler, which will detect and report the error.

```
1      /*  usage: ginevra   filename.[ch]  */
2
3      #include "global.h"
4
5      struct entry *insert();
6      struct entry *lookup();
7
8      main (argc, argv) int argc; char *argv[];
9      {
```

```
10              int     t;
11              char    *sp;
12              char    msg[BUFSIZ];
13              struct entry *p;
14              int     preproc;        /* in preproc statement? */
15
16                  /* process filename */
17              if (argc != 2) {
18                  sprintf (msg, "usage: %s filename.[ch]", argv[0]);
19                  error (msg, PANIC);
20              }
21              sp = argv[1];
22              if (strlen (sp) < 2)
23                  error ("filename must end with .h or .c", PANIC);
24              sp += strlen(sp)-2;
25              if (*sp++ != '.' || !index("ch", *sp))
26                  error ("filename must end with .h or .c", PANIC);
27              sp = argv[1];
28              if ( (yyin = fopen (sp, "r")) == NULL) {
29                sprintf (msg, "cannot open %s.", sp);
30                error (msg, PANIC);
31              }
32
33              preproc = 0;  /* start out not in preproc stmt */
34              while ((t=yygettoken ()) != EOFILE) {
35                  if (yycolumn == 1 && t == '#') {
36                      preproc++;
37                      t = yygettoken (); /* get keyword */
38                      if (t == DEFINE) {
39                          t = yygettoken ();  /* symbol to define */
40                          if (t == EOFILE)
41                              error ("premature end of file.", PANIC);
42                          else if (t == '\n') {
43                              error ("premature end of #define.", CONTINUE);
44                              preproc--;
45                          }
46                          else if (t == IDENT) {
47                              if (lookup(yytext) != NULL) {
48                                  error ("multiple symbol definition.",
49                                      SKIPLINE);
50                              }
51                              p = insert (yytext);
52                              define (p);
53                          }
54                          else
55                              error ("identifier expected after #define",
56                              SKIPLINE);
57                      }
58                      else
59                          error ("warning: # in column 1, but not a #define",
60                              EMITLINE);
61                      preproc--;
62                  }
63                  else if (t == IDENT) {
64                      if ((p=lookup(yytext)) != NULL)
65                          printf (" %s ", p->value);
66                      else
67                          printf (" %s ", yytext);
68                  }
69                  else if (t == '\n')
70                      putchar ('\n');
71                  else    /* write symbol */
72                      printf ("%s", yytext);
73              }
74          }
75
76      define (p)  struct entry *p;     /* determine value of defined symbol */
77      {
78          char    buffer[BUFSIZ];   /* where value is assembled */
79          int     t;                /* current token */
80          struct entry *q;
81          char    *s;
```

```
82
83              buffer[0] = '\0';
84              while (1) {
85                  t = yygettoken ();
86                  if (t == EOFILE)
87                      error ("premature end of file.", PANIC);
88
89                  if (t == IDENT) {
90                      if ((q=lookup(yytext)) != NULL)
91                          strcat (buffer, q->value);
92                      else
93                          strcat (buffer, yytext);
94                      strcat (buffer, " ");
95                  }
96                  else if (t ==  '\n') {
97                      s = (char *) malloc (strlen(buffer)+1);
98                      strcpy (s, buffer);
99                      p->value = s;
100                     return;
101                 }
102                 else
103                     strcat (buffer, yytext);
104             }
105         }
```

The code makes several references to identifiers beginning with "yy". Both *lex* and *yacc* follow this convention for externally visible names. *ginevra* continues in that tradition.

The main program begins by checking whether its single argument has the correct .[*ch*] suffix and then attempting to open it with FILE pointer yyin. It then begins a **while** loop which processes each token in turn. A token is obtained through a call to yygettoken, which returns an integer that uniquely identifies it. Integer valued symbolic constants defined in *global.h* represent special tokens:

Constant	Purpose
EOFILE	end of file
DEFINE	the keyword "define"
IDENT	an identifier
STRING	a single or double quoted character string

ginevra is a one-pass preprocessor, defining symbols as #define statements are encountered, and emitting output on the fly. The loop continues until token EOFILE is reached or a catastrophic error occurs forcing early termination.

A symbol table holds the value of each defined symbol. Storage for it is allocated dynamically and it is searched linearly for simplicity here. Each entry in the table has three fields:

Field Name	Purpose
key	the symbol being defined
value	the value of the defined symbol
next	pointer to next entry in table

The code for it is:

```
1       #include "global.h"
2
3       struct entry *table = NULL;
4
5       struct entry *
6       lookup (s) char *s;
7       {
```

```
 8          struct entry *p;
 9
10          for (p=table; p!=NULL; p=p->next)
11             if (!strcmp (p->key, s))
12                  return p;
13          return NULL;
14      }
15
16      struct entry *
17      insert (s) char *s;
18      {
19          static struct entry *last = NULL;
20          int   i;
21          struct entry *p;
22
23          p = (struct entry *) malloc (sizeof (struct entry));
24          p->key = (char *) malloc (strlen(s)+1);
25          strcpy (p->key, s);
26          p->value = NULL;
27          p->next = NULL;
28
29          if (last == NULL)
30             last = table = p;
31          else {
32             last->next = p;
33             last = p;
34          }
35          return p;
36      }
```

There are just two routines, `lookup`, which searches the table, returning a pointer to its entry if found, `NULL` otherwise; and `insert`, which inserts a string into the table, returning a pointer to the newly created entry.

2.4 LEXICAL ANALYSIS

The scanner is structured as a finite-state machine, examining the text character by character. Based on the symbol it is currently examining, plus knowledge of the text it has previously seen (its state), the scanner determines whether the current character is part of a comment, extraneous white space, the beginning of a new token, the continuation of an old token, or a malformed token. The scanner then takes appropriate action.

```
 1      #include "global.h"
 2      #include <ctype.h>
 3      #include <strings.h>
 4
 5      typedef enum {_START, _IDENT, _INIDENT, _INCOMMENT, _STRING,
 6              _INSQUOTE, _INDQUOTE, _EOF, _EOL, _OTHER, _BAD} state;
 7
 8      int     yylineno = 0;
 9
10      static char   curchar;    /* current character */
11      static char   nextchar;   /* succeeding character */
12      static char *p = NULL;
13      static int    c = 0;
14
15      static char     /* read next character from yyin */
16      getch ()
17      {
18          static int firsttime = 1;
19
20          if ( firsttime || *p=='\n') {
21             if (firsttime)
22                  firsttime--;
23             if ((p = fgets (yyline, BUFSIZ, yyin)) != NULL) {
24                  yylineno++;
25                  c = 1;
26                  nextchar = *(p+1);
```

```
27                      return (curchar = *p);
28                  }
29              else   /* at end of file */
30                    return (curchar = nextchar = '\0');
31          }
32
33          if (p == NULL)  /* at end of file */
34              return (curchar = nextchar = '\0');
35
36          c++;
37          nextchar = *(p+2);
38          return (curchar = *++p);
39      }
40
41      yyemitline ()    /* write out line to stdout */
42      {
43          static char newline = '\n';
44
45          printf ("%s", yyline);
46          p = &newline;
47          getch ();
48      }
49
50      int            /* get the next token from input stream */
51      yygettoken ()
52      {
53          char   msg[BUFSIZ];
54          static int firsttime = 1;
55          state curstate;
56          int    i, done;
57
58          if (firsttime) {
59            getch();
60            firsttime--;
61          }
62
63      start:
64          curstate = _START;
65          yytext[0] = '\0';
66          done = 0;
67
68          while (!done) {
69            switch (curstate) {
70            case _START:
71                yycolumn = c;
72                if (curchar == ' ' || curchar == '\t')
73                    ;
74                else if (curchar == '\0') { /* end of file */
75                  curstate = _EOF;
76                  done++;
77                }
78                else if (curchar == '\n')   /* end of line counts */
79                {
80                  curstate = _EOL;
81                  strncat (yytext, &curchar, 1);
82                  getch();
83                  done++;
84                }
85                else if (curchar == '\'') {
86                  strncat (yytext, &curchar, 1);
87                  curstate = _INSQUOTE;
88                }
89                else if (curchar == '"') {
90                  strncat (yytext, &curchar, 1);
91                  curstate = _INDQUOTE;
92                }
93                else if (isalpha (curchar))
94                { /* beginning of identifier */
95                  strncat (yytext, &curchar, 1);
96                  curstate = _INIDENT;
97
98                else if (curchar == '/' &&
```

```
 99                         nextchar == '*') {   /* comment */
100                         getch ();
101                         curstate = _INCOMMENT;
102                     }
103                     else if (curchar == '\\' &&
104                         nextchar == '\n') { /* continue */
105                         getch ();
106                     }
107                     else {   /* routine symbol */
108                         strncat (yytext, &curchar, 1);
109                         getch ();
110                         curstate = _OTHER;
111                         done++;
112                     }
113                     break;
114                 case _INSQUOTE:
115                     if (curchar == '\'') {
116                         curstate = _STRING;
117                         strncat (yytext, &curchar, 1);
118                         getch ();
119                          done++;
120                     }
121                     else if (curchar == '\\' && nextchar == '\'') {
122                         strcat (yytext, "\\'");
123                         getch ();
124                     }
125                     else if (curchar == '\\' && nextchar == '\n') {
126                             /* skip past backslash newline */
127                         getch();
128                     }
129                     else if (curchar == '\0' || curchar == '\n') {
130                         curstate = _BAD;
131                         done++;
132                     }
133                     else
134                         strncat (yytext, &curchar, 1);
135                     break;
136                 case _INDQUOTE:
137                     if (curchar == '"') {
138                         curstate = _STRING;
139                         strncat (yytext, &curchar, 1);
140                         getch ();
141                         done++;
142                     }
143                     else if (curchar == '\\' && nextchar == '"') {
144                         strcat (yytext, "\\\"");
145                         getch ();
146                     }
147                     else if (curchar == '\\' && nextchar == '\n') {
148                             /* skip past backslash newline */
149                         getch();
150                     }
151                     else if (curchar == '\0' || curchar == '\n') {
152                         curstate = _BAD;
153                         done++;
154                     }
155                     else
156                         strncat (yytext, &curchar, 1);
157                     break;
158                 case _INCOMMENT:
159                     if (curchar == '*' && nextchar == '/') {
160                                 /* end of comment */
161                         getch ();
162                         curstate = _START;
163                     }
164                     else if (curchar == '\0')
165                         error ("unexpected end of input", PANIC);
166                     break;
167                 case _INIDENT:
168                     if (isalnum (curchar)) {
169                         strncat (yytext, &curchar, 1);
170                         break;
```

```
171                  }
172                  curstate = _IDENT;
173                  done++;
174                  break;
175              }
176              if (!done) {
177                  getch();
178              }
179          }
180          switch (curstate) {
181          case _BAD:
182              sprintf (msg, "malformed token \"%s\"", yytext);
183              error (msg, EMITTOKEN);
184              goto start;
185          case _EOF: return EOFILE;
186          case _EOL:
187          case _OTHER: return yytext[0];
188          case _IDENT:
189            if (!strcmp (yytext, "define"))
190                return DEFINE;
191            else
192                return IDENT;
193          case _STRING: return (STRING);
194          }
195      }
```

yygettoken, as the lexical analysis routine is called, can be in one of 10 states as it examines the input stream:

```
typedef enum {_START, _IDENT, _INIDENT, _INCOMMENT, _STRING,
        _INSQUOTE, _INDQUOTE, _EOF, _EOL, _OTHER, _BAD} state;
```

The analyzer always begins in the _START state and stays there while skipping whitespace. If the next character is alphabetical, it enters the _INIDENT state. Similarly, there is an _INSQUOTE state when the scanner is in a single quoted string, _INDQUOTE for double quoted strings, and _INCOMMENT when it is processing a comment. When the analyzer has finished processing the complete token, it will be in a state indicating which token type it found:

State	Significance
_BAD	malformed token
_EOF	end of file
_EOL	end of line
_OTHER	miscellaneous token
_IDENT	identifier
_STRING	single or double quoted string

There is no _COMMENT state since a comment is skipped over. It is never actually part of a token. Unless a token is bad, yygettoken returns, having modified global variables:

Global Variables	Significance
yytext	the actual string matched
yylineno	current line number in input stream
yycolumn	column where current token begins
yyin	input stream

The return value reflects the state of the scanner. For special symbols such as identifiers and strings, yygettoken returns a special defined constant such as IDENT and STRING. These are called *named* tokens or token *groups*. For ordinary one-character tokens, it simply returns yytext[0], the matched string. These are also called *anonymous* tokens. Note that the code does not consider "define" to be an identifier. It is recognized as a reserved keyword causing `yygettoken` to return constant `DEFINE` instead of `IDENT`.

If a token is bad, `yygettoken` handles the error, as shown in lines 181-184. It prints out an error message, emits the token to `stdout`, and begins fresh looking for a token; for example,

```
printf ("this should end with a double quote);
return;
```

evokes:

```
line 1: malformed token "this should end with a double quote);"
 printf ("this should end with a double quote);
 return ;
```

Finally, the lexical analyzer assumes that no sequence of characters in an identifier is ever embedded in another token. *C* violates this assumption with hexadecimal and long constants. Input:

```
#define  x  whoops
#define  L  yech
0x57      /* hexadecimal 57 */
53L       /* 53 long */
```

produces:

```
0 x57
53 yech
```

Augmenting *ginevra* to handle these cases is left as Exercise 5.

2.5 ERROR PROCESSING

Error processing, which is fairly comprehensive, consists of three activities:

Activity	Action
detection	find the error
reporting	tell the user about the error
recovery	continue in the face of error

This general breakdown is used consistently throughout the text. Detection ranges from the purely ad hoc to very systematic. For example, the filename being processed must end with either a *.h* or a *.c*. *ginevra* makes an ad hoc check of the filename at the beginning of execution reporting

```
"filename must end with .h or .c"
```

if there is an error. On the other hand, the lexical analyzer is organized as a finite-state machine, so that an attempted transition to an illegal state is routinely detected.

Error reporting and recovery are handled by the single routine `error`, defined in *error.c*:

```
error (msg, recovery)  char *msg; strategy recovery;
```

`error` first writes `msg` to `stderr` along with the line number on which the error occurred. It then invokes one of five error recovery strategies:

Strategy	Action
PANIC	terminate *ginevra*
SKIPLINE	skip the rest of the line
EMITTOKEN	emit the current token
EMITLINE	emit the current line
CONTINUE	resume execution

PANIC is the simplest recovery strategy. It is used when the error is catastrophic, causing *ginevra* to terminate prematurely with exit code 1. Being unable to open the input file or having an input file name with an incorrect suffix are examples of a catastrophic error.

When the preprocessor is confused to the point where it needs to flush the rest of the current line and begin processing at the beginning of the next line, SKIPLINE is used. If the symbol being defined duplicates a previously defined symbol, there are two sensible actions. The first is to warn the user of a duplicate definition and process the second as if the first never occurred. The second is to treat the redefinition as an error and keep the first. *cpp* adopts the first strategy, while *ginevra* follows the second. SKIPLINE simply skips onto the next line. The text:

```
#define X   Y
#define X   Z
```

leads to:

```
line 2: multiple symbol definition.
```

EMITTOKEN tells *ginevra* to continue processing the current line in the face of error. This occurs when *ginevra* finds a malformed character string; for example, the input

```
printf ("this should end with a double quote);
return;
```

produces:

```
line 1: malformed token ""this should end with a double quote);"
 printf ("this should end with a double quote);
 return ;
```

Error recovery in most cases is decided by higher-level functions such as the main program, main, or the routine that processes a #define statement, define. This is consistent with the view that since the higher-level functions understand the context of the error, they can be smarter about invoking the best recovery. Lexical errors are the exception, handled by the lexical analyzer yygettoken itself. Higher-level functions are never aware that a lexical error has occurred. A malformed token is emitted by yygettoken's call to error with strategy EMITTOKEN.

Finally, EMITLINE is used when *ginevra* wishes to pass the line onto the *C* compiler without further processing. This happens when *genevra* encounters a "#" in column 1 fooling it into thinking it has seen the beginning of a #define statement. If it subsequently encounters "include", for example, it will just emit that whole line and ignore it.

Example 2-2. There are limitations to *ginevra*'s error checking. The input:

```
#include  <stdio.h>      /* This should be ignored
                            but won't completely be */
```

produces:

```
line 1: warning: # in column 1, but not a #define
line 2: malformed token "'t completely be */"
```

```
#include  <stdio.h>    /* This should be ignored
  but won't completely be */
```

Since the rest of the line beginning with `#include` is ignored, so is the start of the comment. The parser does not know that the second line is the continuation of a comment and is fooled into attempting to parse it as a normal expression. This problem can be removed by having *ginevra* complete the scan of lines it does not understand—a task left as Exercise 4.

◆

```
1    #include "global.h"
2
3    error (msg, recovery)  char *msg; strategy recovery;
4    {
5        int t;
6
7        if (yylineno)
8            fprintf (stderr, "line %d: ", yylineno);
9        fprintf (stderr, "%s\n", msg);
10
11       switch (recovery) {
12           case PANIC:  exit(1);
13           case SKIPLINE:
14               while ( (t=yygettoken()) != '\n' && t!=EOFILE); return;
15           case EMITTOKEN:  printf ("%s", yytext);  return;
16           case EMITLINE:  yyemitline(); return;
17           case CONTINUE: return;
18           default:  error ("internal error - bad recovery", PANIC);
19       }
20   }
```

This chapter concludes with the text for *global.h*, whose content was explained as it was needed, but was not actually displayed:

```
1    #include <stdio.h>
2
3            /* error recovery strategies */
4    typedef enum {PANIC, SKIPLINE, EMITTOKEN, EMITLINE, CONTINUE} strategy;
5
6            /* types of tokens.  each is represented by an integer.
7               tokens comprised of a single char are just their ascii
8               representation */
9    #define   DEFINE    256     /*  "define" */
10   #define   STRING    257     /*  character string or char */
11   #define   IDENT     258     /*  an identifier */
12   #define   EOFILE    259     /*  end of file */
13
14           /* global names beginning with "yy" to mirror lex */
15   char      yytext[BUFSIZ];   /* current token */
16   FILE      *yyin;            /* file being scanned */
17   extern int yylineno;        /* current line number */
18   int       yycolumn;         /* line column token begins in */
19   char      yyline[BUFSIZ];   /* current line */
20
21   struct entry {
22       char *key, *value;
23       struct entry *next;
24   };
25
26   extern struct entry *table;             /* symbol table */
```

EXERCISES

1. Write the output of *ginevra* on:

```
#define C "abc"
#define B C "def"   /* comment */
#define D "ghi" B C
A B C D
```

2. Modify *ginevra* so it redefines a symbol when it encounters a second definition, issuing the warning

```
line %d: warning: %s redefined.
```

3. Change *ginevra* so that with the *-C* flag it leaves comments in the output.

4. Change the error handling in *ginevra* so it looks for comments even in preprocessor statements it does not understand. Demonstate your program works correctly on:

```
#include <stdio.h>   /* This should be ignored
                        but won't completely be */
```

5. Modify *ginevra* so it correctly handles hexadecimal and long integer constants.

6. Add the #undef statement to *ginevra*:

```
#undef name
```

which causes the definition of `name` (if any) to be forgotten from that point on. It is not an error to undefine a name that was not previously defined.

7. Add the #include statement to *ginevra*:

```
#include "filename"
#include <filename>
```

which means to include `filename` at that point. Do *not* run the included file through *ginevra*. When the "<`filename`>" notation is used, `filename` is only searched for in standard places:

```
/usr/include
/usr/include/sys
```

8. Modify your implementation of #include statements so it correctly handles nested inclusion; that is, run the included file through *ginevra* as well. Be sure to check for circular inclusion; that is, file *x* includes *y* which includes *x*. This should be reported as a fatal error.

9. Add the #ifdef and #ifndef statements to *ginevra*:

```
#ifdef name
#ifndef name
#endif
```

The lines between #ifdef and #endif will appear in the output only if `name` is defined. The lines between #ifndef and #endif appear in the output only if `name` is not defined. Do not support nested #ifdef or #ifndef statements.

10. Extend your implementation of #ifndef and #ifdef to support nested statements; for example,

```
#ifdef V7
#ifdef VAX
#define MAX 100
#endif
#ifdef PDP
#define MAX 30
#endif
#endif
```

which sets MAX to 100 if both VAX and V7 are defined, to 30 if PDP and V7 are defined and emits nothing if either V7 is undefined or V7 is defined but neither VAX nor PDP are.

11. Extend #define to support *cpp* macros:

```
#define name(arg,...,arg) token-string
```

No spaces are allowed between *name* and '('. Replace subsequent occurrences of *name* followed by '(', a list of comma separated tokens, and ')' by *token-string*, where each occurrence of an *arg* in *token-string* is replaced by the corresponding token in the comma separated list.

Chapter 3
CECILIA: AN EXPRESSION COMPILER

3.1. AN EXPRESSION LANGUAGE AND TRANSLATION

The last chapter uncovered the design and implementation of a translator for *C* preprocessor statements. Fundamentals of lexical analysis, error processing, and parsing were studied along with the basic structure and manipulation of symbol tables. This chapter continues by studying a more sophisticated translator, *cecilia*, which maps assignment statements into a simple imaginary assembly language.

cecilia is more interesting than *ginevra* because it has a much richer parser and the output looks so much different than the input. To keep the example manageable and because the focus in this chapter is on parsing and code generation, the error processing and lexical analysis requirements are simpler than in the last chapter. All errors are fatal—a simple but adequate strategy. Furthermore, the entire program to be translated must fit onto a single line, and there are no comments.

The language to be translated is a series of zero or more *C* assignment statements. The only data type is integer, all variables are declared implicitly by their use, and only unsigned integer literals and variables are allowed in expressions. The four basic operations of addition, subtraction, multiplication, and division are supported. The precedence among operators found in *C* applies, multiplication and division having a higher precedence than addition and subtraction. All operations are left associative. The implicit precedence and associativity can be overridden by parenthesization. An example program which fits onto a single line is

```
black = 2; magic = (black+1)*black*(223-1)/2;
```

The assignment statements are translated into a simple imaginary assembly language which has five major operators: `assign`, `add`, `sub`, `mult`, and `div` with the obvious meanings. In addition, the special assembler pseudo-operation, `.text`, precedes the statement portion of the program, `.data` precedes the data segment, and `.end` physically terminates the whole program. Logical program execution is ended with the `exit` statement which has an integer exit code for its operand. Each statement has the form

```
label?    operator    operand₁?    operand₂?
```

where the label and operand fields are optional, as indicated by the question marks. The meaning of

```
add    operand₁    operand₂
```

is to add $operand_2$ to $operand_1$, storing the result in $operand_1$; similarly, for the other operations. There is no hardware stack or similar architectural feature to be concerned with in this simple machine.

Example 3-1. The translation of the above program is

```
1               .text
2               assign  black   2
```

```
 3                assign   _xxx0   black
 4                add      _xxx0   1
 5                assign   _xxx1   _xxx0
 6                mult     _xxx1   black
 7                assign   _xxx2   223
 8                sub      _xxx2   1
 9                assign   _xxx3   _xxx1
10                mult     _xxx3   _xxx2
11                assign   _xxx4   _xxx3
12                div      _xxx4   2
13                assign   magic   _xxx4
14                exit     0
15                .data
16      black     int
17      magic     int
18      _xxx0     int
19      _xxx1     int
20      _xxx2     int
21      _xxx3     int
22      _xxx4     int
23                .end
```

Note the presence of five new identifiers, _xxx0 through _xxx4. These are created during compilation to hold *temporary* quantities. This reflects the fact that the assembly language does not support complex arithmetic expressions. A complex expression must be broken down into several simpler expressions with the intermediate results stored in temporary variables. This translation could actually be simplified somewhat by optimizing the code generator, but optimization techniques will not be studied until Chapter 11 and optimization is incidental to the purpose of this chapter.

3.2. STRUCTURE OF CECILIA

The implementation of *cecilia* is less than 400 lines of code including comments, broken into files much as was *ginevra*:

File	Purpose
main.c	main program and parser
lex.c	lexical analyzer
table.c	symbol table
error.c	error handling
code.c	code generator
global.h	global declarations

Make

A simple *makefile* for *cecilia* together with its output is in Fig. 3-1.

Error Processing, Lexical Analyzer, and Symbol Table

The error processing, lexical analyzer, and symbol table code are similar to those of *ginevra*; they are presented without further explanation. Error processing will be revisited in the next section where the parser is discussed.

error.c:

```
1       #include "global.h"
2
3       error (msg, recovery)  char *msg; strategy recovery;
```

```
1    cecilia: error.o lex.o table.o code.o main.o
2            cc -O -o cecilia error.o lex.o table.o main.o code.o
3
4    main.o: global.h
5            cc -c -O main.c
6
7    code.o: global.h
8            cc -c -O code.c
9
10   error.o: global.h
11           cc -c -O error.c
12
13   lex.o: global.h
14           cc -c -O lex.c
15
16   table.o: global.h
17           cc -c -O table.c
```

makefile for *cecilia*

```
1    % make
2    cc -c -O error.c
3    cc -c -O lex.c
4    cc -c -O table.c
5    cc -c -O code.c
6    cc -c -O main.c
7    cc -O -o cecilia error.o lex.o table.o main.o code.o
```

Output of *make* on *cecilia*

Figure 3-1. *makefile* and Output of *make* for *cecilia*.

```
4    {
5        if (yycolumn)
6            fprintf (stderr, "in column %d: ", yycolumn);
7        fprintf (stderr, "%s\n", msg);
8
9        switch (recovery) {
10           case PANIC:  exit(1);
11           default:  error ("internal error - bad recovery", PANIC);
12       }
13   }
```

lex.c:

```
1    #include "global.h"
2    #include <ctype.h>
3    #include <strings.h>
4
5    typedef enum {_START, _IDENT, _INIDENT, _EOF, _INT, _ININT, _EOL,
6            _OTHER} state;
7
8    static char curchar;   /* current character */
9    static char nextchar;  /* succeeding character */
10   static char *p;
11   static int  c = 0;
12
13   static char    /* read next character from yyin */
14   getch ()
15   {
16       static int firsttime = 1;
17
18       if (firsttime) {
19           firsttime--;
20           if ((p = fgets (yyline, BUFSIZ, yyin)) != NULL) {
21               c = 1;
22               nextchar = *(p+1);
23               return (curchar = *p);
```

```
24              }
25          else   /* at end of file */
26              error ("null input file", PANIC);
27          }
28
29      if (nextchar == '\0')  /* last character */
30          return (curchar = nextchar = '\0');
31
32      c++;
33      nextchar = *(p+2);
34      return (curchar = *++p);
35  }
36
37  int          /* get the next token from input stream */
38  yygettoken ()
39  {
40      static int firsttime = 1;
41      state curstate;
42      int   i, done;
43
44      if (firsttime) {
45          getch();
46          firsttime--;
47      }
48
49      curstate = _START;
50      yytext[0] = '\0';
51      done = 0;
52
53      while (!done) {
54        switch (curstate) {
55        case _START:
56              yycolumn = c;
57              if (curchar == ' ' || curchar == '\t')
58                  ;
59              else if (curchar == '\0') { /* end of file */
60                  curstate = _EOF;
61                  done++;
62              }
63              else if (curchar == '\n') { /* end of line counts */
64                  curstate = _EOL;
65                  strncat (yytext, &curchar, 1);
66                  getch ();
67                  done++;
68              }
69              else if (isalpha (curchar)) {   /* identifier */
70                  strncat (yytext, &curchar, 1);
71                  curstate = _INIDENT;
72              }
73              else if (isdigit (curchar)) { /* integer */
74                  strncat (yytext, &curchar, 1);
75                  curstate = _ININT;
76              }
77              else {   /* routine symbol */
78                  strncat (yytext, &curchar, 1);
79                  getch ();
80                  curstate = _OTHER;
81                  done++;
82              }
83              break;
84          case _INIDENT:
85              if (isalnum (curchar)) {
86                  strncat (yytext, &curchar, 1);
87                  break;
88              }
89              curstate = _IDENT;
90              done++;
91              break;
92          case _ININT:
93              if (isdigit (curchar)) {
94                  strncat (yytext, &curchar, 1);
95                  break;
```

```
96                  }
97                  curstate = _INT;
98                  done++;
99                  break;
100             }
101             if (!done)  getch();
102         }
103         switch (curstate) {
104         case _EOF: return EOFILE;
105         case _EOL:
106         case _OTHER: return yytext[0];
107         case _IDENT:
108             if (lookup (yytext) == -1)
109                 insert (yytext, NOTLITERAL);
110             return IDENT;
111         case _INT:
112             if (lookup (yytext) == -1)
113                 insert (yytext, LITERAL);
114             return INTEGER;
115         }
116     }
```

table.c:

```
1       #include "global.h"
2
3       int tabsize = 0;
4
5       int
6       lookup (s) char *s;
7       {
8           register int i;
9
10          for (i=0; i<tabsize; i++)
11              if (!strcmp (table[i].key, s))
12                  return i;
13          return NOTFOUND;
14      }
15
16      int
17      insert (s, lit) char *s;  int lit;
18      {
19          char *p;
20
21          if (tabsize == TABSIZE)
22              error ("internal error: symbol table overflow", PANIC);
23          p = (char *) malloc (strlen(s)+1);
24          strcpy (p, s);
25          table[tabsize].key = p;
26          table[tabsize].literal = lit;
27          return (tabsize++);
28      }
```

3.3. PARSING AND MAIN PROGRAM

The parsing of *cecilia* is much more sophisticated than that of *ginevra*. Looking at the program translated in Section 3.

```
black = 2; magic = (black+1)*black*(223-1)/2;
```

some of the reasons for this complexity become apparent. The parser needs to decide whether an assignment statement has the form

```
identifier  '='  expression  ';'
```

where `expression` can be arbitrarily long (provided it fits onto a line). An arithmetic expression can be nested arbitrarily deep in parentheses. The parser must ensure that the parentheses are balanced and enforce the semantics of the parentheses that group subexpressions for evaluation. The implicit higher precedence of multiplication and division over addition and subtraction is enforced by the parser as well as is the fact that operations of the same precedence are performed left to right.

main.c:

```
1      /* usage: cecilia  filename */
2
3      #include "global.h"
4
5      #define STACK 100
6
7      int    opandstk[STACK], optorstk[STACK];
8      int    topoptor = -1, topopand = -1;
9      int    curtoken;
10
11     main (argc, argv) int argc; char *argv[];
12     {
13         char   msg[BUFSIZ];
14         char   *sp;
15
16         /* process filename */
17         if (argc != 2) {
18             sprintf (msg, "usage: %s filename", argv[0]);
19             error (msg, PANIC);
20         }
21         sp = argv[1];
22         if ( (yyin = fopen (argv[1], "r")) == NULL) {
23             sprintf (msg, "cannot open %s", sp);
24             error (msg, PANIC);
25         }
26
27         emit (TEXT, BLANK, BLANK);   /* emit header statement */
28
29         curtoken = yygettoken ();  /* get first token */
30         if (stmts ()) {
31             if (curtoken == '\n' ¦¦ curtoken == EOFILE) {
32                 curtoken = yygettoken ();
33                 if (curtoken == EOFILE) {
34                     emit (EXIT, insert("0"), BLANK);
35                     data ();
36                 }
37             }
38             else
39                 error ("end of file or end of line expected.", PANIC);
40         }
41         exit (0);
42     }
43
44     stmts ()    /* look for a series of statements */
45     {
46         /* a series of stmts is a stmt followed by a series of
47            stmts or nothing */
48         if (curtoken == '\n' ¦¦ curtoken == EOFILE)
49             return 1;
50         if (curtoken == IDENT) {
51             if (stmt())
52                 if (stmts())
53                     return 1;
54         }
55         error ("end of line, end of file, or identifier expected", PANIC);
56     }
57
58     stmt ()    /* look for a single statement */
59     {
60         int rhs;
61
62         /* identifier = expression ; */
63         if (curtoken == IDENT) {
64             pushopand (lookup(yytext));
65             curtoken = yygettoken ();
```

```
66          if (curtoken == '=') {
67              pushoptor (ASSIGN);
68              curtoken = yygettoken ();
69              if (express ()) {
70                  if (curtoken == ';') {
71                      curtoken = yygettoken ();
72                      rhs = popopand ();
73                      emit (popoptor(), popopand(), rhs);
74                      return 1;
75                  }
76                  error ("';' expected.", PANIC);
77              }
78          }
79          error ("'=' expected.", PANIC);
80      }
81      error ("identifier expected.", PANIC);
82  }
83
84  express ()     /* look for expression */
85  {
86      if (curtoken == IDENT || curtoken == INTEGER ||
87              curtoken == '(') {
88          if (term() && expresses())
89              return 1;
90      }
91      error ("identifier, integer, or '(' expected.", PANIC);
92  }
93
94  expresses ()     /* look for second half of expression */
95  {
96      int lhs, rhs, temp;
97
98      if (curtoken == ')' || curtoken == ';')
99          return 1;
100     if (curtoken == '-' || curtoken == '+') {
101         if (curtoken == '-')
102             pushoptor (SUB);
103         else
104             pushoptor (ADD);
105         curtoken = yygettoken ();
106         if (term()) {
107             rhs = popopand ();
108             lhs = popopand ();
109             temp = mktmp();
110             emit (ASSIGN, temp, lhs);
111             emit (popoptor(), temp, rhs);
112             pushopand (temp);
113             if (expresses())
114                 return 1;
115         }
116     }
117     error ("')', ';', '-', or '+' expected.", PANIC);
118 }
119
120 term ()     /* look for multiplicative expression */
121 {
122     if ( curtoken == IDENT || curtoken == INTEGER ||
123             curtoken == '(')
124         if (factor() && terms())
125             return 1;
126     error ("identifier, integer, or '(' expected.", PANIC);
127 }
128
129 terms ()     /* look for second half of multiplicative expression */
130 {
131     int  lhs, rhs, temp;
132
133     if (curtoken == '/' || curtoken == '*') {
134         if (curtoken == '/')
135             pushoptor (DIV);
136         else
137             pushoptor (MULT);
138         curtoken = yygettoken ();
```

```
139                 if (factor()) {
140                     rhs = popopand ();
141                     lhs = popopand ();
142                     temp = mktmp();
143                     emit (ASSIGN, temp, lhs);
144                     emit (popoptor(), temp, rhs);
145                     pushopand (temp);
146                     if (terms())
147                         return 1;
148                 }
149             }
150             else if ( curtoken == '+' || curtoken == '-' ||
151                     curtoken == ')' || curtoken == ';')
152                 return 1;
153             error ("'/', '*', '+', '-', ')' or ';' expected.", PANIC);
154         }
155
156     factor ()      /* look for string derived from factor */
157     {
158         if (curtoken == '(') {
159             curtoken = yygettoken ();
160             if (express ()) {
161                 if (curtoken == ')') {
162                     curtoken = yygettoken ();
163                     return 1;
164                 }
165                 error ("')' expected.", PANIC);
166             }
167         }
168         if (curtoken == INTEGER || curtoken == IDENT) {
169             pushopand (lookup(yytext));
170             curtoken = yygettoken();
171             return 1;
172         }
173         error ("'(', integer, or identifier expected.", PANIC);
174     }
175
176     pushopand (i) int i;
177     {
178         if (++topopand == STACK)
179             error ("internal error: operand stack overflow", PANIC);
180         opandstk[topopand] = i;
181     }
182
183     int
184     popopand ()
185     {
186         if (topopand == -1)
187             error ("internal error: operand stack underflow.", PANIC);
188         return (opandstk[topopand--]);
189     }
190
191     pushoptor (i)  int i;
192     {
193         if (++topoptor == STACK)
194             error ("internal error: operator stack overflow.", PANIC);
195         optorstk[topoptor] = i;
196     }
197
198     int
199     popoptor ()
200     {
201         if (topoptor == -1)
202             error ("internal error: operator stack underflow.", PANIC);
203         return (optorstk[topoptor--]);
204     }
205
206     int
207     mktmp ()
208     {
209         static int  seed = 0;
210         char name[BUFSIZ];
```

```
211
212             sprintf (name, "_xxx%d", seed++);
213             return (insert (name, NOTLITERAL));
214        }
```

Recursive Descent Parsing

The parser used here is called *recursive descent* because it is written as a set of recursive functions which logically descend down the syntactic structure of the source string. This method of parsing, studied formally in Chapter 5, is used quite often for hand-generated parsers, that is, parsers that do not take advantage of a translator-writing system. This is because it operates in an intuitive manner and is relatively straightforward to build. However, for sizable languages, such as all of *C* or Pascal, a recursive descent parser can become quite large and consequently difficult to debug and maintain. The parsing methods presented in Chapter 7 have a much more compact specification.

The primary purpose of the parser is to manipulate two stacks: opandstk and optorstk. The former is a stack of operands encountered in arithmetic expressions. The latter is an analogous stack of operators. The parser pushes the operands and operators onto the stack as they are encountered using functions pushopand and pushoptor. At the "correct moment" the parser pops one operator and two operands off the stack using popopand and popoptor and emits an assembly language instruction which performs the indicated operation by calling emit. When the assignment statement has been completely scanned, all operators and operands will have been pushed and popped, and all assembly code corresponding to that statement emitted. When the entire source program has been scanned, code for all its statements emitted, and the end of file token reached, *cecilia* emits the data section of the object code by scanning the symbol table for variables encountered and created during the scan of the source program (call to data).

Example 3-2. The execution of *cecilia* on the sample program, displaying the manipulation of stacks and code emission, is in Fig. 3-2 (p. 40).

♦

The structure of the source language is embedded in the parser through a series of recursive functions representing major grammatical categories; for example, the entire program is a series of statements. The parser reflects this in lines 30–40:

```
30          if (stmts ()) {
31             if (curtoken == '\n' || curtoken == EOFILE) {
32                curtoken = yygettoken ();
33                if (curtoken == EOFILE) {
34                   emit (EXIT, insert("0"), BLANK);
35                   data ();
36                }
37             }
38          else
39             error ("end of file or end of line expected.", PANIC);
40          }
```

Function stmts returns 1 ("true") if the source program is a series of statements. stmts itself emits all of the object code produced by *cecilia* on those statements. The parser then checks whether the current and next tokens are '\n' and EOF. If so, it emits the terminating exit assembly language statement, emits all data declarations, and terminates execution.

stmts in turn tests whether the current token is '\n' or EOF. If so, it returns immediately since the end of the source program has been reached. Otherwise, the current token should be an identifier since any assignment statement begins with an identifier. If it does not find one, an error has occurred and program execution is terminated with the message from line 55:

```
"end of line, end of file, or identifier expected"
```

Otherwise, it looks for a single assignment statement (in function stmt) followed by another series of zero or more statements:

```
50              if (curtoken == IDENT) {
51                  if (stmt())
52                      if (stmts())
53                          return 1;
54              }
```

`stmt` in turn pushes onto `opandstk` the symbol table index of the identifier on the left-hand side of the assignment operator `'='` (line 64), pushes a defined constant representing the assignment operator onto `optorstk` (line 67), and calls `express` to process the expression on the right-hand side of the assignment statement (line 69). `express` will leave the token pointing to the result of evaluating the expression on top of `opandstk`. If the next token is `';'`, `stmt` pops the assignment operation and two operands off `optorstk` and `opandstk`, respectively, emitting the appropriate code (lines 72–73).

opandstk	optorstk	next symbol	code emitted
			.text
		black	
black		=	
black	=	2	
2 black	=	;	assign black 2
		magic	
magic		=	
magic	=	(	
magic	=	black	
black magic	=	+	
black magic	+ =	1	
1 black magic	+ =	)	assign _xxx0 black
			add _xxx0 1
_xxx0 magic	=	*	
_xxx0 magic	* =	black	
black _xxx0 magic	* =	*	assign _xxx1 _xxx0
			mult _xxx1 black
_xxx1 magic	* =	(	
_xxx1 magic	* =	223	
223 _xxx1 magic	* =	–	
223 _xxx1 magic	– * =	1	
1 223 _xxx1 magic	– * =	)	assign _xxx2 223
			sub _xxx2 1
_xxx2 _xxx1 magic	* =	/	assign _xxx3 _xxx1
			mult _xxx3 _xxx2
_ xxx3 magic	/ =	2	
2 _xxx3 magic	/ =	;	assign _xxx4 _xxx3
			div _xxx4 2
			assign magic _xxx4
		EOF	exit 0 ...

Figure 3-2. Execution of cecilia.

Analysis of arithmetic expressions is more interesting because expressions are broken into a "front-end" and "back-end" called `term` and `expresses`, respectively. A `term` leads to singleton operands (an integer or an identifier or a parenthesized expression) or to whole arithmetic triples (*operand operator operand*) that have multiplication or division operations. `expresses` is a partial expression (*operator operand*) that begins with `'+'` or `'–'` or else is the null string. As long as there are multiplicative subexpressions, `terms`, which is called from `term` is recursively invoked. The first time the operator becomes `'+'` or `'–'`, or the expression terminates, the recursion ends, and `expressions` is called.

The series of calls to these functions can be represented in a *parse tree*, reflecting the grammatical structure of the string. Parsing will be studied formally in Chapter 5, but the tree is introduced in passing here to help understand why *cecilia* works.

Example 3-3. The parse tree for the sample program is in Fig. 3-3.

◆

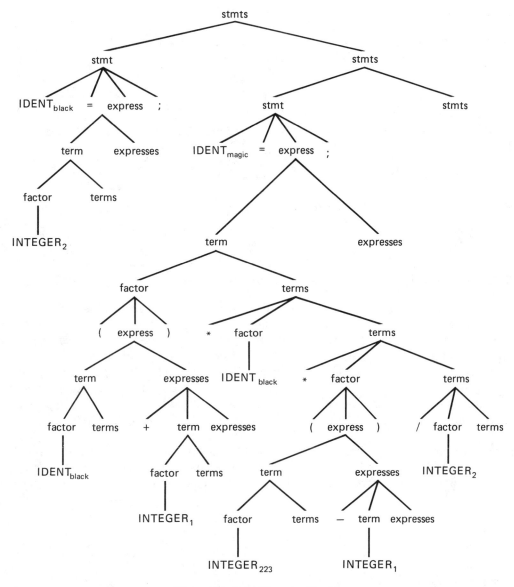

Figure 3-3. Parse Tree for Magic.

Error Processing

There are many calls to `error` in the parser. Each function such as `stmt` or `express` begins with a *guard* which checks whether the current token could legitimately appear at that point in the derivation. For example, the guards of `stmts` are in lines 48 and 50:

```
48          if (curtoken == '\n' || curtoken == EOFILE)

50          if (curtoken == IDENT) {
```

The first is appropriate for the end of a program; the second for the beginning of a new statement. Each statement begins with an identifier. If the current token is not an identifier, this string cannot possibly be a sentence. The error response is in line 55:

```
55          error ("end of line, end of file, or identifier expected", PANIC);
```

This would happen on input

```
1=2;
```

which produces

```
in column 1: end of line, end of file, or identifier expected
```

For input

```
a=1+20*);
```

a right parenthesis appears where an operand or a left parenthesis is allowed. The error message generated is

```
in column 8: '(', integer, or identifier expected.
```

Figure 3-4 shows the parse tree and the sequence of function calls that lead up to issuing the error message.

3.4. CODE GENERATION

The translator developed in the last chapter took an extended *C* and mapped it into standard *C*. The translation performed by *cecilia* is more radical because it maps *C* assignment statements into a completely different assembly language. The assembly language is for an imaginary simple computer which performs operations on memory locations. It has no addressable stack or registers.

Information about the assembly language operations is kept in a simple table `optable`. Since the set of operations is constant, the indices into the table are all represented by defined constants in *global.h*; for example, the name of the multiplication operation is `MULT`, whose value 3, is the index into `optable`, where the string `"mult"` is found. This string is emitted in the opcode field of an assembly instruction.

The separate symbol table contains an entry for each identifier and integer literal found in the input. Each entry also indicates whether the symbol is an identifier or an integer. The table holds information on up to 100 symbols. Since the entire program must appear on a single line, this seems adequate.

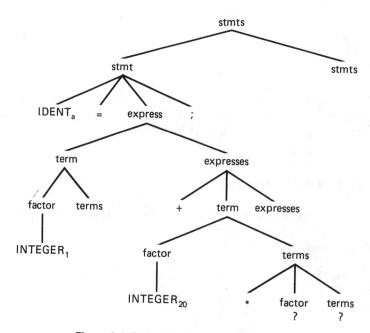

Figure 3-4. Parse Tree for "a=1+20*);".

code.c:

```
1      #include "global.h"
2
3      static char *optable[] = { "sub", "add", "div", "mult", ".end",
4              ".text", "assign", "exit", ".data"};
5
6      emit (opcode, op1, op2)  int opcode, op1, op2;
7      {
8          printf ("%-6s  %-6s  %-6s  %-6s\n", "", optable[opcode],
9              op1==-1?"":table[op1].key, op2==-1?"":table[op2].key);
10     }
11
12     data ()
13     {
14         register int i;
15
16         emit (DATA, BLANK, BLANK);
17
18         for (i=0; i<tabsize; i++)
19             if (!table[i].literal)
20                 printf ("%-6s  %-6s\n", table[i].key, "int");
21
22         emit (END, BLANK, BLANK);
23     }
```

Again, *global.h* is listed at the end of the chapter:

```
1      #include <stdio.h>
2
3          /* error recovery strategies */
4      typedef enum {PANIC} strategy;
5
6          /* types of tokens.  each is represented by an integer.
7             tokens comprised of a single char are just their ascii
8             representation */
9      #define    IDENT      256      /*  an identifier */
10     #define    INTEGER    257      /*  an integer */
11     #define    EOFILE     258      /*  end of file */
12
13     #define    NOTLITERAL  0       /*  symbol is not a literal */
14     #define    LITERAL     1       /*  symbol is a literal */
15
16     enum {SUB, ADD, DIV, MULT, END, TEXT, ASSIGN, EXIT, DATA} opcodes;
17
18     #define    BLANK      -1       /* field is blank */
19
20          /* global names beginning with "yy" to mirror lex */
21     char         yytext[BUFSIZ];   /* current token */
22     FILE        *yyin;             /* file being scanned */
23     int          yycolumn;         /* line column token begins in */
24     char         yyline[BUFSIZ];   /* current line */
25
26     #define  TABSIZE    100
27
28     struct entry {
29         char  *key;
30         int    literal;  /* literal or identifier? */
31     }  table[TABSIZE];
32
33     extern int tabsize;
34
35     #define NOTFOUND    -1    /* value when lookup fails */
```

EXERCISES

1. Translate by hand the expressions:

(a) today = yesterday+1; tomorrow = yesterday+2;
(b) x = (y+1)/(220/(3+x));
(c) y = (((z+1))); z = 1/((y));

2. Trace through the execution of *cecilia* until it finds an error in the following expressions. Show how much code is produced up through the point when the error is found and the state of the two stacks when it is detected:

   (a) `1`
   (b) `today = yesterday 1;`
   (c) `x = ((z)));`
   (d) `z = 1/((y+));`

3. Write a statement that will cause (a) `opandstk` to overflow; (b) `optorstk` to overflow.

4. Replace the linear search algorithm in `lookup` with a hash algorithm.

5. Modify *cecilia* so it supports the Pascal operators `":="` and `"div"` instead of *C*'s `"="` and `"/"`. The keyword `"div"` should be reserved.

6. Add the square operator `"^"` operator to *cecilia* so that

   ```
   ^4=16   ^3=9   ^(x+1)=16 if x=3
   ```

   Do it in such a way that the target language is not changed.

7. Only one assignment operator is allowed per statement in *cecilia*. Extend it so that any number of assignments can be made in a single statement as in *C*; for example, the statement

   ```
   black = white = red = 1;
   ```

   should be legal.

8. Allow octal and hexadecimal in addition to decimal integer constants where an octal constant is a zero followed by any number of digits in the range `0-7` and a hexadecimal constant is a `0x` or `0X` followed by any number of digits in the range `0-9` plus the extended digits `a-f` and `A-F`.

9. Allow character constants of the form `'c'` where *c* is any character except a backslash or a quote. Arithmetic on characters should be allowed as in *C*, for example,

   ```
   lowercase = uppercase+'a'-'A';
   ```

   converts an uppercase ASCII letter to its lowercase equivalent.

10. Extend the implementation done in the last exercise to support character constants of the form: `'\''`, `'\\'`, `'\n'`, `'\b'`, `'\f'`, `'\r'`, and `'\t'` with their normal *C* interpretation.

11. Extend error handling so that instead of panicking when it finds an erroneous token, *cecilia* starts skipping tokens until it finds one that is expected at the point where the error occurred. *cecilia* should print an appropriate error message such as

    ```
    in column %d: %s unexpected. skipping until column %d
    ```

12. Extend *cecilia* so it handles programs on an arbitrary number of lines.

13. *ginevra* and *cecilia* should be able to work together. Demonstate how the output of *ginevra* can become the input to *cecilia* in

    ```
    #define MAX 100
    #define MAXMAX MAX*MAX
    huge = 2*(MAX*3)+MAXMAX;
    ```

    What is the value of `huge` when the code is executed?

Chapter 4
Lexical Analysis

4.1. REGULAR GRAMMARS

A *regular grammar* is a way to specify how to generate strings that can be recognized by a finite-state machine. A regular grammar has several desirable properties:

1. It is compact and easily understood by people.
2. It can be algorithmically converted into a finite-state machine that recognizes the strings the grammar generates.
3. It is relatively straightforward to represent most lexical information using regular grammars.

A regular grammar consists of four parts:

1. A finite alphabet of *terminals*.
2. A finite set of lexical categories or *nonterminals*.
3. A distinguished nonterminal called the *axiom*.
4. A finite set of *rules* telling how to generate strings.

The set of both terminals and nonterminals is sometimes called the *vocabulary*. The rules are alternatively called *productions*.

The axiom is the seed from which strings are produced using the rules. Each rule has one of four basic forms:

1. *b*: X *c*
2. *b*: *c*
3. *b*:
4. *b*: X

where *b* and *c* are nonterminals, and X is a terminal. At least one of the rules should have the axiom on the left-hand side of ' : '. The third rule form is sometimes called a *null rule* because the right-hand side is empty.

The first sample grammar, *longid*, specifies that an identifier is an arbitrarily long string of alphanumeric characters beginning with an alphabetic character. The axiom is *id*, the terminals are the upper- and lowercase letters 'a'−'z' and 'A'−'Z' and the digits '0'−'9', and the nonterminals are just *id* and *alphanum*:

```
1.    id: 'a' alphanum
2.    id: 'b' alphanum
        . . .
52.    id: 'Z' alphanum
53.    alphanum: 'a' alphanum
54.    alphanum: 'b' alphanum
```

```
        . . .
104.    alphanum:  'Z' alphanum
105.    alphanum:  '0' alphanum
106.    alphanum:  '1' alphanum
        . . .
114.    alphanum:  '9' alphanum
115.    alphanum:
```

The number of rules is so large because there are so many characters in the alphabet. The generation of identifier `Tiger` from the rules begins with the axiom

(a) *id*

Next, rule 46 is applied, replacing *id*, which appears on the left-hand side of the rule, by the symbols on the right-hand side:

(b) 'T' *alphanum*

The generation continues with rule 61:

(c) 'T' 'i' *alphanum*

then rules 59, 57, and 75:

(d) 'T' 'i' *alphanum*
(e) 'T' 'i' 'g' *alphanum*
(f) 'T' 'i' 'g' 'e' *alphanum*
(g) 'T' 'i' 'g' 'e' 'r' *alphanum*

Finally, rule 115 is applied, which simply erases `alphanum` (replace `alphanum` by nothing):

(h) 'T' 'i' 'g' 'e' 'r'

There are four notational simplifications that can be made to reduce the amount of writing to specify this language:

1. (Reduction) Replace rules of the form:

$$b: X_1\ b_1$$
$$b_1: X_2\ b_2$$
$$\ldots$$
$$b_{n-1}: X_n\ b_n$$
$$b_n: X_{n+1}\ c$$

where b_1 through b_n are not used in other rules by

$$b: X_1\ X_2\ \ldots\ X_{n+1}\ c$$

2. (Alternation) Replace rules of the form

$$b: e_1$$
$$b: e_2$$
$$\ldots$$
$$b: e_n$$

by

$$b: e_1 \mid e_2 \mid \ldots \mid e_n$$

where e_i is an expression.

3. (Sequencing) Suppose there are rules of the form

```
b: e₁ X₁ e₂
b: e₁ X₂ e₂
   . . .
b: e₁ Xₙ e₂
```

where X_1, ..., X_n are an ascending sequence of characters in a known alphabet (for the sake of example assume ASCII). Replace these rules by

```
b: e₁ [X₁ - Xₙ] e₂
```

4. (Negation) Suppose there are rules of the form:

```
b: e₁ X₁ e₂
b: e₁ X₂ e₂
   . . .
b: e₁ Xₙ e₂
```

where X_1, X_2, ..., X_n are the entire terminal alphabet except for Y_1, Y_2, ..., Y_m. Replace these rules by

```
b: e₁ ~[Y₁ Y₂ . . . Yₘ] e₂
```

Using these four shorthand notations, the example grammar can be rewritten as *shortid* with the same terminals, axiom, and nonterminals, but with only two rules:

```
1.   id: [a-z] alphanum ¦ [A-Z] alphanum
2.   alphanum: [a-z] alphanum ¦ [A-Z] alphanum ¦ [0-9] alphanum ¦
```

Reduction and negation are not needed for this example, but will be used later.

The experienced Unix user will recognize the notation that uses square brackets to demarcate a sequence of characters. It is found in a number of Unix tools including *egrep* (search for patterns in a file) and *ed* (a line editor). In fact these are *regular expressions*, which are an alternative way to represent regular languages. At the end of this chapter when *lex* is studied, regular expressions will be revisited in depth. There are still further notational shortcuts which could be defined for *ginevra*, but they add nothing conceptual to the material.

Grammar *gram-ginevra* to generate the tokens recognized by *ginevra* is significantly more complex. The axiom is *token*. The other nonterminals and terminals can be inferred from the rules:

```
1.    token:  '\n' ¦ other ¦
2.    other: misc ¦ ident ¦ integer ¦ dstring ¦ sstring
3.    misc: ';' ¦ '+' ¦ '-' ¦ '*' ¦ '/' ¦ '=' ¦ ...
4.    ident: [a-z] alphanum ¦ [A-Z] alphanum
5.    alphanum: [a-z] alphanum ¦ [A-Z] alphanum ¦ [0-9] alphanum ¦
6.    integer: [0-9] inttail
7.    inttail: [0-9] inttail ¦
8.    dstring: '"' dtail
9.    dtail: ~["\\] dtail ¦ '\' dslash ¦ '"'
10.   dslash: '\' dtail ¦ '"' dtail
11.   sstring: '\"' stail
12.   stail: ~['\\] stail ¦ '\' sslash ¦ '\''
13.   sslash: '\' stail ¦ '\'' stail
```

The lexical category `misc` stands for all of the characters that can appear in a *C* program which are not part of identifiers and integers. They are not actually all listed here for the sake of brevity. Nonterminals `ident` and `integer`, which generate identifiers and integers, respectively, operate in much the same manner as did `id` in grammar *shortid*. The handling of single and double quoted strings is more interesting for two reasons:

1. Strings have an explicit beginning and ending delimiter.

2. Preceding the delimiting character by a backslash causes it to be treated as part of the string rather than as a delimiter.

4.2. FINITE-STATE MACHINES

A *finite-state machine* (FSM) has one purpose—to accept or reject input strings. It processes the input string one character at a time. As each character is processed, the machine either steps to a new *state* or rejects the string. If, when the last character has been processed, the machine is in one of a designated number of *final* states, the string is accepted; otherwise, it is rejected.

Converting a regular grammar into a finite-state machine that recognizes the strings generated by that grammar is straightforward. For every FSM there is a regular grammar that generates the strings recognized by that machine and conversely. The algorithm for converting from a grammar to a machine is first presented using the basic notation for grammars defined at the beginning of the last section; then it is modified to accommodate the notational shortcuts.

A FSM consists of five components:

1. A finite alphabet of *terminals*.
2. A finite set of machine *states*.
3. A distinguished *start* state.
4. A finite set of state *transitions*.
5. A set of *final* states.

The machine always begins recognition in the start state. The input string is always followed by an end of token character. Each transition has the form

```
s   X   t
```

where *s* and *t* are states (called the *source* and *target* states, respectively) and X is a terminal. The sequence of states the machine can assume is determined by the state transitions. If the machine is in state *s*, the terminal character being processed is X, and there is a transition rule *sXt*, then the machine changes to state *t* and continues processing with the next input character. If there is no legal transition rule *sXt*, the machine halts and rejects the string. If there is a sequence of legal transitions that process up through the last character before the end of token character, and the machine is then in a final state, the string is accepted; otherwise, it is rejected.

This simple execution strategy is compounded by the possibility of having more than one legal transition at any instant. This happens if there are two or more transition rules with the same source state and terminal:

```
s  X  t₁
s  X  t₂
  . . .
s  X  tₙ
```

In this case the machine is said to be *nondeterministic*, and is said to accept an input string if there is *any* sequence of legal state transitions that cause it to be in a final state when the last character is processed. A machine that is not nondeterministic is said to be *deterministic*. There is an algorithm, not shown here, which maps a nondeterministic FSM into an equivalent deterministic FSM.

The first sample machine, *mach-longid*, recognizes the identifiers generated by grammar *longid*. Its start state is `id`; the terminals are the same as those of *longid*; the states are `id` and `alphanum`; `alphanum` is the sole final state; the end of token character is newline; the transitions are:

```
  1.    id   'a'   alphanum
  2.    id   'b'   alphanum
             . . .
 52.    id   'Z'   alphanum
 53.    alphanum   'a'   alphanum
 54.    alphanum   'b'   alphanum
             . . .
104.    alphanum   'Z'   alphanum
105.    alphanum   '0'   alphanum
106.    alphanum   '1'   alphanum
             . . .
114.    alphanum   '9'   alphanum
```

mach-longid is deterministic.

The relationship between *longid* and *mach-longid* is simple. The axiom of the grammar becomes the start state of the machine. Each rule of the grammar with form

    b: X c

becomes transition

    b   X   c

A rule of the form

    b:

has no corresponding transition. Furthermore, if there were rules of the form

    b: c

in the grammar, they would be mapped to

    b   c

which is the *null* transition. This means that if the machine is in state *b*, it can change to state *c* without regard to what the current input character is provided that character is a legal terminal. Rules of the form

    b: X

would be mapped to

    b   X   final

where *final* is an implicit final state of every FSM.

This machine is pictured as a *state transition diagram* in Fig. 4-1. Each state is a circle. The start state is a double circle. The arrow leading into it has no tail. The final state is shaded (if there were more than one final state, all would be shaded), and transition *s* X *t* is shown as an arrow from the circle representing state *s* to the circle representing state *t* with an X labeling the arrow.

Figure 4-2 is a sequence of snapshots of the machine as it recognizes identifier "Tiger" followed by a newline. The machine begins in start state id. It transitions to state alphanum over the arrow labeled by 'T' when the 'T' is seen. It then transitions to state alphanum again over the arrow labeled by 'i' when 'i' is seen. Similar transition steps are made for 'g', 'e', and 'r'. At this point there are no more characters in the string to be recognized, and alphanum is a final state. The machine stops and accepts "Tiger".

Since the notational shortcuts for regular grammars can all be mapped back to the basic notation, each has a well-defined mapping to a finite-state construct. For alternation there is no notational shortcut for

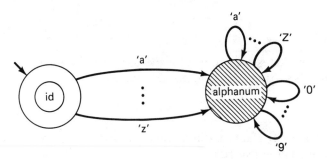

Figure 4-1. State Transition Diagram for *mach-longid*.

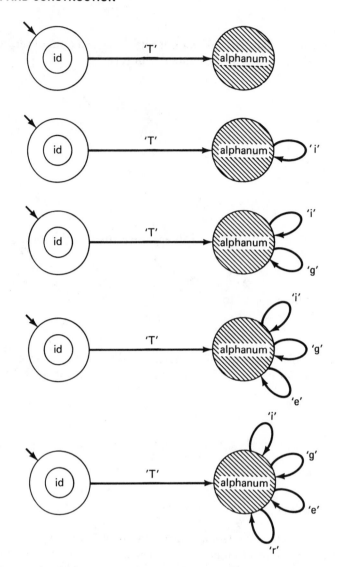

Figure 4-2. *mach-longid* Recognizing "Tiger".

transition rules defined; however, for the other three, the syntax for transition rules is extended to allow more compact specification of machines. A rule using reduction

$$b: X_1 \; X_2 \; \ldots \; X_n \; c$$

is mapped to several transitions

```
b  X₁  t₁
t₁  X₂  t₂
   . . .
tₙ₋₂  Xₙ₋₁  tₙ₋₁
tₙ₋₁  Xₙ  c
```

where t_1, t_2, $\ldots$, t_{n-1} are states created just for the purpose of stepping through the string $X_1 . . X_n$. As a notational shortcut, these transitions can be abbreviated by

$$b \quad X_1 \; \ldots \; X_n \; c$$

Wherever $[X-Y]$ or $\tilde{} [X_1 . . X_n]$ appears in a grammar, use the same symbol in the corresponding transition; for example, map grammar rule

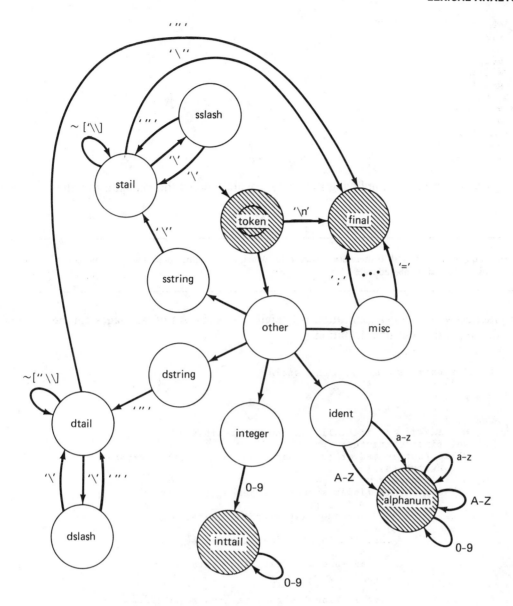

b: ¹x¹ [1-9] ⁻[ab] c

to

b ¹x¹ [1-9] ⁻[ab] c

with the obvious interpretation—if the machine is in state b and the input string continues with an ¹x¹ followed by any character in the sequence ¹1¹ through ¹9¹ followed by any characters except ¹a¹ or ¹b¹, then change to state c.

mach-ginevra is pictured in Fig. 4-3.

4.3. IMPLEMENTATION OF FINITE-STATE MACHINES

The high-level design of an FSM implementation is shown next where *start* is the start state, $\{s_1, \ldots, s_n\}$ are all of the states, $\{F_1, \ldots, F_m\}$ are the final states, and the transition rules are

$$s_1 \quad e_{1,1} \quad t_{1,1}$$
$$s_1 \quad e_{1,2} \quad t_{1,2}$$
$$\ldots$$
$$s_1 \quad e_{1,m_1} \quad t_{1,m_1}$$
$$s_2 \quad e_{2,1} \quad t_{2,1}$$
$$s_2 \quad e_{2,2} \quad t_{2,2}$$
$$\ldots$$
$$s_2 \quad e_{2,m_2} \quad t_{2,m_2}$$
$$\ldots$$
$$s_n \quad e_{n,1} \quad t_{n,1}$$
$$\ldots$$
$$s_n \quad e_{n,m_n} \quad t_{n,m_n}$$

This design makes a major simplifying assumption which forces the machine to behave deterministically:

> The transition rules are ordered. If there are several rules which the machine could follow at any particular transition, it always takes the lowest numbered rule.

From a practical view, this simplification is benign. The same set of languages can be recognized by suitably modifying the machine definition.

```
1    typedef enum {s₁, s₂, ..., sₙ} state;
2
3    state s;
4
5    FSM () {
6        s = start;  /* initially in the start state */
7        get first character;
8        while (not at end of token marker or end of input stream) {
9            switch (s) {
10               case s₁:
11                   if (input stream matches e₁,₁) {
12                       s = t₁,₁;
13                       advance past matching characters;
14                   }
15                   else if (input stream matches e₁,₂) {
16                       s = t₁,₂;
17                       advance past matching characters;
18                   }
19                       ...
20                   else if (input stream matches e₁,ₘ₁) {
21                       s = t₁,ₘ₁;
22                       advance past matching characters;
23                   }
24                   else
25                       reject string;
26                   break;
27               ...
28               case sₙ:
29                   if (input stream matches eₙ,₁) {
30                       s = tₙ,₁;
31                       advance past matching characters;
32                   }
33                   else if (input stream matches eₙ,₂) {
34                       s = tₙ,₂;
35                       advance past matching characters;
36                   }
37                       ...
38                   else if (input stream is eₙ,ₘₙ) {
39                       s = tₙ,ₘₙ;
40                       advance past matching characters;
41                   }
42                   else
43                       reject string;
```

```
44                break;
45            default:
46                error ("Illegal state transition.", PANIC);
47            }
48        }
49    if (s is in {F₁, ..., Fₙ} and at end of token marker)
50        accept string;
51    else
52        reject string;
53    }
```

A complete implementation of a deterministic version of an FSM for *mach-shortid* follows. It reads one line from stdin, accepting the line if it contains exactly one identifier followed by whitespace; otherwise, it rejects it. Note how the sequence "[x-y]" is mapped to the test in an **if** statement "(curchar >= 'x' && curchar <= 'y')".

```
1    /* 1.  id: [a-z] alphanum | [A-Z] alphanum
2
3        2.  alphanum: [a-z] alphanum | [A-Z] alphanum | [0-9] alphanum |
4    */
5    #include <stdio.h>
6    #include "globals.h"
7
8    typedef enum {id, alphanum, final} state;
9
10   state s;
11
12   char curchar;
13
14   main () {
15       curchar = getchar();
16       s = id;
17       while ((curchar != '\n' && (curchar != NULL)) {
18           switch (s) {
19           case id:
20               if (curchar >= 'a' && curchar <= 'z') {
21                   s = alphanum;
22                   curchar = getchar ();
23               }
24               else if (curchar >= 'A' && curchar <= 'Z') {
25                   s = alphanum;
26                   curchar = getchar ();
27               }
28               else
29                   error ("bad transition from id: reject string", PANIC);
30               break;
31           case alphanum:
32               if (curchar >= 'a' && curchar <= 'z') {
33                   s = alphanum;
34                   curchar = getchar ();
35               }
36               else if (curchar >= 'A' && curchar <= 'Z') {
37                   s = alphanum;
38                   curchar = getchar ();
39               }
40               else if (curchar >= '0' && curchar <= '9') {
41                   s = alphanum;
42                   curchar = getchar ();
43               }
44               else
45                   error ("bad transition from alphanum: reject string",
46                           PANIC);
47               break;
48           default:
49               error ("Illegal state transition", PANIC);
50           }
51       }
52
53       if ((s == alphanum) && (curchar == '\n'){
54           printf ("accept string\n");
```

```
55          exit (0);
56      }
57      else {
58          printf ("not in final state: reject string\n");
59          exit (1);
60      }
61  }
```

4.4. DESIGN OF *GIOCONDA*

The lexical analyzers in the last two chapters were based on finite-state machines and seem to have much structure and even detail in common. It is natural to ask whether there is a way to systematize this commonality and write one program that can be used to support many lexical analyzers. The answer, of course, is "yes". *gioconda*, whose design and partial implementation is shown here, is a *lexical analyzer generator*; that is, the input to *gioconda* is the specification of a lexical analyzer. Its output is a lexical analyzer written in *C*. This process is shown in Fig. 4-4. *gioconda* has two major subsystems, *gen-gioconda* and *skel-gioconda*. *gen-gioconda* is the generator which takes an analyzer specification written by a programmer and converts it into a series of *C* statements stored in several *.h* files. These statements are inserted into an incomplete (skeletal) program, *skel-gioconda*. *skel-gioconda* represents the common aspects of a lexical analyzer. When *skel-gioconda* is completed by inserting into it the statements generated by *gen-gioconda*, the result is the source code for a full working lexical analyzer. Additionally, there may be several auxiliary source files written by the programmer to support the actions called out in the specification. A lexical analyzer generated in this way can be included in a still larger program such as a compiler.

The paradigm of identifying commonality across different implementations and writing a tool to extract and support that commonality is very powerful. It is repeated in the next few chapters where parsing tools are developed and is the basis for much current work in software engineering for improving programmer productivity through software reuse. Both *lex* and *yacc*, the commercially used translator-writing tools found on Unix, follow this paradigm.

The last section showed how to write an FSM which recognizes individual tokens. This model can be generalized into a lexical analyzer which examines an arbitrarily long input stream, breaking it into individual tokens and skipping over whitespace and comments. The lexical analyzers developed using *gioconda* make several common underlying assumptions which simplify the presentation. They can be further generalized as exercises:

1. It is possible to decide whether the current character belongs to the current token, is whitespace, or begins a new token by examining no further in the input stream than the next character. This simplifies the state transition function since the transition is based only on the current and next character rather than on characters arbitrarily far down in the input stream.
2. A token is always the longest possible sequence of characters which could be in that token; for example, the sequence "longid " would be a single identifier six characters long followed by a space, not identifier "long", followed by identifier "id", followed by a space.

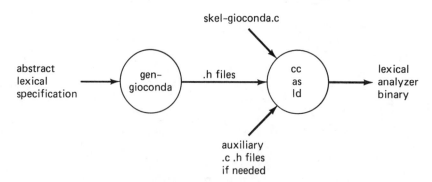

Figure 4-4. Generating Lexical Analyzer Using *gioconda*.

3. The lexical analyzer is always a function called `yylex` which returns the state of the analyzer when it completes recognition of the token and sets the actual string recognized in global variable `yytext`. `yylexerr` is set to 1 if a lexical error is discovered; otherwise it is 0.
4. The lexical analyzer itself does not alter the symbol table. Independent code that uses the return value of `yylex` and `yytext` will make appropriate entries in the symbol table as required by the larger application into which the analyzer fits.

FORTRAN is a good example of a language that violates the first restriction. The lines

```
DO10I=1,20
```

and

```
DO10I=1.20
```

are identical except for the eighth character. Blanks are not token delimiters in FORTRAN (a consequence of having been designed in the mid-1950s before the implications of readability were understood). In fact, a legal program can be written with no intertoken spaces at all, even though it would be rather silly to do so. Rewriting these two lines with a space between each token yields

```
DO 10 I = 1 , 20
```

and

```
DO10I = 1.20
```

The first is the beginning of a `DO` loop, which is similar in purpose to a `for` loop in *C*. The second is an assignment statement, assigning the real value `1.20` to variable `DO10I`. A lexical analyzer for FORTRAN would have to scan up through the eighth character to determine the first token's endpoint for these statements.

Grammars have been viewed as generating individual tokens. This view is now extended to one where they generate a sequence of tokens separated by zero or more whitespace characters. The grammar must specify the rules for generating both the legal tokens and the legal whitespace sequences.

To illustrate how *skel-gioconda* works, *shortids* will be revisited. The language of identifiers is extended to be an arbitrarily long sequence of identifiers, separated by spaces, tabs, and newlines. The rules for *shortids*, including one for whitespace between tokens, are:

```
1   token: id
2   id: [a-z] alphanum ¦ [A-Z] alphanum
3   alphanum: [a-z] alphanum ¦ [A-Z] alphanum ¦ [0-9] alphanum ¦ ident
4   whitespace: '\n' whitespace ¦ ' ' whitespace ¦ '\t' whitespace ¦
5   ident:
```

The axiom of any grammar is always `token`. Nonterminal `whitespace` is treated specially. It is used to demarcate the end of a token and the beginning of whitespace. For example, the following steps would generate the string

```
Tiger  Panda
```

where the two identifiers are separated by two spaces:

```
1   token
2   id
3   'T' alphanum
4    ...
5   'T' 'i' 'g' 'e' 'r' alphanum
6   'T' 'i' 'g' 'e' 'r' ident
7   'T' 'i' 'g' 'e' 'r'
8   'T' 'i' 'g' 'e' 'r' whitespace
```

```
 9    'T' 'i' 'g' 'e' 'r' ' '  whitespace
10    'T' 'i' 'g' 'e' 'r' ' ' ' '  whitespace
11    'T' 'i' 'g' 'e' 'r' ' ' ' '
12    'T' 'i' 'g' 'e' 'r' ' ' ' ' ' '  token
13    ...
14    'T' 'i' 'g' 'e' 'r' ' ' ' ' ' 'P' 'a' 'n' 'd' 'a'  alphanum
15    'T' 'i' 'g' 'e' 'r' ' ' ' ' ' 'P' 'a' 'n' 'd' 'a'  ident
16    'T' 'i' 'g' 'e' 'r' ' ' ' ' ' 'P' 'a' 'n' 'd' 'a'
```

If this grammar were input to *gen-gioconda*, the completed analyzer resulting from inserting its output into *skel-gioconda* would be

```
 1    #include <stdio.h>
 2    #include "global.h"
 3
 4    #define _token        0
 5    #define _id           1
 6    #define _alphanum     2
 7    #define _whitespace   3
 8    #define _ident        4
 9
10    static char   nextchar, curchar;
11    static int    yycurstate;
12    char   yytext[BUFSIZ];
13    static char *p;
14
15    yygetchar () {
16        static firsttime = 1;
17        static char line [BUFSIZ];
18
19        if (firsttime || index ("\n\f\r", *p)) {
20            if (firsttime) firsttime--;
21            if ( (p=gets (line, BUFSIZ)) != NULL) {
22                nextchar = *(p+1);
23                return (curchar = *p);
24            }
25            else
26                return (curchar = nextchar = '\0');
27        }
28
29        if (p == NULL)
30            return (curchar = nextchar = '\0');
31
32        nextchar = *(p+2);
33        return (curchar = *++p);
34    }
35
36    yylex () {
37        int   i, done;
38
39        yycurstate = _whitespace;      /* first look for whitespace */
40        yytext[0] = '\0';
41        done = 0;
42        while (!done && (curchar != '\0')) {
43            switch (yycurstate) {
44                case _whitespace:
45                    if (curchar == '\n') {
46                        yycurstate = _whitespace;
47                        yygetchar ();
48                    }
49                    else if (curchar == ' ') {
50                        yycurstate = _whitespace;
51                        yygetchar ();
52                    }
53                    else if (curchar == '\t') {
54                        yycurstate = _whitespace;
55                        yygetchar ();
56                    }
57                    else
58                        done++;
59                    break;
```

```
60              default:
61                  error ("Internal error.", PANIC);
62          }
63
64      done = 0;     /* now look for token -- skipped whitespace */
65      yycurstate = _token;
66      while (!done && (curchar != '\0')) {
67          switch (yycurstate) {
68              case _token:
69                  yycurstate = _id;
70                  break;
71              case _id:
72                  if (curchar >= 'a' && curchar <= 'z') {
73                      yycurstate = _alphanum;
74                      strncat (yytext, curchar, 1);
75                      yygetchar ();
76                  }
77                  else if (curchar >= 'A' && curchar <= 'Z') {
78                      yycurstate = _alphanum;
79                      strncat (yytext, curchar, 1);
80                      yygetchar ();
81                  }
82                  else  /* illegal token */
83                      done++;
84                  break;
85              ...
86              default:
87                  error ("Illegal state transition.", PANIC);
88          }
89
90      if (yycurstate != _ident)   /* error */
91          yylexerr = 1;
92      else
93          yylexerr = 0;
94      return yycurstate;
95  }
```

The defined constants in lines 4–8 represent the states of the machine. There is one defined constant for each grammar nonterminal. The person writing the grammar should guarantee that the rules are structured so that the final state selected for each token will be meaningful to the parser. For example, yycurstate is always _ident when yylex returns after seeing an identifier. The parser could use this fact to know it has seen a member of the token group _ident.

Additional "temporary" states beyond those found in the grammar itself could be generated, but are not needed for this example. The states are referenced by name in the body of the code. The analyzer looks for the beginning of the token by first skipping past whitespace. Once a non-whitespace character is found, the analysis of the next token begins in earnest. Do note, though, that the scheme for handling whitespace and tokens is uniform. Both are expressed using regular grammars and both are implemented in the same way using a finite-state transition model.

gen-gioconda produces four files which will be included by *skel-gioconda* at the appropriate places:

1. _state.h: the set of states in the machine inferred from examining the grammar; these are the defined constants at the beginning of the program.
2. _token.h: the switch statement case elements which define the machine's state transitions while it is recognizing a token.
3. _white.h: the switch statement case elements which define the machine's state transitions while it is recognizing whitespace.
4. _final.h: the if statement at the end of yylex which tests whether the analyzer is in a final state or has encountered an erroneous character.

From the example just presented, it should be fairly clear how to construct *gen-gioconda*. Its details are left as an exercise.

Relatively few errors can be discovered by the scanner because it operates at such a low level that it is unable to determine whether what it sees is erroneous. It can detect:

1. An error internal to the scanner such as attempting to transition to an illegal state. This should never happen, but of course it will if the scanner itself has bugs.
2. An illegal special symbol such as `'%'` in Pascal. This could happen if someone were to accidentally type `'%'` instead of `'5'` (`'%'` is above a `'5'` on the keyboard of many terminals) in the Pascal statement:

```
count := count+%;
```

instead of:

```
count := count+5;
```

3. A malformed multi-character token such as a string in *C* which does not have a closing double quote.

gioconda supports recovery for these three error types. The most reasonable recovery for internal errors for a scanner that is part of a compiler is to panic and terminate execution of the program to which the scanner belongs. Line 87 calls `error` with second argument `PANIC` in just such a case. Even if a more sophisticated recovery strategy could be developed, it probably would not be worth the effort. Compilers are not normally expected to be robust in the face of internal error. On the other hand, if the scanner is part of a real-time control process, for example, a program that reads telemetry data on an airplane to help navigate, a more elegant recovery strategy is probably needed, although there is no standard method for dealing with internal program errors.

Illegal special symbols are passed onto the parser which invoked the scanner. A parser has available to it the context in which the illegal symbol appeared. In some cases, the parser may want to "guess" the programmer's intent based on this context, replacing it with what statistically the programmer likely intended. This is especially true in student-oriented batch compilers which want to continue processing as much of a program as possible. The parser can always choose to discard the illegal symbol by simply calling `yylex` again, `yylexerr` will equal 0 if `yylex` found a legal token and 1 if it did not. `yytext` and the return value of `yylex` are available for further analysis when the parser finds out that `yylex` failed.

Malformed multi-character tokens are especially troublesome to recover from because the error usually is the lack of a token terminator, making it impossible to reliably find the real end of token. Any strategy that guesses where the token should have ended will necessarily be wrong much of the time. The rules in the regular grammar which specify the correct form of a multi-character token such as a string should treat encountering a newline as an error. Ignoring escaped characters, the following four rules define the correct form of strings:

```
1    token:  ... ¦ string ¦ ...
2    string: '"'  tailstring
3    tailstring: ˉ["\n] tailstring ¦ '"' goodstring
4    goodstring:
```

One of the most reasonable approaches is to terminate the token when the newline is discovered. Termination of the call to `yylex` when the newline is encountered is automatic with these rules. When a legal string is recognized, the scanner is in state `_goodstring` and `yylexerr=0`. If end of line is reached while the scanner is still looking for the end of a string, it will be in state `_tailstring` instead and `yylexerr=1`.

4.5. LEX: A LEXICAL ANALYZER GENERATOR

gioconda is useful as a first example of a scanner generator, but has limited capabilities. A full feature alternative is *lex*, the lexical analyzer generator which is available as a standard tool in virtually all versions of Unix. Originally developed at Bell Labs, *lex* supports powerful lexical pattern matching, producing fairly efficient analyzers (although there are pathological cases for which *lex* produces very large code). In fact, it not only simplifies writing scanners, but allows arbitrary programmer-defined action to be taken as each token is identified. It really is a mini-translator-writing system in which the analysis of the input is highly constrained. For example, it is easy to write *lex* specifications for filters that map uppercase letters to their lowercase equivalents, count the number of lines, words, and characters in a file (like the standard Unix command *wc*), remove extra blanks and blank lines from a file, and so on. Rather exotic *lex* programs can be written by heaping enough complexity into the action code performed during recognition, but exploring them here would set the poor example of using the wrong tool to solve a problem.

Basic Operation: Replace

The first *lex* example is just two lines. It replaces all uppercase letters with lowercase letters.

```
1   %%
2   [A-Z]    putchar(yytext[0]+'a'-'A');
```

A *lex* specification consists of up to three parts. Part 2 is mandatory; the others are optional. Parts are separated by "%%" in columns 1 and 2. In this example only part 2, which contains *patterns* and *actions*, is present. The fact that line 1 is "%%" indicates that part 1 is null. Part 2 follows it. If part 3 is omitted, it is not necessary to terminate part 2; hence, "%%" is omitted at the end of the specification. Each entry in part 2 has the form

    pattern   *action*

In the example above, there is just one entry in which the pattern is "[A-Z]" and the action is "putchar(...);". Patterns are regular expressions similar to those found in *ed*, *ex*, and other Unix tools. The general set of pattern matching facilities in *lex* is extensive. Suppose P and Q are patterns. Some of the rules governing patterns are:

1. Letters, digits, and most special characters match themselves.
2. '.' matches any character except newline.
3. Square brackets, '[' and ']', enclosing a sequence of characters define a *character class*, which matches any enclosed character. If the first character in the class is '^', the pattern matches any character not in the class. Within a class, '-' between two characters denotes inclusive range.
4. $P*$ matches zero or more occurrences of P.
5. '^' matches the beginning of a line.
6. '$' matches the end of a line.
7. $P+$ matches one or more occurrences of P.
8. $P?$ matches either zero or one occurrence of P.
9. Tab, newline, and formfeed are represented by their C equivalents: '\t', '\n', and '\f'.
10. Special symbols can be escaped by double quoting them or using backslash as in C.
11. Patterns may be grouped with parentheses '(' and ')' with the obvious interpretation.
12. '¦' indicates alternation. $P ¦ Q$ matches either P or Q.
13. '/' is the *look-ahead* operator. P/Q matches P if it is followed by Q; for example, ab/cd matches "ab" only if it is followed by "cd".
14. "{ }" is the *up through* operator. $P\{i,j\}$ matches from i up through j occurrences of P.

See [Lesk and Schmidt 83] for a more complete description of *lex*.

By these definitions, pattern [A-Z] matches any character between 'A' through 'Z' inclusive. When it is matched, the indicated action code is executed, causing character yytext[0]+'a'-'A' to be written to stdout. As in *gioconda*, yytext contains the string matched in the pattern. Here that would be the particular uppercase character seen. Assuming the ASCII character set is used, yytext[0]+'a'-'A' replaces the matched uppercase character with its lowercase equivalent, which is written to stdout.

This specification, stored in file *replace.l* (by convention *lex* file names end with *.l*), is converted into a running C program by typing the shell commands:

```
% lex replace.l
% cc -o replace lex.yy.c -ll
```

lex produces a code segment in *lex.yy.c*. The *lex* library is invoked by the −ll flag to *cc*, which reads in a default main program and other support routines to complete the analyzer. Running *replace* on

```
aBcDeFgHiJk
LmNoPqRsTuV
wXyZ
```

produces

```
abcdefghijk
lmnopqrstuv
wxyz
```

The down side of *lex* is easily illustrated by modifying this example slightly. *lex* is not very friendly, producing rather cryptic messages. When the input specification is modified slightly

```
1   %%
2   [A-Z]
```

to omit any action, *lex* does not visibly object. Yet when the resulting *lex.yy.c* file is compiled, the output in Fig. 4-5 results. To say the least, this is disconcerting, but with practice a programmer can become familiar enough with the quirks of *lex* to know how to decipher such arcane messages. [Schreiner and Friedman 85] provide much practical insight into the use of *lex*.

```
% lex badreplace.l
% cc -o badreplace lex.yy.c -ll
"lex.yy.c", line 31: case not in switch
"lex.yy.c", line 32: illegal break
"lex.yy.c", line 33: duplicate default in switch
"lex.yy.c", line 35: syntax error
"lex.yy.c", line 35: warning: old-fashioned initialization: use =
"lex.yy.c", line 35: warning: old-fashioned initialization: use =
"lex.yy.c", line 37: warning: undeclared initializer name yyvstop
"lex.yy.c", line 37: warning: old-fashioned initialization: use =
"lex.yy.c", line 40: cannot recover from earlier errors: goodbye!
```

Figure 4-5. *lex* Processing of *badreplace.l*.

Second Example: Count

The second example has all three parts and illustrates much of the power of *lex*:

```
1    %{
2      int  numchar=0, numword=0, numline=0;
3    %}
4
5    %%
6
7    \n            {numline++; numchar++;}
8    [^ \t\n]+     {numword++; numchar += yyleng;}
9    .             {numchar++;}
10
11   %%
12
13   main ()
14   {
15       yylex();
16       printf ("%d\t%d\t%d\n", numchar, numword, numline);
17   }
```

When this is processed by *lex*, compiled, and run against *count.l*, the specification itself, the result is:

```
% lex count.l
% cc -o count lex.yy.c -ll
% cat count.l ¦ count
248     29      17
```

The first part contains global declarations defining variables which are referenced in the actions associated with the patterns in the second part. It also has other uses revealed in the next section.

The second part has three patterns in lines 7–9. The first pattern matches a newline, the second matches one or more occurrences of a string consisting of characters other than blank, tab, and newline, and the third pattern matches any character except newline. There is an implicit rule that causes any character not otherwise matched by a pattern to be written to `stdout`.

lex effectively tries to match all three patterns concurrently with a simple tie-breaking strategy:

1. Always match the longest possible input string.
2. If two patterns match the same string, use the first one in the list.

Hence, on string

```
"a bc \n"
```

count would match `"a"` and `"bc"` with the second pattern, the two spaces with the third pattern, and the newline with the first pattern.

lex actually implements pattern matching by first constructing a non-deterministic FSM to represent the patterns and then converting it into a deterministic machine that accepts the same language. Such a conversion guarantees that the analyzer can process the input string in a linear function of the length of the input; however, the conversion from non-deterministic to deterministic FSM can lead to an exponential growth in the number of machine states. Hence, in some cases *lex* produces very large (but fast) analyzers.

The third part of the example has a user-defined main program which appears in place of the default main program supplied in the *lex* library. The analyzer function produced by *lex* is called `yylex` as was the one produced by *gioconda*. It normally reads characters from `stdin` and assigns values to several global variables when it returns including:

Global Variable	Purpose
`char yytext[]`	actual string matched
`int yylineno`	line number of string matched
`int yyleng`	length of `yytext`

`yylex` returns 0 unless action code explicitly returns another value. Information necessary for error recovery can be passed to the calling routine using global variables or through encoding error information in the return value for `yylex`. The state of the lexical analyzer equivalent to `yycurstate` in *gioconda* can also be explicitly assigned to a global variable in action code or can be passed to the calling routine in the return value for `yylex`.

Lexical Analyzer for Ginevra

The final example recasts the lexical analyzer for *ginevra* into a *lex* specification. The original specification appeared in Section 2.4:

```
1   %{
2
3       #include "token.h"
4       #include "table.h"
5
```

```
 6    int     preproc;
 7    int     i;
 8    int     ateof=0;
 9
10    %}
11
12    %%
13
14    [ \t]+                         ;
15
16    [\n]                      return (yytext[0]);
17
18    \'([^'\n]¦\\['\n])+\' return (STRING);
19
20    \"([^"\n]¦\\["\n])*\" return (STRING);
21
22    "/*""/"*([^*/]¦[^*]"/"¦"*"[^/])*"*""*"*/"    ;
23
24    define              return (DEFINE);
25
26    [A-Za-z][A-Za-z0-9]+  return (IDENT);
27
28    .                     return (OTHER);
29
30    %%
31
32    yywrap ()
33    {
34       ateof = 1;
35       return 1;
36    }
```

The first pattern matches whitespace which is simply one or more blanks or tabs. Since the action does not include a **return** statement, after whitespace has been matched, yylex simply tries to match another pattern, precisely, the action desired.

The second pattern matches newlines. In this case, however, a token has been successfully found and yylex returns the value '\n'.

The third pattern matches single-quoted character literals. It accounts for the fact that a quote can be escaped by preceding it with backslash \ and continued onto another line if the newline is escaped with backslash. It is rather interesting and should be understood before continuing. The fourth pattern, for double-quoted character strings, is just a slight variation on the third.

Comments are defined in the fifth pattern, by far the most challenging presented so far, worthy of careful examination. The pattern correctly deals with /*/, which is not a comment, correctly notes that /*////*/ is a comment (i.e., that the embedded /* does not begin a new comment), and that /**/ is a comment. It also correctly handles multiple-line comments, which, unlike strings, are continued without special escapes. Comments begin with /*. They are followed by any number of slashes, "/"*. At this point there are three alternative continuations which can appear zero or more times ((..¦..¦..)*). The first is any character except a star or slash, [^*/]. It is the ordinary case. The second is any character except a star, but followed by a slash, [^*]"/". This slash does not end a comment since it was not preceded by a star. The third is a star followed by any character except a slash. This also does not end the comment. These are followed by any number of stars followed by a final star followed by a slash, *"*"*/. Whew! Note that unlike the delimiters for character and string literals, it is not possible to escape the meaning of star and slash in a comment. The other patterns are straightforward mappings from the original code in Section 2.4.

The major remaining issue is the handling of end of file. Unfortunately, *lex* has what can fairly be considered a significant design flaw in that it does not allow a rule to explicitly handle end of file. Instead of having a special pattern symbol such as "@" match end of file, the function yywrap is automatically invoked by yylex when it cannot read any further input characters (to "wrap up" processing). The default yywrap does nothing but return the value 1, indicating that there is no special action to take on end of file. The user can write his or her own yywrap which sets an end of file flag and then explicitly check for it after yylex returns. In this example, integer variable ateof is used for this purpose. If ateof is 1 when yylex returns, the current token should be assigned EOFILE; otherwise, it should remain whatever value was returned by yylex.

Finally, *lex* can be made to read from a file other than `stdin` by reassigning the globally accessible `FILE` pointer `yyin`. With slight additional tweeks left as exercises, the original *ginevra* can integrate smoothly with this *lex* specification.

4.6. LEXICAL ANALYZERS FOR PASCAL AND C

To more fully illustrate *lex*'s use in compilers, scanners for full Pascal and *C* are presented. For each token the scanner writes a line that indicates the integer returned by `yylex`, the length of the token, and the actual string in `yytext`.

Keywords are distinguished from other identifiers. There is a `lookup` function for each scanner which determines whether the current token is a keyword. If so, it returns a unique integer for that keyword; otherwise, it returns its argument. To establish the unique number for each token group and keyword, *yacc* is used. Although *yacc* will not formally be introduced until Chapter 8, it is enough to know that it generates file *y.tab.h* of defined constants that associate a unique integer with each multi-character token, token group, and keyword. The *lex* specification includes *y.tab.h*.

Pascal

In Pascal ([Jensen and Wirth 85]) upper- and lowercase letters are not distinct in identifiers; for example,

```
Hello   HELLO   HeLlO
```

are all the same identifier. This also holds true for keywords, which is reflected in the call to `lower` in `lookup`. `lower` returns its argument with all uppercase letters replaced by their lowercase equivalents:

```
1    %{
2    #include "y.tab.h"      /* generated by yacc */
3
4    #define token(x)    x
5    %}
6
7    alpha       [a-zA-Z_]
8    alphanum    [a-zA-Z_0-9]
9    comment     "{"[^}]*"}"
10   exponent    e([+-])?[0-9]+
11   string      \'([^'\n]¦\'\')+\'
12   unsignedint [0-9]+
13   whitespace  [ \t\n]
14
15   %%
16
17   ">="                         return token(GE);
18   "<="                         return token(LE);
19   "<>"                         return token(NE);
20   ":="                         return token(ASSIGN);
21   ".."                         return token(DOTDOT);
22
23   {alpha}{alphanum}*           return lookup(IDENT);
24
25   {unsignedint}                return token(INT);
26
27   {unsignedint}\.{unsignedint}({exponent})?  return token(REAL);
28
29   {unsignedint}{exponent}?     return token(INT);
30
31   {string}                     return token(STRING);
32
33   {whitespace}+                ;
34
35   {comment}+                   ;
36
37   .                            return token(yytext[0]);
38
39   %%
```

```
40
41    main ()
42    {
43        int t;
44
45        while (t = yylex())
46            printf ("token %d with length %d is \"%s\"\n", t, yyleng,
47                    yytext);
48    }
```

It correctly handles Pascal comments and character strings, including the somewhat bizzare:

```
''''
```

which is a string containing a single quote. There is no null string literal in Pascal. The last specification reveals another *lex* feature. Part 1 defines several named patterns in lines 7–13 which are referenced in curly brackets in part 2. Named patterns such as whitespace improve readability and modifiability of *lex* specifications as do defined constants in *C*.

lookup and its supporting code is:

```
1     #include <stdio.h>
2     #include <ctype.h>
3     #include "y.tab.h"
4     #define   token(x)    x
5
6     char yytext[];
7
8     static struct keyword {
9            char  *name;          /* actual symbol in source text */
10           int   token_yylex;    /* value to return from scanner */
11     } keytable[] = {
12     "and",          token(AND),
13     "array",        token(ARRAY),
14     "begin",        token(_BEGIN),
15     "case",         token(CASE),
16     "const",        token(CONST),
17     "div",          token(DIV),
18     "do",           token(DO),
19     "downto",       token(DOWNTO),
20     "else",         token(ELSE),
21     "end",          token(END),
22     "file",         token(_FILE),
23     "for",          token(FOR),
24     "function",     token(FUNCTION),
25     "goto",         token(GOTO),
26     "if",           token(IF),
27     "in",           token(IN),
28     "label",        token(LABEL),
29     "mod",          token(MOD),
30     "nil",          token(NIL),
31     "not",          token(NOT),
32     "of",           token(OF),
33     "or",           token(OR),
34     "packed",       token(PACKED),
35     "procedure",    token(PROCEDURE),
36     "program",      token(PROGRAM),
37     "record",       token(RECORD),
38     "repeat",       token(REPEAT),
39     "set",          token(SET),
40     "then",         token(THEN),
41     "to",           token(TO),
42     "type",         token(TYPE),
43     "until",        token(UNTIL),
44     "var",          token(VAR),
45     "while",        token(WHILE),
46     "with",         token(WITH),
47     0,              0
48     };
```

```
49
50   char *
51   lower (n)  char *n;
52   {
53        static char name[128];
54        register char *p;
55
56        p = (char *)name;
57        while (*n) {
58             isupper(*n) ? (*p++ = *n++ +'a'-'A') : (*p++ = *n++);
59        }
60        *p = '\0';
61        return (char *)name;
62   }
63
64   lookup (t) int t;  /* ignore case of identifier */
65   {
66
67        register struct keyword *p;
68
69        p = keytable;
70
71        while (p->name)
72             if (!strcmp(lower(yytext), p->name))
73                  return p->token_yylex;
74             else
75                  p++;
76        return t;
77   }
```

_BEGIN is used in line 14 because *lex* uses BEGIN internally as a defined constant. FILE, of course, is taken by *stdio.h. y.tab.h*, produced by *yacc*, is:

```
1    # define AND 257
2    # define ARRAY 258
3    # define _BEGIN 259
4    # define CASE 260
5    # define CONST 261
6    # define DIV 262
7    # define DO 263
8    # define DOWNTO 264
9    # define ELSE 265
10   # define END 266
11   # define _FILE 267
12   # define FOR 268
13   # define FUNCTION 269
14   # define GOTO 270
15   # define IF 271
16   # define IN 272
17   # define LABEL 273
18   # define MOD 274
19   # define NIL 275
20   # define NOT 276
21   # define OF 277
22   # define OR 278
23   # define PACKED 279
24   # define PROCEDURE 280
25   # define PROGRAM 281
26   # define RECORD 282
27   # define REPEAT 283
28   # define SET 284
29   # define THEN 285
30   # define TO 286
31   # define TYPE 287
32   # define UNTIL 288
33   # define VAR 289
34   # define WHILE 290
35   # define WITH 291
36   # define IDENT 292
37   # define INT 293
```

```
38   # define REAL 294
39   # define STRING 295
40   # define ASSIGN 296
41   # define NE 297
42   # define GE 298
43   # define LE 299
44   # define DOTDOT 300
```

Numbering starts with 257, which guarantees there is no conflict with any character literally returned in the "." pattern in line 37 of the *lex* specification. A sample Pascal program containing `real` literals with and without exponents, character strings, comments, and numerous keywords appears in Fig. 4-6. The keywords have been written with a mix of upper-and lowercase to demonstrate that the scanner will recognize them. Partial output of the scanner on *sqrt* is:

```
1    token 281 with length 7 is "Program"
2    token 292 with length 4 is "sqrt"
3    token 40 with length 1 is "("
4    token 292 with length 5 is "input"
5    token 44 with length 1 is ","
6    token 292 with length 6 is "output"
7    token 41 with length 1 is ")"
8    token 59 with length 1 is ";"
9    token 261 with length 5 is "Const"
10   token 292 with length 3 is "Eps"
11   token 61 with length 1 is "="
12   token 294 with length 6 is "0.1e-4"
13   token 59 with length 1 is ";"
14   token 289 with length 3 is "Var"
15   token 292 with length 1 is "X"
16   token 44 with length 1 is ","
17   token 292 with length 2 is "X0"
18   token 44 with length 1 is ","
19   token 292 with length 2 is "X1"
     ...
64   token 44 with length 1 is ","
65   token 292 with length 1 is "X"
66   token 44 with length 1 is ","
67   token 295 with length 4 is "'is'"
68   token 44 with length 1 is ","
69   token 292 with length 2 is "X0"
70   token 41 with length 1 is ")"
71   token 59 with length 1 is ";"
72   token 266 with length 3 is "End"
73   token 46 with length 1 is "."
```

C's analyzer is similar to Pascal's but there are several major differences including the fact that *C* has fewer keywords but many more operators, upper-and lowercase letters are distinct, character and string

```
1    Program sqrt (input, output);    {Newton's Method}
2    Const
3         Eps = 0.1e-4;
4    Var
5         X, X0, X1: Real;
6    Begin
7         Readln (X);
8         X1 := X;
9         Repeat
10            X0 := X1;
11            X1 := (X0 + X/X0)*0.5
12        Until abs(X1-X0) < Eps*X1;
13        writeln ('sqrt of ', X, 'is', X0);
14   End. {sqrt}
```

Figure 4-6. Sample Pascal Program *sqrt*.

literals have different forms, there are several numeric constant forms, and comments are bracketed by "/*" and "*/". The *lex* specification is:

```
1    %{
2    #include "y.tab.h"       /* generated by yacc */
3
4    #define token(x)    x
5    %}
6
7    alpha              [a-zA-Z_]
8    alphanum           [a-zA-Z_0-9]
9    char               \'([^'\n]¦\\[ntbrf'\n]¦\\0[0-7]{0,2})+\'
10   comment            "/*""/"*([^*/]¦[^*]"/"¦"*"[^/])*"*"*"*/"
11   exponent           [eE][-+]?[0-9]+
12   string             \"([^"\n]¦\\["\n])*\"
13   unsignedint        [0-9]+
14   whitespace         [ \t\n]
15
16   %%
17
18   ">="                               return token(GE);
19   "<="                               return token(LE);
20   "=="                               return token(EQ);
21   "!="                               return token(NE);
22   "->"                               return token(ARROW);
23   "+="                               return token(PLUSEQ);
24   "-="                               return token(SUBEQ);
25   "*="                               return token(MULTEQ);
26   "/="                               return token(DIVEQ);
27   "%="                               return token(MODEQ);
28   ">>="                              return token(SHREQ);
29   "<<="                              return token(SHLEQ);
30   "&="                               return token(ANDEQ);
31   "¦="                               return token(OREQ);
32   "^="                               return token(EOREQ);
33   "++"                               return token(PP);
34   "--"                               return token(MM);
35
36   {string}                           return token(STRING);
37
38   {char}                             return token(CHARLIT);
39
40   {alpha}{alphanum}*                 return lookup(IDENT);
41
42   0[xX][0-9a-fA-F]*[lL]?             return token(HEX);
43
44   0[0-7]*[lL]?                       return token(OCTAL);
45
46   {unsignedint}[lL]?                 return token(DECIMAL);
47
48   {unsignedint}\.{unsignedint}?({exponent})?   return token(FLOATLIT);
49
50   \.{unsignedint}({exponent})?   return token(FLOATLIT);
51
52   {whitespace}+                      ;
53
54   {comment}+                         ;
55
56   .                                  return token(yytext[0]);
57
58   %%
59
60   main ()
61   {
62       int t;
63
64       while (t = yylex())
65           printf ("token %d with length %d is \"%s\"\n", t, yyleng,
66                   yytext);
67   }
```

The specification does not complain about a character constant that is longer than one character. It does specifically recognize (but does not use) the various escaped sequences in characters such as ' \ n ' and ' \ 0 '. They were included to illustrate more exotic patterns. Note the distinction between octal, hexadecimal, and decimal constants. The ' x ', ' X ', ' l ', and ' L ' really are part of the constant. The *yacc* specification used to produce *y.tab.h* is:

```
 1    /* enough of yacc grammar for C to support lex */
 2
 3    /* keywords */
 4
 5    %token AUTO   BREAK  CASE   CHAR   CONTINUE  DEFAULT  DO   DOUBLE
 6    %token ELSE  ENUM  EXTERN  FLOAT   FOR   GOTO   IF   INT   LONG   REAL
 7    %token REGISTER  RETURN  SHORT  SIZEOF  STATIC  STRUCT  SWITCH
 8    %token TYPEDEF  UNION  UNSIGNED   WHILE
 9
10    /* token groups other than operators -- distinguish between types
11       of numeric literals */
12
13    %token IDENT   STRING   CHARLIT  OCTAL   DECIMAL   HEX   FLOATLIT
14
15    /* operators */
16    %token GE              /* >= */
17    %token LE              /* <= */
18    %token EQ              /* == */
19    %token NE              /* != */
20    %token ARROW           /* -> */
21    %token PLUSEQ          /* += */
22    %token SUBEQ           /* -= */
23    %token MULTEQ          /* *= */
24    %token DIVEQ           /* /= */
25    %token MODEQ           /* %= */
26    %token SHREQ           /* >>= */
27    %token SHLEQ           /* <<= */
28    %token ANDEQ           /* &= */
29    %token OREQ            /* |= */
30    %token EOREQ           /* ^= */
31    %token PP              /* ++ */
32    %token MM              /* -- */
33
34    %%
35    program:
36            ;
```

lookup, not shown here, must be modified so it no longer folds upper- and lowercase letters. The partial output of the scanner run on *lookup.c* is in Fig. 4-7.

```
  1    token 35 with length 1 is "#"
  2    token 286 with length 7 is "include"
  3    token 287 with length 9 is ""y.tab.h""
  4    token 35 with length 1 is "#"
  5    token 286 with length 6 is "define"
  6    token 286 with length 5 is "token"
  7    token 40 with length 1 is "("
  8    token 286 with length 1 is "x"
  9    token 41 with length 1 is ")"
 10    token 286 with length 1 is "x"
         ...
270    token 286 with length 1 is "p"
271    token 297 with length 2 is "->"
272    token 286 with length 11 is "token_yylex"
273    token 59 with length 1 is ";"
274    token 265 with length 4 is "else"
275    token 286 with length 1 is "p"
276    token 308 with length 2 is "++"
277    token 59 with length 1 is ";"
278    token 276 with length 6 is "return"
279    token 286 with length 1 is "t"
280    token 59 with length 1 is ";"
281    token 125 with length 1 is "}"
```

Figure 4-7. Partial Output of Scanner on *lookup.c*.

EXERCISES

1. Write regular grammars for the following languages:

   (a) any number of 1's followed by any number of 0's
   (b) *C* octal constants
   (c) *C* hexadecimal constants
   (d) Pascal real numbers which is an optional sign, followed by one or more digits, a decimal point, one or more digits, optionally followed by an exponent consisting of an 'e', an optional sign, and one or more digits
   (e) all strings of digits with no digit repeated
   (f) all strings of digits that do not have two adjacent digits repeat
   (g) all strings of letters with the vowels in alphabetical order
   (h) all strings of letters with the vowels in any order
   (i) all strings of letters that have at most five vowels

2. Draw deterministic FSMs to recognize the languages of Exercise 1.

3. Construct *lex* programs for parts (a), (e)–(i) of Exercise 1.

4. Describe the following languages which have been written as *lex* patterns:

   (a) `[+-][0-9]+`
   (b) `[A-Z][A-Z]{0,6}`
   (c) `(00|11)+((01|001|110)|1)*`
   (d) `0*1*(0|1)*1*0*`

5. Construct FSMs to recognize the languages of Exercise 4.

6. (a) Write a *lex* program that reads dates of the form:

   mm/*dd*/*yy*

   where *mm* (month) is 01-12, *dd* (day) is 01-31, and *yy* (year) is 00-99, mapping them into their verbose equivalents; for example, 07/04/86 is mapped into

   ```
   July 4, 1986
   ```

   Do not check whether the date is legal; that is, the date "02/31/86" would be mapped into

   ```
   February 31, 1986
   ```

   (b) Add error checking to your specification so that only legal dates are accepted. Check for leap year when deciding if "02/29/??" is legal using the rule that every year divisible by 4 is a leap year except those divisible by 400.

7. Write a *lex* program that correctly recognizes the tokens in FORTRAN assignments and DO loops. Make sure the program correctly handles the two cases:

   ```
   DO10I=1,10
   DO10I=1.10
   ```

8. Write a *lex* program that reads in a FORTRAN program, replacing all occurrences of the token "REAL" with "DOUBLE PRECISION".

9. Write a *lex* program that prints out a character whenever it appears twice in a row; for example,

   ```
   "abbcbaa"
   ```

   would print out:

   ```
   b
   a
   ```

No character should be counted more than once; for example,

    aaa

would print out:

    a

and not count the first and second 'a' as one pair and the second and third 'a' as a second pair.

10. Change the program from the last exercise so that characters can be counted twice; that is, the string "aaa" would match twice.

11. Revise the scanner for *C* given in Section 4.6 so that keywords are distinguished in *lex* patterns rather than through lookup. Compare the object code size and run times for the two versions. Account for the differences.

12. Write a *lex* program that recognizes the tokens of FORTRAN, writing out a line similar to that for the Pascal and *C* scanners in Section 4.6.

13. Write a *lex* program that reverses each line in a file.

14. Write a *lex* program that implements the #define statement of Chapter 2.

15. Extend the program of the last exercise to also support the #undef statement.

16. Prove that a language can be recognized by a FSM if and only if it can be generated by a regular expression constructed from

Operation	Notation
concatenation	PQ
alternation	P ¦ Q
grouping	(P)
closure	P*

17. Prove that a language can be generated by a regular expression if and only if it can be generated by a regular grammar.

18. Prove that a language can be recognized by a nondeterministic FSM if and only if it can be recognized by a deterministic FSM.

Chapter 5
RECURSIVE DESCENT PARSING

5.1. EXPRESS: A LANGUAGE OF ARITHMETIC EXPRESSIONS

Just as regular grammars provide a model for specifying lexical analyzers, a more powerful grammatical form, the *context-free grammar* (CFG), can be used to specify parsers. Originally motivated by studies of natural language [Chomsky 56, Chomsky 59], the CFG, in one variant or another, is the primary formal tool used by language designers to specify language syntax. The descriptions produced using a CFG are well behaved, easy to understand, relatively concise, and completely rigorous.

Unfortunately, the context-free model is limited. Programming languages have features that cannot be modeled by any context-free grammar; for example, there is no context-free grammar for C which will generate all and only programs that declare each referenced variable exactly once. It is not a question of cleverness on the part of the grammar designer, but a provable inadequacy of the context-free model. However, a context-free grammar can be written which approximates the desired language. By tweaking the parser and by using ad hoc techniques during semantic analysis to restrict the programs accepted, the correct language is obtained.

Sometimes a feature that could be captured grammatically should be handled elsewhere in order to simplify the overall compiler structure. Whitespace is particularly notorious in this respect. A context-free grammar could be written which accounts for whitespace token separators, but such a grammar would appear cluttered. Since one of the motivations for a formal grammar is clarity, the handling of whitespace and other relatively simple but clumsy forms such as comments and character string literals are pushed onto the scanner. Since the scanner's job is relatively simple compared to that of the parser, increasing the scanner's complexity slightly to off-load the parser seems like a wise trade-off.

Recognizing the inadequacies of English for precisely stating restrictions on the form of programs, various researchers have proposed rigorous augmentations of the context-free grammar. Among the most important are the *Van Wijngaarden grammar* [Van Wijngaarden et al, 69, Cleaveland and Uzgalis 77] used to define the semantics of Algol 68, the *Vienna Definition Language* in which PL/1 was formally defined [Lucas and Walk 69], *attribute grammars* [Knuth 68] subsequently used by a variety of authors for exploring compiler construction, especially [Lewis, Rosenkrantz, and Stearns 76], and *denotational semantics*, first developed by Dana Scott and Christopher Strachey [Tennent 76, Stoy 77]. The latter is especially interesting because it lends itself well to mathematical analysis of programming language properties. One of the earliest modelers of language semantics, Tony Hoare, played a fundamental role in the evolution of Pascal by using Pascal as the vehicle for exploring semantic issues [Hoare and Wirth 73]. However, the added precision that formal semantic models offer is more than offset here by the increased complexity inherent in their notations. No formal semantic models will be employed here.

The language chosen to illustrate the context-free grammar is *express*, whose elements are some of the legal arithmetic expressions of *C*. A CFG has four parts just as a regular grammar does: nonterminals, terminals, axiom, and rules. However, context-free rules take on a more general form than those in regular grammars, allowing the production of more interesting strings. A rule has the form

$b: x_1 \ x_2 \ \ldots \ x_n$

or

```
b:
```

where $x_1, \ldots, x_n$ are either terminals or nonterminals. As before, the second form of rule is called a *null rule*. The difference between regular and context-free rules is that there can be any number of nonterminals in a context-free rule and they can appear anywhere on the right-hand side. In regular rules only one nonterminal could appear, and it had to be the right-most symbol.

Example 5-1. The fundamental consequence of generalizing the form of rules in CFGs is best illustrated by noting that a trivial CFG can generate strings of correctly nested parentheses, while no regular grammar can:

```
()    (())    ((()))    (((())))    ((((()))))    ...
```

This language is generated by the CFG, *paren*, with two terminals ' (' and ') ', one nonterminal *p* which is also the axiom, and two rules:

```
1.  p: '('  p  ')'
2.  p: '('  ')'
```

The derivation of " ((( ))) " is

```
1   p                                    - axiom
2   '('  p  ')'                          - rule 1
3   '('  '('  p  ')'  ')'                - rule 1
4   '('  '('  '('  ')'  ')'  ')'         - rule 2
```

Each line in the derivation is called a *sentential form*.
◆

In future examples, quotes around terminals will be omitted where there is no risk of confusion.

The essential reason why no regular grammar can generate properly nested parentheses is summarized in the name of the machine model that recognizes regular language—*finite*-state. A finite-state machine can remember only a limited (finite) amount of information about what it has previously seen. Intuitively, it is like having a counter with a limited number of digits which is incremented by one for each ' (' and decremented by one for each ') ' seen. If it never sees any ' (' after it sees the first ') ', and the counter is 0 after the last parenthesis is seen, the string is in the language. When a string is seen with more left parentheses than the counter can hold, the machine cannot reliably track how many parentheses there really are. When right parentheses are finally seen, it cannot count down accurately to guarantee there is one right parenthesis for every left one.

Grammar *gram-express* generates the arithmetic expressions of interest. There are two nonterminals, *e* (expression) and *o* (operator), and seven terminals:

```
(   )   +   -   *   /   INTEGER
```

Terminal **INTEGER** is special. It is a *named* terminal, so called because it is an identifier that represents one or more actual terminals, in this case the set of integer literals. Any token longer than one character is named, a style motivated by *lex*. For example, the Pascal assignment operator " : = " might appear as the named token **ASSIGN** in a grammar. Named token **INTEGER** can appear anywhere in *gram-express* where an integer can appear in the language.

gram-express has two productions, each with several alternatives:

```
1.  e:  e o e  ¦  ( e )  ¦  INTEGER  ¦  - INTEGER  ¦  - ( e )

2.  o:  +  ¦  -  ¦  *  ¦  /
```

Note the use of **INTEGER**. This grammar generates properly parenthesized arithmetic expressions over the four basic arithmetic operations. Operands are either signed or unsigned integer literals.

```
1    e
2    e   o   e
3    1   o   e
4    1   +   e
5    1   +   e   o   e
6    1   +   20   o   e
7    1   +   20   *   e
8    1   +   20   *   -   2
```

Figure 5-1. Derivation of "1+20*-2" using *gram-express*.

Derivations

Example 5-2. A derivation of "1+20*-2" is in Fig. 5-1. This derivation can be represented graphically in a *derivation tree* which explicitly shows each replacement step. The derivation tree for "1+20*-2" is in Fig. 5-2.

A string will in some cases have more than one derivation tree associated with it. A second derivation tree for the same string is shown in Fig. 5-3.

♦

If every string generated by a grammar has exactly one parse tree, that grammar is said to be *unambiguous*. *paren* is unambiguous. If one or more strings in the language of a grammar has two parse trees, that grammar is said to be *ambiguous*. *gram-express* is ambiguous because the sentence "1+20*-2" has two distinct parse trees.

Ignoring the fact that *C* arithmetic expressions actually have a well-defined evaluation order, the string "1+20*-2" could reasonably be evaluated in either of two ways: addition can be performed before multiplication, or conversely. The answer computed will vary depending on the order in which these two operations are performed. In the former case the value is −42, in the latter it is −39. If "1+20*-2" were rewritten as a fully parenthesized expression, then the choice in ordering the evaluation of operations would disappear. Each expression would have just one interpretation:

```
((1+20)*-2)          (1+(20*-2))
```

The first derivation tree groups "1" and "20" together under the addition operator, while the second tree groups "20" and "-2" together under the multiplication sign. Viewing these groupings within a derivation tree as being logically equivalent to parenthesizing the string, the first tree corresponds to the first evaluation, while the second tree represents the second evaluation. Obviously it is desirable to have the derivation reflect the evaluation order.

There are an infinite number of distinct grammars for any language; some will be ambiguous, while others will not. There are some languages that are *inherently ambiguous*, that is, have no unambiguous grammars. They are not, however, of practical concern. For more information on these peculiar languages see [Hopcroft and Ullman 69].

Grammars that drive the parser of a compiler are usually unambiguous. In this way, each string has a unique grammatical description. Alternatively, the compiler writer might use a grammar that is ambigu-

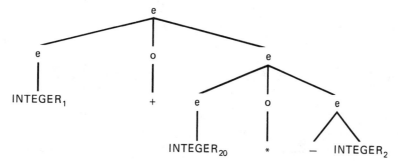

Figure 5-2. Derivation Tree for "1+20*-2".

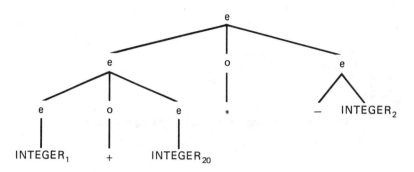

Figure 5-3. Second Derivation Tree for "1+20*-2".

ous, but apply some extra-grammatical means to *disambiguate* it, that is, remove the ambiguity. The parser is, in effect, augmented with special information to tell it how to disambiguate.

Unambiguous Grammars

The next example is an unambiguous grammar for *express*. In addition, the derivation trees of this new grammar, *unambig-express*, express all of the implicit precedence in *C*. Multiplication and division are performed before addition and subtraction scanning left to right across an expression. The terminals are the same as for *gram-express*. The nonterminals are e (express), t (term), ao (additive operator), mo (multiplicative operator), and f (factor):

```
1.  e:  t  ¦  e  ao  t
2.  t:  f  ¦  t  mo  f
3.  f:  ( e )  ¦  INTEGER  ¦  - INTEGER  ¦  - ( e )
4.  ao:  +  ¦  -
5.  mo:  *  ¦  /
```

The unique derivation tree of "1+20*-2" is pictured in Fig. 5-4. Even though *unambig-express* is unambiguous, it still has certain undesirable properties which will be studied in the next section.

5.2. TOP-DOWN RECURSIVE DESCENT PARSING

The previous discussion explained what a derivation tree is, but did not address how to actually construct the derivation tree for a string. The rest of this chapter and all the next analyzes one particular class of parsers called *top-down*, so called because they construct the derivation tree from the root to the frontier, and by custom, the root of the tree is always its top. Chapter 7 explores the other common approach, called *bottom-up* parsing.

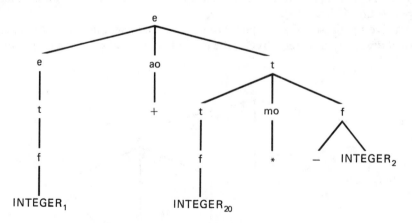

Figure 5-4. Unique Derivation Tree of "1+20*-2".

Example 5-3. Some of the problems that arise in parsing are illustrated by trying to parse "1+20*-2" using *unambig-express*. If the leftmost nonterminal is replaced in each step of a derivation, that derivation is said to be *leftmost*. One non-leftmost derivation of "1+20*-2" using *unambig-express* is in Fig. 5-5. It is not leftmost because '+' is derived from *ao* before *e* is expanded in the third line. The leftmost derivation of the same string is in Fig. 5-6.

◆

Each derivation tree has a unique leftmost derivation associated with it; thus, the leftmost derivation is a normal form for arbitrary derivations. Many parsing algorithms generate a leftmost derivation of a sentence; in particular, the top-down parsing algorithm described in this chapter does so.

The *recursive descent* parsing method is so called because it is implemented by a set of recursive procedures, one to correspond to each nonterminal of the grammar. This was illustrated in Chapter 3 where *cecilia* was presented. Such a parser descends the tree, actually constructing the tree during the descent. In general, the recursive descent parser is too inefficient for practical use; however, under special conditions it becomes quite efficient and practical.

Consider the problem of generating the leftmost derivation of "1+20*-2" with respect to grammar *unambig-express*. The operating principle of brute force recursive descent parsing is to guess which rule should be applied in constructing the leftmost derivation, try it, backtrack out of the consequences of that choice if it proves to be wrong, then try another guess. This trial and error is repeated until the derivation is produced or there are no more alternatives to try.

All leftmost derivations begin with the axiom, *e*, so initially the leftmost derivation of "1+20*-2" must be just the single symbol:

    1   *e*

At this point, there are two alternative rules which can be applied, rules 1.1 (first alternative of rule 1) and 1.2 (second alternative of rule 1). Having no other basis upon which to decide at this time, the first alternative is selected; if that fails to lead to the desired derivation, and that failure can be recognized, the erroneous step will be undone and rule 1.2 will be tried instead:

    2   *t*

Rule 2.1 replaces *t* by *f*:

    3   *f*

which in turn leads to

    4   (*e*)

In order for "1+20*-2" to eventually be derived from (e), the longest leading substring of terminal symbols must also be a leading substring of "1+20*-2". The longest such substring is " (". Matching this against "1+20*-2", it is clear that this derivation is incorrect.

At this point the parser can backtrack out of its guess in step 4 that rule 3.1 was correct and try rule 3.2, giving

    4'   1

```
 1    e
 2    e    ao   t
 3    e    +    t
 4    t    +    t
 5    t    +    t    mo   f
 6    f    +    t    mo   f
 7    1    +    t    mo   f
 8    1    +    t    *    f
 9    1    +    f    *    f
10    1    +    20   *    f
11    1    +    20   *    -    2
```

Figure 5-5. Derivation of "1+20*-2" Using *unambig-express*.

```
 1     e
 2     e   ao   t
 3     t   ao   t
 4     f   ao   t
 5     1   ao   t
 6     1   +    t
 7     1   +    t    mo   f
 8     1   +    f    mo   f
 9     1   +    20   mo   f
10     1   +    20   *    f
11     1   +    20   *    -    2
```

Figure 5-6. Leftmost Derivation of "1+20*-2" Using *unambig-express*.

This derivation matches the first token of "1+20*-2" correctly; unfortunately, there are no nonterminals left in the sentential form, but there are more tokens in "1+20*-2". A sentential form consisting solely of terminals can only derive itself. This fact triggers rejection of this derivation.

Backing out of the selection of rule 3.2 leads to the trial and rejection of the rest of the alternatives of rule 3. Hence, the erroneous guess must have come earlier than the choice of rule 2.1 in derivation step 3. Trying rule 2.2 instead of 2.1 produces

```
 2'    t   mo   f
```

This choice too is wrong because the original choice of rule 1.1 in step 1 was wrong; however, the parser as described using the two rejection strategies:

1. Reject a derivation if the longest leading substring of terminals of the current sentential form is not a leading substring the string being parsed.
2. Reject a derivation if there are no more nonterminals in the sentential form and the form is not equal to the string being parsed.

will never discover its error! The parser will continue searching indefinitely for a leftmost derivation; the partial history of this unsuccessful search, shown in Fig. 5-7, reveals why: failure to find the derivation of "1+20*-2" results from a special property of *unambig-express*. It is *left recursive*. Production *b:w* is said to be *directly left recursive* if *w* has form *bz* where *z* is not null. Such a rule leads to derivations of the form:

```
b
bz
bzz
. . .
```

An arbitrary number of *z*'s can be pushed off to the right without ever terminating the derivation. If there is a derivation:

```
e
t
f
(   e   )                        *backtrack*
1                                *backtrack*
-   INTEGER                      *backtrack*
-   (   e   )                    *backtrack*
t   mo   f
f   mo   f
(   e   )   mo   f               *backtrack*
1   mo   f
-   INTEGER   mo   f             *backtrack*
-   (   e   )   mo   f           *backtrack*
      . . .
```

Figure 5-7. Unsuccessful Search for "1+20*-2".

b
w
...
bz

where z is not null, then rule $b : w$ is said to be *indirectly left recursive*. Such a rule can also lead to derivations that push an arbitrary number of z's to the right without terminating the derivation. A rule that is either directly or indirectly left recursive is said to be *left recursive*. The left-hand side of a left recursive rule is a *left recursive nonterminal*. A grammar that has one or more left recursive nonterminals is itself a *left recursive grammar*. The next section develops an algorithm that eliminates left recursion from any grammar.

5.3. ELIMINATING LEFT RECURSION

Since left recursion causes a problem for recursive descent parsing, the obvious step is to eliminate left recursion. A left recursive grammar can be modified into one which generates the same language but is not left recursive.

Algorithm 5-1. `directelim`.
Purpose: Eliminate direct left recursion for rules with left-hand side b.
Steps: Replace the original productions:

$b: \quad b \ w_1 \ \vert \ b \ w_2 \ \vert \ \ldots \ \vert \ b \ w_m \ \vert \ v_1 \ \vert \ \ldots \ \vert \ v_k$

by

$b: \quad v_1 \ C \ \vert \ v_2 \ C \ \vert \ \ldots \ \vert \ v_k \ C$
$C: \quad w_1 \ C \ \vert \ w_2 \ C \ \vert \ \ldots \ \vert \ w_m \ C \ \vert$

where C is a new nonterminal.

◆

The second algorithm eliminates general left recursion, whether direct or not. It makes multiple passes over the grammar, essentially removing one level of indirection of left recursion between two nonterminals in each pass. If the grammar originally had rules $b : dw$ and $d : bz$, then after one pass it would instead have $b : bzw$ and $d : bz$ instead. Now the direct left recursion of production $b : bzw$ can be eliminated. If there are n nonterminals, then after n-1 passes, all left recursion will have been eliminated.

Algorithm 5-2. `genelim`.
Purpose: Eliminate general left recursion from grammar G.
Input: Grammar G with ordered nonterminals $b_1, b_2, \ldots, b_m$.
Output: Grammar equivalent to G, but without left recursion.
Steps

```
1    genelim () {
2        int i,j;
3
4        for (i=1; i≤m; i++) {   /* for each nonterminal */
5            for (j=1; j<i; j++) { /* for each nonterm with lesser index */
6                for (each rule b₁:bⱼw and bⱼ:z) {
7                    remove rule b₁:bⱼw;
8                    add rule b₁:zw;
9                }
10           }
11           directelim (b₁);
12       }
13   }
```

◆

`genelim` assumes that the grammar has no *cyclic nonterminals*, that is, no nonterminals that derive themselves in one or more steps as in

```
b
w
...
b
```

It also assumes there are no null productions. There are algorithms that eliminate both null productions and cyclic nonterminals from arbitrary context-free grammars. These can be applied to a grammar before trying to eliminate left recursion; their specification is left as Exercises 7 and 10.

Left recursion can be removed from *unambig-express* using algorithm `genelim`. This grammar has no null rules or cyclic nonterminals. In fact, *unambig-express* does not really require the full power of `genelim`; if the nonterminals are ordered,

```
e   t   f   ao   mo
```

then there are no rules of the form

```
b₁:   bⱼ  w
```

where $i < j$, so that `directelim` suffices.

Example 5-4. Suppose the nonterminals in *unambig-express* have the order shown above. Calling `directelim(e)` yields a grammar with

```
e: t  ¦  e  ao  t
```

replaced by:

```
e:   t  es
es:  ao  t  es  ¦
```

where *es* is a new nonterminal. Invoking `directelim(t)` similarly causes

```
t:  f  ¦  t  mo  f
```

to be replaced by

```
t:  f  ts
ts:  mo  f  ts  ¦
```

with new nonterminal *ts*. Since none of the other nonterminals are left recursive, further calls to `directelim` have no effect. The resulting grammar is *norec-express*:

```
1.   e:   t  es
2.   es:  ao  t  es  ¦
3.   t:   f  ts
4.   ts:  mo  f  ts  ¦
5.   f:   ( e )  ¦  INTEGER  ¦  - INTEGER  ¦  - ( e )
6.   ao:  +  ¦  -
7.   mo:  *  ¦  /
```

The leftmost derivation of "1+20*-2" with respect to *norec-express* is in Fig. 5-8.

♦

Example 5-5. To illustrate the full power of `genelim` the nonterminals are reordered, interchanging *t* and *e*:

```
t  e  f  ao  mo
```

Initialize i to 1 and j to 1 in lines 4 and 5. Since j = i, the **for** loop in lines 5–10 is skipped, leading to the invocation of `directelim(t)`. The alternative productions of *t* are:

```
t:  f  ¦  t  mo  f
```

which are replaced by

```
t:   f  ts
ts:  mo  f  ts  ¦
```

The second time through the outer loop, i = 2, forcing the examination of rules

```
e:  t  ¦  e  ao  t
```

Since the index of *t* = 1 and the index of *e* = 2, the inner loop is entered. Rule *e : t* is removed and rule

```
e:  f  ts
```

is added. Calling `directelim(e)` forces the replacement of

```
e:  e  ao  t
```

by

```
e:   f  ts  es
es:  ao  t  es  ¦
```

At this point the grammar rules are

```
e:   f  ts  es  ¦  f  ts
es:  ao  t  es  ¦
t:   f  ts
ts:  mo  f  ts  ¦
f:   ( e )  ¦  INTEGER  ¦  -  INTEGER  ¦  -  ( e )
ao:  +  ¦  -
mo:  *  ¦  /
```

Additional steps of the algorithm will not produce any further changes. Note that this grammar differs from *norec-express* because the rules with left-hand side *e* are distinct. The ordering of the nonterminals

```
 1   e
 2   t  es
 3   f  ts  es
 4   1  ts  es
 5   1  es
 6   1  ao  t  es
 7   1  +  t  es
 8   1  +  f  ts  es
 9   1  +  20  ts  es
10   1  +  20  mo  f  ts  es
11   1  +  20  *  f  ts  es
12   1  +  20  *  -  2  ts  es
13   1  +  20  *  -  2  es
14   1  +  20  *  -  2
```

Figure 5-8. Leftmost Derivation of " ' 1+20*-2" Using *norec-express*.

affects the grammar produced by algorithm `genelim`; however, all grammars produced are equivalent, in that they generate the same language, and all grammars produced are free of left recursion.

◆

With the elimination of left recursion, the brute force recursive descent parser will always find a leftmost derivation of a string if, indeed, one exists at all. If there is no leftmost derivation, the parser will halt and reject the string as not belonging to the language.

5.4. A PARSER FOR EXPRESS

The implementation of `parse-express`, the recursive descent parser modeled after *norec-express*, is now presented. It prints the line ''is a sentence'' if the string is successfully parsed, otherwise, it prints ''is not a sentence''.

Each rule of *norec-express* is represented by a single function; that is, there is a function e, *es*, *t*, and so on. The flow of control in each procedure maps cleanly from the structure of the right-hand side of the alternative rules it represents. It is easy to see how the derivation tree is virtually constructed as the recursive functions are invoked. The scanner is not shown, but is assumed to have been constructed using *lex* with the two conventions that (1) when the end of file is reached, integer variable `_ateof` is set to 1, otherwise it is 0; and (2) `yylex` returns the type of token encountered such as integer, asterisk, etc. There are defined constants for these states with the obvious names: `_INTEGER`, `_ASTERISK`, and so on.

```
1       /* parse-express */
2       int token;
3
4       main()
5       {   _ateof = 0;   /* not at end of file initially */
6           token = yylex ();   /* get first token */
7           if (e() && _ateof) {
8               printf ("is a sentence\n");
9               exit (0);
10          }
11          else {
12              printf ("is not a sentence\n");
13              exit (1);
14          }
15      }
16
17      e()   /* look for a string derived from e */
18      {
19          if (t() && es())   /* rule 1 */
20              return 1;
21          return 0;
22      }
23
24      es()   /* look for a string derived from es */
25      {
26          if (ao() && t() && es())   /* rule 2.1 */
27              return 1;
28          return 1;   /* rule 2.2 */
29      }
30
31      t()   /* look for a string derived from t */
32      {
33          if (f() && ts())   /* rule 3 */
34              return 1;
35          return 0;
36      }
37
38      ts()   /* look for a string derived from ts */
39      {
40          if (mo() && f() && ts())   /* rule 4.1 */
41              return 1;
42          return 1;   /* rule 4.2 */
```

```
43          }
44
45          f()     /* look for a string derived from f */
46          {
47              if (token == _LEFTPAREN) { /* rule 5.1 */
48                  token = yylex ();
49                  if (e ())
50                      if (token == _RIGHTPAREN) {
51                          token = yylex ();
52                          return 1;
53                      }
54              }
55              else if (token == _INTEGER) { /* rule 5.2 */
56                  token = yylex ();
57                  return 1;
58              }
59              else if (token == _MINUS) { /* rule 5.3 */
60                  token = yylex ();
61                  if ((token == _INTEGER) {
62                      token = yylex ();
63                      return 1;
64                  }
65              }
66              else if (token == _MINUS) { /* rule 5.4 */
67                token = yylex ();
68                if (token == _LEFTPAREN) {
69                    token = yylex ();
70                    if (e())
71                        if (token == _RIGHTPAREN) {
72                            token = yylex ();
73                            return 1;
74                        }
75                }
76              }
77              return 0;
78          }
79
80          ao()    /* look for a string derived from ao */
81          {
82              if (token == _PLUS) { /* rule 6.1 */
83                  token = yylex ();
84                  return 1;
85              }
86              else if (token == _MINUS) { /* rule 6.2 */
87                  token = yylex ();
88                  return 1;
89              }
90              return 0;
91          }
92
93          mo()    /* look for a string derived from mo */
94          {
95              if (token == _ASTERISK) {  /* rule 7.1 */
96                  token = yylex ();
97                  return 1;
98              }
99              else if (token == _SLASH) {  /* rule 7.2 */
100                 token = yylex ();
101                 return 1;
102             }
103             return 0;
104         }
```

A trace of parse-express on string "1+20" is in Fig. 5-9 (the trace on "1+20*-2" is too long to show). The caret marks the current input token. The line number where each function call is made is indicated to the right of the function name.

parse-express is actually quite special because it turns out that the parser will never actually need to backtrack out of a bad choice. This is a consequence of it being an LL(1) grammar, the topic of the next chapter. In general though, a parser built on a non-left recursive grammar that is not LL(1) may need to backtrack an arbitrary amount of choices.

```
        INPUT       NESTED  CALLS

 1.   ^1+20       e#7
 2.   ^1+20       e#7   t#19
 3.   ^1+20       e#7   t#19   f#33
 4.   ^1+20       e#7   t#19   f#33    match 1#55   return 1#57
 5.   1^+20       e#7   t#19   ts#33
 6.   1^+20       e#7   t#19   ts#33   mo#40
 7.   1^+20       e#7   t#19   ts#33   mo#40   fail return 0#103
 8.   1^+20       e#7   t#19   ts#33   return 1#42
 9.   1^+20       e#7   t#19   return 1#34
10.   1^+20       e#7   es#19
11.   1^+20       e#7   es#19   ao#26
12.   1^+20       e#7   es#19   ao#26   match +#82 return 1#84
13.   1+^20       e#7   es#19   t#26
14.   1+^20       e#7   es#19   t#26   f#33
15.   1+^20       e#7   es#19   t#26   f#33    match 20#55 return 1#57
16.   1+20^       e#7   es#19   t#26   ts#33
17.   1+20^       e#7   es#19   t#26   ts#33   mo#40
18.   1+20^       e#7   es#19   t#26   ts#33   mo#40   fail return 0#103
19.   1+20^       e#7   es#19   t#26   ts#33   return 1#42
20.   1+20^       e#7   es#19   t#26   return 1#34
21.   1+20^       e#7   es#19   es#26
22.   1+20^       e#7   es#19   es#26   ao#26
23.   1+20^       e#7   es#19   es#26   ao#26   fail return 0#90
24.   1+20^       e#7   es#19   es#26   return 1#28
25.   1+20^       e#7   es#19   return 1#27
26.   1+20^       e#7   return 1#20
```

Figure 5-9. Trace of `parse-express` on `"1+20"`.

Example 5-6. Consider the following simple unambiguous grammar with terminals W, X, Y, and Z:

```
1   e:  X   f   ¦   X   g
2   f:  X   h   ¦   X   i
3   h:  Z
4   i:  W
5   g:  X   Y
```

In recognizing string `"XXY"` the corresponding parser would make the following choices with the rule selected shown in parentheses:

```
 1.   e         (1.1)
 2.   X   f     (2.1)
 3.   X   X   h   (3)
 4.   X   X   Z   *fail—backtrack
 5.   X   f     (2.2)
 6.   X   X   i   (4)
 7.   X   X   W   *fail—backtrack twice
 8.   e         (1.2)
 9.   X   g     (5)
10.   X   X   Y
```

◆

The parser must backtrack out of a bad choice several times which forces it to not only unwind from the recursive function calls, it must also back up in the input string and "unsee" the tokens it has already processed. Obviously, this is quite expensive and very undesirable. Aside from the storage cost in having to buffer the entire input string, the execution time for a recursive descent parser can, in general, be rather abysmal. In the worst case it requires $O(k^n)$ time, for some integer constant k, where n is the length of the string being parsed. This long execution time arises from the need to constantly recover from erroneous guesses.

A second problem with the recursive descent approach is the need to mar the grammar's appearance to eliminate left recursion. Grammar *norec-express* does not look as natural as *unambig-express* even though they are equivalent. Unfortunately, there is no way to avoid marring the grammar's appearance and still retain the needed parsing power using top-down approaches. The method described in the next chapter reduces parsing time to $O(n)$ for a certain class of languages which seem to encompass all programming languages of interest, but only parses grammars of a special, somewhat unnatural form; for example, they may not be left recursive.

The method described in the next chapter requires a more obscure grammar for the sake of efficiency; however, it is not necessary to have just one version of a grammar available. A clear natural version can be made available for documentation. A second, more obscure version, can be used for parsing. This becomes especially reasonable when the grammar suitable for parsing is algorithmically derived from the natural grammar, thus assuring their equivalence.

EXERCISES

1. Consider the context-free grammar:

```
1  s: ( b ) ¦ X
2  b: X , s ¦ Y
```

(a)

- **(i)** What are the terminals?
- **(ii)** What are the nonterminals?
- **(iii)** What is the start symbol?
- **(iv)** Is the grammar left recursive?
- **(v)** Is the grammar ambiguous?

(b) Draw parse trees for the following strings:

- **(i)** X
- **(ii)** (Y)
- **(iii)** (X , (X , (Y)))

(c) Construct a leftmost derivation for each string.

(d) Implement a recursive descent parser for the grammar.

2. Consider the grammar:

```
1  s: ( b ) ¦ X
2  b: s , X ¦ s s
```

(a) Is the grammar left recursive? Ambiguous?

(b) Draw parse trees for the following strings:

- **(i)** X
- **(ii)** (((X , X) X) , X)
- **(iii)** (X (X (X , X)))

(c) Construct a leftmost derivation for each string.

(d) Implement a recursive descent parser for the grammar.

3. Trace the execution of *parse-express* on the following strings:

- **(a)** 1−3
- **(b)** (1)
- **(c)** (1*−3) / (4−2)

4. Write a context-free grammar for the following languages. Tell which are regular.

- **(a)** Strings of the form 0*x*1 where *x* is any sequence of 0s and 1s.
- **(b)** Strings with an unequal number of 0s and 1s.
- **(c)** Strings with an equal number of 0s and 1s.
- **(d)** Strings of the form *xy* where *y* is the reverse of *x*.
- **(e)** Implement a recursive descent parser for each of the previous languages.

5. Just as the notation for regular grammars was extended in the last chapter, so can the notation for context-free grammars be extended.

(a) Rigorously define extensions for sequencing and negation.
(b) Define extensions for the *, +, and ? operators found in regular expressions.
(c) Rewrite the grammars from the last exercise using this new notation.

6. The HAL/S language [Intermetrics 76] has a most unusual feature. Subscripts and superscripts can be represented in both single-line and *multi-line mode*; for example,

    X^{T+2}

can either be coded traditionally on one line as

    X**(T+2)

or more exotically on two lines as

    E   T+2
    M X

The "E" in column 1 indicates "T+2" is an exponent, while the "M" indicates that line is main-line code. Placement of characters on the line is important. The similar

    E T+2
    M X

is illegal. Nothing on the E and M lines may overlap. Write a lexical analyzer and parser to handle such expressions assuming the only operator is "+", and the only operands are identifiers and integer constants.

7. A *null* production has the form $b:$.

    (a) Develop an algorithm for eliminating null productions from a grammar.
    (b) Apply your algorithm to

        1 s: a 1 b ¦ b
        2 a: □ a ¦
        3 b: 1 s ¦ b ¦

8. A production is *useless* if it is not in the derivation of at least one sentence.

    (a) Develop an algorithm for eliminating useless productions from a grammar.
    (b) Apply your algorithm to

        1 s: □ ¦ (a)
        2 b: a s ¦ s b ¦ s
        3 a: a s ¦ a

9. Given the following grammar with named terminals INT and REAL:

        1 dcls: dcls dcl ¦
        2 dcl: idents : type ;
        3 idents: ident ¦ idents , ident
        4 type: INT ¦ REAL

    (a) Draw a parse tree for the string

        ab,cd : INT; de,ef,gh : REAL;

    (b) Eliminate left-recursion from the grammar.
    (c) Implement a recursive descent parser for the left-recursion free version of the grammar.
    (d) Draw the new parse tree for the string from (a).

10. A *cycle-free* grammar has no derivations of the form:

$$b$$
$$w$$
$$\ldots$$
$$b$$

for any nonterminal *b*.

(a) Develop an algorithm to eliminate cycles from a grammar.
(b) Try your algorithm on

```
1  s: s s ¦ ( b ) ¦ s ¦ b
2  b: s ¦ b ¦
```

Chapter 6
LL(1) PARSING

6.1. TOP-DOWN PARSING WITHOUT BACKTRACKING

The utility of recursive descent parsing is clear, but the last chapter also showed that its performance can grow arbitrarily bad. Fortunately, there is a modification to the basic recursive descent parsing method which always allows the correct choice among alternative rules. This reduces the execution time to a linear function of the length of the string being parsed, making it quite practical. This modification requires a careful preanalysis of the grammar. Since the grammar analysis is done once, but an arbitrary number of strings will subsequently be parsed, overall there is a tremendous savings.

Assume there is a leftmost derivation from axiom S

```
S
 ...
wBz
 ...
wbr
```

where w is a non-empty sequence of tokens, b is a token, B is a nonterminal, and z and r are possibly empty sequences of tokens. Imagine that at this point sentential form wBz has been derived, and the goal is to determine how to generate wbr from it. Since the derivation is top down, left to right, nonterminal B must be expanded next. Suppose there are two alternative rules that could be applied here,

```
1   B:   v
2   B:   y
```

where v and y are an arbitrary sequence of vocabulary symbols. If none of the sentences derivable from vz began with token b, while at least one sentence derivable from yz did, then rule 2 must be the correct choice; rule 1 could not possibly be correct. The LL parsing method formalizes this observation.

For v, an arbitrary nonempty sequence of vocabulary symbols, define `genfrom(v)` to be the set of all sequences of tokens derivable from v. Since v need not be the axiom, these strings might not be sentences. Define `first(v)` to be the set of leading tokens in `genfrom(v)`. For CFG, G, if it is always true that whenever there are two leftmost derivations

```
S              S
 ...            ...
wBz            wBz
wyz            wuz
 ...            ...
ws             wv
```

where s and v are token sequences, that $u \neq y$ implies that `first(s)` $\neq$ `first(v)`, that grammar is *LL(1)*. The importance of a grammar being LL(1) is captured by the following:

> **An LL(1) grammar can always be parsed top-down without backtracking.**

Given a set of alternative rules, looking at the next token tells which to apply.

The term "LL(1)" comes from the fact that the string being parsed is scanned from *L*eft to right, that the decision as to which rule to apply is made by examining the *L*eftmost tokens that rule will derive, and that to make that choice the *first* token which must still be derived is examined. In the example shown above, this symbol is b, which is also called the *lookahead* token. The lookahead token can be expanded to be a lookahead token sequence of any length k. This gives rise to the definition of LL(k) grammars. Here it is enough to consider such grammars when $k = 1$.

There is an algorithm which tells whether an arbitrary grammar is LL(1), and, in addition, tells which alternative rule to choose in any particular situation. A *selection set* of tokens is computed for each rule. The selection set, `select(B:y)`, of rule $B:y$ is the set of all terminals in `first(yz)` such that there is a derivation

```
S
  ...
wBz
wyz
```

where w is a possibly empty sequence of tokens and z is a possibly empty sequence of vocabulary symbols.

Example 6-1. *norec-express*, constructed in the last chapter, is not quite an LL(1) grammar. (Why not?) It is rewritten here slightly modified as *ll-express*. New nonterminal p (primary) is introduced. In addition, the selection set for each rule appears to the right in square brackets. The symbol EOF stands for end of file.

```
1   e:   t  es                [INTEGER ( ]
2   es:  ao  t  es             [- +]
         |                     [) EOF]
3   t:   f  ts                 [INTEGER ( ]
4   ts:  mo  f  ts             [/ *]
         |                     [EOF - ) +]
5   f:   p                     [( INTEGER ]
         |  -  p                [-]
6   ao:  +                     [+]
         |  -                   [-]
7   mo:  *                     [*]
         |  /                   [/]
8   p:   ( e )                 [( ]
         |  INTEGER            [INTEGER ]
```

◆

The importance of selection sets is clear from the following statement:

> **If the selection sets of alternative rules are mutually disjoint, that grammar is LL(1).**

The selection sets of alternative rules in *ll-express* are mutually disjoint; therefore, it is LL(1). If a grammar is LL(1), the next token in the string being parsed will be in the selection set of at most one alternative rule of the nonterminal being expanded. If there is such a unique rule, it is the correct rule to apply; if not, the string being parsed is not a sentence.

llparse-express

The following program, *llparse-express*, is similar to *parse-express* presented in the last chapter, except that it explicitly uses selection sets to guide the selection among alternate productions. There are no guesses:

```
1    /* llparse_express */
2    int  token;
3
4    main()
5    {
6        token = yylex ();   /* get first token */
7        if (e() && _ateof) {
8            printf ("is a sentence\n");
9            exit (0);
10       }
11       else {
12           printf ("is not a sentence\n");
13           exit (1);
14       }
15   }
16
17   e()  /* look for a string derived from e */
18   {
19       if ((token == _INTEGER ¦¦ /* rule 1 */
20           token == _LEFTPAREN) && t() && es())
21           return 1;
22       return 0;
23   }
24
25   es()   /* look for a string derived from es */
26   {
27       if ((token == _MINUS ¦¦ token == _PLUS) &&
28           ao() && t() && es())  /* rule 2.1 */
29           return 1;
30       else if (token == _RIGHTPAREN ¦¦ ateof)
31           return 1;  /* rule 2.2 */
32       else
33           return 0;
34   }
35
36   t()   /* look for a string derived from t */
37   {
38       if ((token == _INTEGER ¦¦ token == _LEFTPAREN) /* rule 3 */
39           && f() && ts())
40           return 1;
41       return 0;
42   }
43
44   ts()   /* look for a string derived from ts */
45   {
46       if ( (token == _SLASH ¦¦ token == _ASTERISK) &&
47           mo() && f() && ts())  /* rule 4.1 */
48           return 1;
49       else if (ateof ¦¦ token == _MINUS ¦¦ token == _RIGHTPAREN
50           ¦¦ token == _PLUS)
51           return 1;  /* rule 4.2 */
52       else
53           return 0;
54   }
55
56   f()   /* look for a string derived from f */
57   {
58       if ((token = _LEFTPAREN ¦¦ token == _INTEGER)
59           && p()) /* rule 5.1 */
60           return 1;
61       else if (token == _MINUS) { /* rule 5.2 */
62           token = yylex ();
63           if (p ())
64               return 1;
65       }
66       return 0;
67   }
68
69   ao()   /* look for a string derived from ao */
70   {
71       if (token == _PLUS) { /* rule 6.1 */
72           token = yylex ();
```

```
73              return 1;
74          }
75          else if (token == _MINUS) { /* rule 6.2 */
76              token = yylex ();
77              return 1;
78          }
79          return 0;
80      }
81
82      mo()    /* look for a string derived from mo */
83      {
84          if (token == _ASTERISK) {   /* rule 7.1 */
85              token = yylex ();
86              return 1;
87          }
88          if (token == _SLASH) {   /* rule 7.2 */
89              token = yylex ();
90              return 1;
91          }
92          return 0;
93      }
94
95      p()     /* look for a string derived from p */
96      {
97          if (token == _LEFTPAREN) {   /* rule 8.1 */
98              token = yylex ();
99              if (e())
100             if (token == _RIGHTPAREN) {
101                 token = yylex ();
102                 return 1;
103             }
104         }
105         else if (token == _INTEGER) { /* rule 8.2 */
106             token = yylex ();
107             return 1;
108         }
109         return 0;
110     }
```

A grammar may be non-left recursive and still not be LL(1); however, subject to a simple restriction, no left recursive grammar is ever LL(1). The restriction is that there not be any *useless* rules; that is, each rule must be in the leftmost derivation of at least one sentence. The proof that no left recursive grammar with this restriction is LL(1) is left as Exercise 10.

There is a standard set of transformations that are applied to convert non-LL(1) grammars into LL(1) grammars. The removal of left recursion is one such grammar transformation. For most programming languages these transformation rules work; however, they are heuristic and not guaranteed to always succeed. Despite these limitations, real programming languages either have LL(1) grammars or can be approximated by LL(1) grammars. If only an approximation to the intended language can be defined by an LL(1) grammar, then extra-grammatical means can be applied to weed out offending strings.

Apart from their relative efficiency, LL(1) parsers enjoy another desirable property. Errors are detected at the earliest possible moment in a left to right scan of the source string. String *w* of vocabulary symbols is said to be a *viable prefix* if there is a sentential form *wz*; that is, *w* can begin a sentential form. An LL(1) parser scans the candidate string from left to right, rejecting a string as soon as the prefix it has examined so far is not viable. Clearly, it could not reject the candidate any earlier than this using a left to right scan. LL(1) parsing is therefore said to have the *viable prefix property*. Some archaic parsing methods lack this property. For them, error detection may come quite late after much wasted parsing effort.

6.2. COMPUTING SELECTION SETS

The algorithm for computing the selection set of each production is not complex, but it is tedious. A more efficient scheme is presented in the next section, but the one presented here is more appropriate as a first approach.

Central to this algorithm are the notions of *nullable* nonterminal, production, and string. A string is nullable if it can derive the null string. A production is nullable if its right-hand side is nullable, and a nonterminal is nullable if it is the left-hand side of a nullable production. If there were no nullable productions, the computation of selection sets would primarily center on computing relation `first` of the right-hand side of each production.

Example 6-2. Grammar *SG* has rules:

```
1   s:   x  B  C  ¦   y   C
2   x:   A  x  ¦   B
3   y:   C
```

`first(xB) = {A,B}` and `first(yC) = {C}`. These are disjoint as are the two alternatives for rule 2. Consequently, *SG* is LL(1) and can be rewritten with its selection sets:

```
1   s:   x  B  C       [A B]
         ¦  y  C        [C]
2   x:   A  x          [A]
         ¦  B           [B]
3   y:   C  x          [C]
```

◆

From Example 6-2 it is easy to see how to compute `first` of the right-hand side of a production when nothing is nullable. In what follows suppose x and y are arbitrary vocabulary symbols, and w and v are possibly empty vocabulary strings, then

```
select (B:xw) = first (x)
```

For example,

```
select (s:xBC) = first(x) = first(A) ∪ first(B) = {A,B}
```

`first` of a token is the token itself, while `first` of a nonterminal is the set containing first of the leftmost symbol on the right-hand side of each rule that has that nonterminal on the left-hand side.

Added complexity arises from handling nullable symbols and productions. The simpler case occurs when an initial sequence of symbols on the right-hand side of a production are nullable, but the entire production is not. Suppose $B:xw$ is not nullable, but x is. Then $first(xw) = first(x) \cup first(w)$. Similarly, if the leftmost symbol of $w=yv$ is nullable, then $first(w) = first(y) \cup first(v)$. Generalizing, if the right-hand side of a non-nullable production is $x_1 \ldots x_k$, and $x_1, \ldots, x_{r-1}$ are all nullable for $r-1<k$, then $first(x_1 \ldots x_k) = first(x_1) \cup \ldots \cup first(x_r)$. $select(B:x_1 \ldots x_k) = first(x_1 \ldots x_k)$.

The most complex case arises when a production is nullable. Now $select(B:x_1 \ldots x_k) = first(x_1 \ldots x_k) \cup follow(B)$, where $follow(B)$ is the set of tokens that can immediately follow a B in a sentential form. If B is nullable, the members of $follow(B)$ are the tokens that can legitimately occur at that point in the derivation where there is a choice whether or not to use $B:x_1 \ldots x_k$. Consequently, there can be at most one nullable production among alternatives for a single nonterminal in an LL(1) grammar.

`select` can be derived from several relationships among tokens and nonterminals. Each relationship R is represented by a matrix, where $R[i,j] = 1$ if i is related to j and $R[i,j] = 0$ otherwise. The advantage of a matrix representation is that the transitive closure of a relation can be computed in a straightforward manner through matrix multiplication.

Suppose the nonterminals are $\{b_1, \ldots, b_n\}$, the tokens are $\{T_1, \ldots, T_m\}$, and there are p rules.

Algorithm 6-1. Compute the nullable symbols.

```
1   int  nullablenont[n];
2   int  i, changed;
```

```
 3
 4    for (i=0; i<n; i++)  /* assume nothing nullable til proven otherwise */
 5        nullablenont[i] = 0;
 6
 7    for (i=0; i<p; i++)  /* lhs of null productions are nullable */
 8        if (rule i=bⱼ:z, is a null rule)
 9            nullablenont[j] = 1;
10
11    changed = 1;          /* keep looking for new nullable symbols */
12    while (changed) {
13        changed = 0;
14        for (i=0; i<p; i++)
15            if (in rule i = bⱼ:x₁...xₙ, all x are nullable
16                && !nullablenont[j]) {
17                nullablenont[j] = 1;
18                changed++;
19            }
20    }
```

Nonterminal b begins_directly_with vocabulary symbol x if there is a rule $b:wxz$, where w is nullable. Token x begins_directly_with x.

Algorithm 6-2. Compute begins_directly_with.

```
 1    int  begins_directly_with[n+m, n+m];
 2    int  i,j;
 3
 4    for (i=0; i<n; i++)  /* nonterminals first */
 5        if (there is a rule b₁:wTⱼz)
 6            begins_directly_with[i,j] = 1;
 7        else
 8            begins_directly_with[i,j] = 0;
 9
10    for (i=n; i<n+m; i++)  /* now tokens */
11        for (j=n; j<n+m; j++)
12            if (i != j)
13                begins_directly_with[i,j] = 0;
14            else
15                begins_directly_with[i,j] = 1;
```

The reflexive transitive closure of begins_directly_with is begins_with, from which first can be directly computed. first(b) are the tokens b begins with. For each null rule, $b:$, first($b:$) = {}. For each rule, $b:x_1...x_k$, first($b:x_1...x_k$) = first(x_1) ∪ ... ∪ first(x_r) where $x_1, ..., x_{r-1}$ are nullable symbols.

To compute follow, several simpler relations must first be calculated. x is_direct_end_of b if there is a rule $b:wxz$, where z is nullable. x is_end_of y if it is in the reflexive transitive closure of is_direct_end_of. Intuitively, x is_end_of y if in a derivation from y, x is the rightmost symbol. Symbol x is_followed_directly_by y if there is a rule $b:wxvyz$, where v is nullable. Finally, x is_followed_by y if and only if there is a string derived from the axiom in which xy is a substring. This is computed by multiplying:

    is_end_of × is_followed_directly_by × begins_with

The generation of selection sets using this algorithm will be illustrated on the familiar example *ll-express*.

Example 6-3. There are two nullable nonterminals: *es* and *ts*. Productions 2.2 and 4.2 are nullable. The various relations are shown in Figs. 6-1 through 6-8.

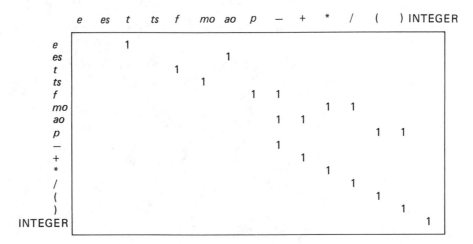

Figure 6-1. begins_directly_with.

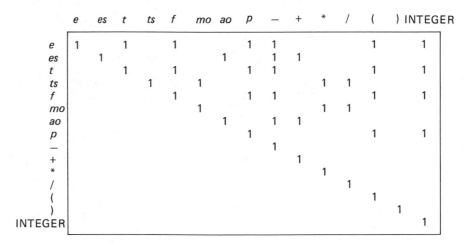

Figure 6-2. begins_with.

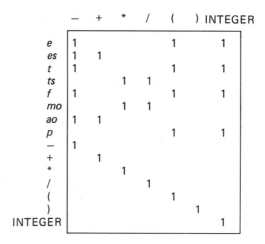

Figure 6-3. first of each Symbol.

Production	*first*
e: t es	— (INTEGER
es: ao t es	— +
⋮	NULL
t: f ts	— (INTEGER
ts: mo f ts	* /
⋮	NULL
f: p	(INTEGER
⋮ — p	—
ao: +	+
⋮ —	—
mo: *	*
⋮ /	/
p: (e)	(
⋮ INTEGER	INTEGER

Figure 6-4. `first` of Each Production.

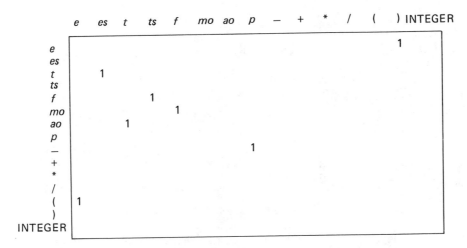

Figure 6-5. is_followed_directly_by.

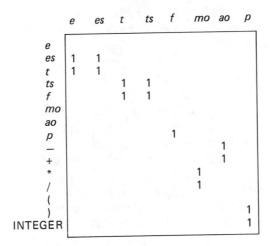

Figure 6-6. is_direct_end_of.

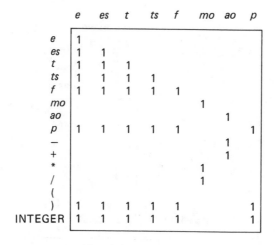

	e	es	t	ts	f	mo	ao	p
e	1							
es	1	1						
t	1	1	1					
ts	1	1	1	1				
f	1	1	1	1	1			
mo						1		
ao							1	
p	1	1	1	1	1			1
−							1	
+							1	
*						1		
/						1		
(								
)	1	1	1	1	1			1
INTEGER	1	1	1	1	1			1

Figure 6-7. is_end_of.

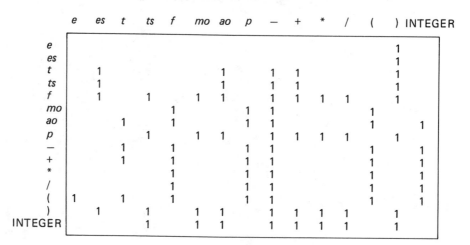

	e	es	t	ts	f	mo	ao	p	−	+	*	/	(	)	INTEGER
e														1	
es														1	
t		1					1		1	1				1	
ts		1					1		1	1				1	
f		1		1		1	1		1	1	1	1		1	
mo					1			1					1		1
ao			1		1			1					1		1
p		1		1		1	1		1	1	1	1		1	
−			1		1			1					1		1
+			1		1			1					1		1
*					1			1					1		1
/					1			1					1		1
(	1		1		1			1					1		1
)		1		1		1	1		1	1	1	1		1	
INTEGER		1		1		1	1		1	1	1	1		1	

Figure 6-8. is_followed_by.

LL(1) parsing is one method to eliminate backtracking. The overhead of computing the selection set of each production in advance is significant − $O(n^3)$, where n is the size of the grammar. However, this computation is done only once and used repeatedly in parsing strings. The overhead in parsing is then reduced to a linear function of the length of the input. The computational overhead in selecting a production is quite small. The selection set of each alternative production must be examined. For any practical grammar, there will typically be only a handful of alternate productions which can be searched quite rapidly using standard lookup techniques. In most cases, the number of alternatives will be less than 10 so that a linear search is adequate.

Efficiently Computing first and follow

The algorithm in the last section required a number of matrix multiplications to compute `first` and `follow` of each production. A more efficient method using a graph search algorithm was presented in [Backhouse 79] and in one form or another has become somewhat standard in actual implementations. Improvements appear in [Gough 85] and [Dwyer 85] which are quite similar in character but differ in detail from that of Backhouse. This section highlights the graph search approach taken by Backhouse in part to illustrate how graph search techniques have application in unexpected places.

Given grammar G, consider a graph that has a node for each terminal plus `EOF` and a node representing `first` of each nonterminal. There is an arc from node A to B if and only if there is a production $B: vAy$ where v is nullable, that is, if B `begins_directly_with` A. Such a graph is called a *first graph* because there is a path from node C to D if and only if C is in `first(D)`. A cycle in the graph would indicate the grammar is left recursive.

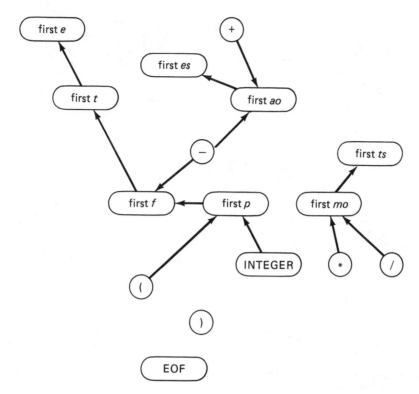

Figure 6-9. *first* **Graph for** *ll-express.*

Example 6-4. The `first` graph for *ll-express* is in Fig. 6-9. It has no cycles since *ll-express* is not left recursive.

♦

`follow` can be summarized by a set of equations readily derived from the set of nullable nonterminals and the productions. If there is a production $B: vCyDz$ then `follow(C)` contains `first(y)`. If y is nullable, it also contains `first(D)`. If yDz is nullable, it also contains `follow(B)`. This information can also be represented in a graph in which there is a node for each term in the equations and an arc from A to B if and only if A is on the right-hand side and B is on the left-hand side of an equation.

Example 6-5. For *ll-express*, the equations for `follow` are:

```
follow(e) = {)} + EOF
follow(t) = first(es) + follow(es) + follow(e)
follow(es) = follow(e) + follow(es)
follow(ts) = follow(ts) + follow(t)
follow(f) = first(ts) + follow(ts) + follow(t)
follow(ao) = first(t)
follow(mo) = first(f)
follow(p) = follow(f)
```

The `follow` graph is shown for *ll-express* in Fig. 6-10.

♦

Again it follows quite simply that there is a path from A to B if and only if A is in `follow(B)`.

Finally, these two graphs can be combined to produce a *first/follow* graph such that there is a path from a node labeled by terminal b to a node labeled by `follow(B)` if and only if b is in `follow(B)`.

Example 6-6. Fig. 6-11 shows the combined `first/follow` graph for *ll-express*.

♦

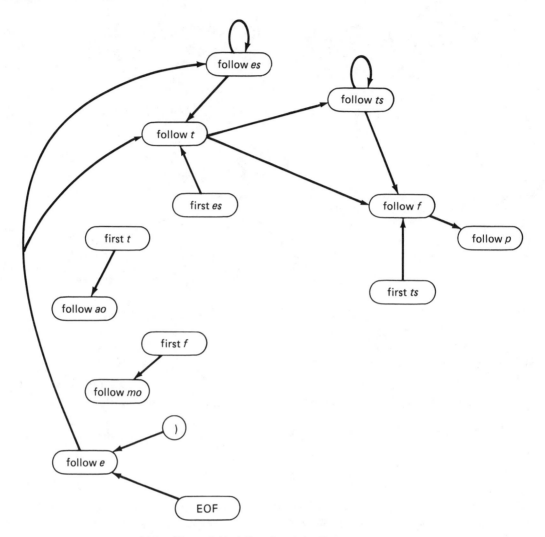

Figure 6-10. *follow* **Graph for** *ll-express.*

The computation of `first` and `follow` has been reduced to the efficient search for a path between two nodes in a graph.

Algorithm 6-3. Graph search.
Input: A graph with nodes $N = \{n_1, n_2, ..., n_k\}$ and selected node n.
Output: All nodes reachable from n.
Steps

```
1     setofnodes  reached, frontier;
2     node  f;
3
4     reached = frontier = {n};
5     f = n;
6     while (f != NULL && frontier != NULL) {
7         remove f from frontier;
8         for (each arc r with tail f)
9             if (head of r is not in reached)
10                add head of r to reached;
11        select f from frontier;
12    }
```

This search algorithm is quite efficient if properly implemented using, for example, a bitmap to decide whether a node is in a set. It only adds an element to the set once, and having added a node never deletes it. The details of implementing this algorithm are left as Exercise 5.

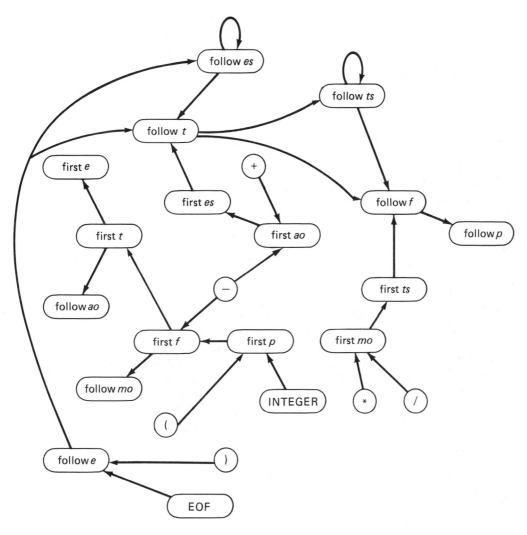

Figure 6-11. Combined *first*/*follow* Graph.

6.3. DESIGN OF *MARLI*

The parsers shown earlier take on the "shape" of the underlying grammar by including one function per grammar rule. This style requires starting from scratch and rewriting the entire parser every time a new grammar is used. Such reinvention is costly and turns out to be unnecessary. The same reasons that earlier motivated a lexical analyzer generator prompts the design of *marli*, an LL(1) parser generator. (This presentation is based on an LL(1) translator-writing system, *zuse*, produced by the author [Pyster 81]. *zuse* is itself written in Berkeley Pascal and produces compilers written in Pascal.) *marli* is a pair of programs: *gen-marli* and *skel-marli*, fashioned after *gen-gioconda* and *skel-gioconda* studied in Chapter 4. Figure 6-12 shows how they work together to support parser writing.

skel-marli is missing the axiom, nonterminals, tokens, and rules that vary from grammar to grammar. When that information is provided, *skel-marli* is complete and the resulting program will parse candidate strings with respect to the original context-free grammar. *gen-marli* can take a very human-readable expression of a CFG and map it into a set of data types, variables, and constants which can be used by *skel-marli* to parse input strings.

To simplify the discussion of *skel-marli*, the lexical analyzer will not be explicitly discussed and no symbol table will be used.

The design of *skel-marli* centers around comparing the current sentential form with the current token in the input stream. The comparison is always of the leftmost symbol *x* in the sentential form. If *x* is a token, it must match the current token *t* in the input stream. In that case, *x* is dropped off of the left end

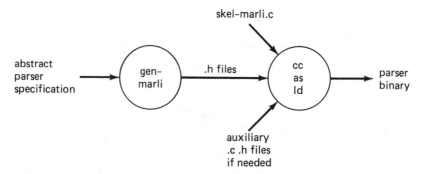

Figure 6-12. Using *marli* to Generate an LL(1) Parser.

of the sentential form since it has been "matched" and can never be revisited (since there is no backtracking with LL(1) parsers). Since input token t has also been "matched," the parser reads the next token from the input stream. If x does not match t, the input stream is not a sentence and the parser can terminate (or take some more reasonable error recovery).

If x is a nonterminal, then the selection sets of the alternative rules of x are examined for the one that contains t. If none do, then again the input stream is not a sentence and the parser can terminate. On the other hand, if one rule does contain t, its right-hand side replaces x in the sentential form. Since t has not yet been matched by a symbol in the sentential form, it is left as the current token.

The sentential form is an array of structures, each containing two elements: `selector` and `value`. `selector` is 0 or −1 if the symbol is a terminal. If it is 0, then `value` is the actual token expected. If it is −1, `value` is the name of the expected token. If `selector` is positive, the symbol is a nonterminal, and the `selector` actually indicates which nonterminal. There is a unique mapping from each nonterminal to a positive integer defined in *grammar.h*, the file that fills the hole in *skel-marli* that is included when *skel-marli* is compiled.

Algorithm 6-4. *skel-marli.*

```
1    /* skel-marli */
2    #include <lex.h>
3
4    #define SENTMAX     k
5    #define TERMINAL    0
6    #include "_grammar.h"    /* definition of grammar including:
7                                tokens, nonterminals and their indices,
8                                axiom, and rules. */
9    #define AXIOM       1    /* axiom always has index 1 */
10
11   typedef struct {
12       int   selector, state;
13       char value[BUFSIZ];
14   } symbol;
15   int   token;
16   symbol    sentform[SENTMAX];       /* sentential form */
17
18   main()
19   {
20       int   i;
21       int   outcome = 0; /* was input stream a sentence? */
22
23            /* first symbol in sentential form should be axiom */
24       sentform[1].selector = AXIOM;
25
26       token = yylex ();  /* get first token. */
27
28       while (!_ateof) {   /* not at end of input */
29           if (sentform[0].selector == TERMINAL)
30               if (token == sentform[0].state) {
31                   drop sentform[0] off shifting sentform left;
32                   token = yylex ();
33               }
```

```
34              else /* input is not a sentence */
35                   break;
36          else if (there is a rule with left-hand side ==
37                   sentform[0] && yytext is in its selection
38                   set)
39              replace sentform[0] with right-hand side of selected
40                   rule, adjusting sentsize appropriately;
41          else  /* input is not a sentence. */
42              break;
43      }
44      if (_ateof && sentform is empty)
45              /* reached end of candidate at the same time reached end
46                   of sentential form */
47          outcome++;  /* input is a sentence. */
48
49      if (outcome) {
50          printf ("is a sentence\n");
51          exit (0);
52      }
53      else {
54          printf ("is not a sentence\n");
55          exit (1);
56      }
57  }
```

The components of a parser which vary from grammar to grammar are yylex and the information in _grammar.h. Everything else remains the same.

Example 6-7. Figure 6-13 shows the parsing action on "1+20*-2".

◆

This parser is generated by writing the grammatical information of *ll-express* into the required form in *grammar.h* and merging it with *skel-marli*.

The design of *gen-marli* can be patterned after that used in *gen-gioconda*. In this case, however, the input format is a specification of the axiom, the nonterminals, tokens and token names, and the rules. Using the algorithm shown in the last section, *gen-marli* can compute the selection set for each production and determine whether the grammar is LL(1). If it is not, it should reject the grammar. Finally, it should emit appropriate datatypes, variables, and constants to reflect this information. The details of *gen-marli*'s design are left as an important exercise or the reader is urged to look at [Pyster 81]. It is

Sentential Form	Current Token	Selected Rule
e	1	1
t es	1	3
f ts es	1	5.1
p ts es	1	8.2
1 ts es	+	4.2
1 es	+	2.1
1 ao t es	+	6.1
1 + t es	20	3
1 + f ts es	20	5.1
1 + f p es	20	8.2
1 + 20 ts es	*	4.1
1 + 20 mo f ts es	*	7.1
1 + 20 * f ts es	2	5.2
1 + 20 * - p ts es	EOF	8.2
1 + 20 * - 2 ts es	EOF	4.2
1 + 20 * - 2 es	EOF	2.2
1 + 20 * - 2	EOF	outcome=1

Figure 6-13. LL(1) Parsing of "1+20*-2".

suggested that the general input format in Fig. 6-14 which is patterned much after the format used by *yacc* be used. This format breaks the specification into four sections, one for each grammar component except basic tokens plus named tokens. Using keywords prefixed by "%" in column 1 simplifies parsing of the specification itself. A section continues onto subsequent lines until the next keyword delimiter is found. Whitespace should generally be ignored and *C* style comments should be allowed. If minimal error checking is attempted, a working implementation of both parts of *marli* should total between 1000 and 1500 lines of *C* code.

```
%axiom    B
%nonterminals    B₁ B₂ ... Bₖ
%token-names    G₁ G₂ ... Gₘ
%rules
B₁:  W₁;
B₂:  W₂;
    ...
Bₖ:  Wₖ;
```

Figure 6-14. Format for *gen-marli*.

6.4. ERROR PROCESSING

There are few errors that a lexical analyzer can detect because it lacks the context in which the lexemes appear. The parser, on the other hand, has a much richer view of what is "correct" and can detect errors relating to the order of tokens. The parser also finds it more difficult to recover from errors because even a single erroneous character can badly botch the overall program structure.

Example 6-8. Consider the correct program *count* in Fig 6-15 which computes the number of characters and complete lines in stdin, writing the result on stdout. Innocently changing the left curly bracket '{' in line 10 to a right curly bracket '}' provokes the following response from *cc*:

```
"count.c", line 10: syntax error
"count.c", line 15: syntax error
"count.c", line 15: illegal character: 043 (octal)
"count.c", line 15: cannot recover from earlier errors: goodbye!
```

It properly recognizes that the while statement is incomplete when '}' is encountered, causing the first error message. However, at this point, it gets so befuddled about how to continue that by the time line 15 is reached, it does not recognize that '#' (octal 043) is part of a character string, and just gives up. The '}' in line 10 terminates the declaration of the main function so that the subsequent statements are outside the context of a function declaration. This compiler cannot gracefully deal with that condition. In fact, submitting the single statement

```
 1    /*  number of characters and complete lines in stdin  */
 2
 3    #include <stdio.h>
 4
 5    main ()
 6    {
 7        char c;
 8        int  ccount, lcount = 0;
 9
10        while ((c=getchar()) != EOF) {
11            ccount++;
12            if (c == '\n')
13                lcount++;
14        }
15        printf ("# of chars = %d, # of lines = %d\n",
16            ccount, lcount);
17    }
```

Figure 6-15. *count*: Counting Characters and Lines.

```
printf ("# hello world\n");
```

to *cc* produces similar complaints:

```
"printf.c", line 1: syntax error
"printf.c", line 1: illegal character: 043 (octal)
"printf.c", line 1: cannot recover from earlier errors: goodbye!
```
◆

A compiler should keep processing in the face of error if only to uncover more errors in the input. Parsing errors are broken into three severity levels depending on how difficult it is for the parser to continue in their presence:

1. **minor:** a syntactic violation for which the parser believes it has a correction that is likely to be what the programmer intended. It fixes the program and continues processing with a very high probability it "guessed" right.
2. **major:** a violation for which the parser has no reliable correction. It will attempt to continue the parse, but will probably have to skip over part of the input or take some other exceptional action to do so. There is a significant risk it "guessed" wrong.
3. **panic:** things are so fouled up, the parser cannot continue. It terminates execution.

From its name alone, *panicking* seems very undesirable and should be used only for the most severe errors. It is an admission of defeat by the parser (writer) normally reserved for internal errors within the parser or when one of the parser's resources, such as a stack or buffer, is exceeded. Panicking is also common when the parser gets so confused about the state of the parse it cannot figure out how to continue. This was illustrated earlier.

A compiler should be able to generate executable code if it encounters only minor syntactic errors. The programmer's intent is likely preserved by the error correction (although the programmer should verify his or her intentions really were understood) which allows the programmer to execute the code and perform run-time debugging. Generating code in the presence of major errors, however, is almost certainly useless since the programmer's intent cannot be reconstructed. Continuing compilation in their presence only helps detect more errors, speeding the overall debugging process.

Minor and major errors are repaired by modifying either the input stream or the sentential form that represents the current state of the parse. It is possible to back up in the input stream or undo parsing decisions as part of error recovery. This section explores backing out parsing decisions, but never backs up the input stream.

Several simple major and minor recovery strategies are possible:

1. **skip token:** skip the current token, pretending it was never there. The current symbol in the sentential form is unchanged.
2. **skip symbol:** skip the current symbol in the sentential form if it is a terminal, pretending it was matched. The current token is left unchanged.
3. **replace token:** replace the current token with one that legitimately might have appeared there. The current symbol in the sentential form is unchanged.
4. **match token:** pretend the current token matches the current symbol if it is a terminal.
5. **insert token:** push an additional token in front of the erroneous one. The current symbol remains unchanged.

Example 6-9. The first strategy, ignoring the erroneous token, only works well if that token truly was extra; for example, in the Pascal assignment statement

```
i := i ** 1
```

is the second `"*"` superfluous or was an operand accidentally omitted? The Pascal compiler *pi* on 4.2BSD assumes the latter and produces the message

```
            i := i ** 1
E -------------------^--- Inserted identifier
```

The uppercase "E" at the beginning of the message indicates that *pi* views this error as a major one. Insertion of an imaginary identifier to act as a placeholder allows the parser to continue, but reasonable object code cannot be generated after this point.

◆

Skipping a terminal symbol in the sentential form is the same as pretending that terminal appeared in the input stream. It is useful when the current token could legitimately follow the next symbol but not the current one.

Replacing a bad token with a legal one is frequently done in student-oriented compilers that work very hard to force a program to become legal. Of course, this is probabilistic since the person writing the parser can never be certain what the programmer actually intended. Relatively safe replacement is the substitution of ":=" for "=" in the malformed Pascal assignment statement

```
x = y;
```

Pretending the current token really matches the current terminal symbol is a specialized form of token replacement.

Inserting a new token in front of the offending one guarantees that the parser will be able to continue through at least one more token before encountering another error. Again, it is probabilistic whether the insertion is correct. One of the most common insertions is a statement terminator such as ";".

Example 6-10. When the program in Fig. 6-16 is run through *pi*, the following message is produced:

```
      6      i := i+1
e ----------^--- Inserted ';'
```

This insertion allows the compilation to proceed to normal conclusion and produce executable code. *pi* classified this problem as a minor error, indicated by the lower case "e" at the beginning of the message. The compiler will generate runnable object code since it believes the correction captures the programmer's intent.

◆

Insertion becomes a much more arguable strategy when there is more than one likely candidate such as in

```
x = y+ ;
```

There is no reasonable way for the parser to know what token was intended as the second argument of the addition. Insertion of an identifier under these conditions patches the program to allow compilation to continue in order to find other errors, but no executable code can be produced.

These recovery strategies are all easily implemented. Suppose *marli* were extended to support the *skip token* recovery strategy.

```
1    program helloworld (output);
2    var
3        i: integer;
4    begin
5        writeln ('Hello world')
6        i := i+1
7    end.
```

Figure 6-16. Pascal Program Missing ";" in Line 5.

Example 6-11. Consider the partial parse of string `"2**3"` by grammar *ll-express*:

	String	Sentential Form
1	^2**3	^e
2	^2**3	^t es
3	^2**3	^f ts es
4	^2**3	^p ts es
5	^2**3	^INTEGER ts es
6	2^**3	2 ^ts es
7	2^**3	2 ^mo f ts es
8	2^**3	2 ^* f ts es
9	2*^*3	2 * ^f ts es

f cannot be expanded since there is no production for f whose selection set contains `"*"`. Dropping `"*"` as superfluous leads to

10	2*^3	2 * ^f ts es
11	2*^3	2 * ^p ts es
	...	

♦

Example 6-12. Consider recovering `"3)+4"`:

	String	Sentential Form
1	^3)+4	^e
2	^3)+4	^t es
3	^3)+4	^f ts es
4	^3)+4	^p ts es
5	^3)+4	^INTEGER ts es
6	3^)+4	3 ^ts es
7	3^)+4	3 ^es
8	3^)+4	3 ^

The error is finally recognized after all symbols have been erased from the sentential form (by expanding them to the null string). At this point the parser can do nothing more than skip past all of the remaining tokens in the input.

♦

Skipping past tokens clearly is a weak recovery in this case because nonterminals in the sentential form were expanded based on a token (`")"`) that was subsequently discarded as erroneous. The solution is to allow the parser to backtrack to step 6, the state of the parse when the offending token was first seen and skip `")"` at that time. This would lead to

7'	3^+4	3 ^ts es

from which the parse could continue normally. Note that in the previous example, the parser detected the erroneous token before making any false expansions, so that no backtracking was necessary.

Recall that the chief advantage of LL(1) parsing over general recursive descent is the avoidance of backtracking. It might seem that having to back out the parsing steps is a major concession, but that is not really true. Backtracking only has to be done when an error occurs, not during the parsing of correct programs. In practice the ratio of erroneous characters to valid ones in a program is very small, so the overall performance penalty is minimal.

No one strategy is correct for all circumstances. A flexible parser should allow the grammar writer to specify what action to take at each point and adopt a default strategy when none is specified. This allows the grammar writer to perform special recovery for unusual cases such as when "=" is seen but ":=" is expected in Pascal. The grammar writer should be able to specify that ":=" is to replace "=". *marli* can be extended to allow just that.

Consider *ll-assign*, a simple extension of *ll-express* that generates a series of Pascal-like assignment statements terminated by semicolons. The new nonterminals are *s* (statement) and *ss* (statements). There is a new named token, ASSIGN representing ":=":

```
 1    ss: s  ss                        [IDENT]
         |                             [EOF]
 2    s: ident  ASSIGN  e  ;           [IDENT]
 3    e: t  es                         [INTEGER (]
 4    es: ao  t  es                    [- +]
         |                             [) ;]
 5    t: f  ts                         [INTEGER (]
 6    ts: mo  f  ts                    [/ *]
         |                             [; - ) +]
 7    f: p                             [( INTEGER]
         |  - p                        [-]
 8    ao: +                            [+]
         |  -                          [-]
 9    mo: *                            [*]
         |  /                          [/]
10    p: ( e )                         [(]
         |  INTEGER                    [INTEGER]
         |  IDENT                      [IDENT]
```

Suppose the following recovery strategies are desired:

1. If "=" is encountered, substitute ":=" (minor error).
2. If an operand is found, but a binary operator could have been expected, insert the operator "+" (major error).
3. If "+" is encountered where the unary operator "-" could appear, substitute "-" (major error).
4. If a statement does not begin with an identifier, skip tokens until after the next ";" or EOF is reached (major error).
5. In all other circumstances, follow the standard *skip token* recovery (major error).

ll-assign is augmented with special error code to indicate this. The selection sets have been omitted to avoid clutter:

```
 1    ss  {e do {
                  skiptoken();
                } until (token == _SEMICOLON) || _ateof);
             skiptoken();
          }
        :  s  ss  |
 2    s: ident   ASSIGN
             {e if (token == _EQUAL)
                   replacetoken (_ASSIGN);}
          e ;
 3    e {e if (token == _PLUS)
                   replacetoken (_MINUS); }
          :  t  es
 4    es  {e if (token == _IDENT || token == _INTEGER)
                   inserttoken (_PLUS);}
          :  ao  t  es  |
 5    t {e if (token == _PLUS)
                   replacetoken (_MINUS);}
          :  f  ts
 6    ts  {e if (token == _IDENT || token == _INTEGER)
                   inserttoken (_PLUS);}
          :  mo  f  ts  |
 7    f {e if (token == _PLUS)
                   replacetoken (_MINUS);}
```

```
            :  p
            ¦  -  p
 8   ao:  +  ¦  -
 9   mo:  *  ¦  /
10   p {e if (token == _PLUS)
                  replacetoken (_MINUS);}
          :  ( e )  ¦  INTEGER  ¦  IDENT
```
◆

A recovery strategy is written as

```
{e   strategy  }
```

It can appear to the right of any symbol in a production, including the nonterminal on the left-hand side. Normally it is ignored during parsing. When an error occurs, the parser takes the following steps:

1. If there is an error specification immediately to the right of the symbol which it is trying unsuccessfully to match (terminal) or expand (nonterminal), that code is executed. When that code has completed execution, if it modified either the input stream or the sentential form, the parser continues as if nothing unusual had occurred; otherwise, the parser invokes the default error recovery (to avoid an infinite loop).
2. If there is no error specification to the right of the current symbol and that symbol is a terminal, the default recovery action is taken.
3. If there is no error specification to the right of the current symbol and that symbol is a nonterminal, the parser checks whether there is an error specification to the right of the production which has that symbol as its left-hand side. If not, the default recovery action is taken. If so, that code is executed. When that code has completed execution, if the input stream or the sentential form has been modified, the parser continues as if nothing unusual had occurred; otherwise, it invokes the default error recovery.

To support special error handling, several predefined functions are added, including skiptoken, replacetoken, and inserttoken which have the obvious effects.

Example 6-13. Using augmented *ll-assign* to parse the rather badly botched string "x=)1;y:=+3;1+2;"'' demonstrates the various error recovery strategies in Fig. 6-17.
◆

This general recovery approach, while quite powerful in dealing with errors that can be corrected by adjusting the input stream, is limited. It cannot deal with code that is so badly botched it is necessary to skip forward in the sentential form; for example, there is no way using this strategy to simply declare defeat on an entire statement and skip to the comfort of a semicolon except when the problem occurs at the highest level in the parse; that is, when ss is the current symbol. This arises from the fact the token following a semicolon coincidentally begins a statement. It would not be possible to take the same tack when the current symbol is ":=" and the current token is "=" in rule 2. No matter how many tokens are skipped, the parser will still look for ":=e;". The solution to this problem is to add still another error recovery mechanism called *resynchronization*. Resynchronization allows the parser to skip arbitrarily far into the sentential form as well as skip tokens in the input stream. To indicate that when ":=" is not encountered in an assignment, the parser should abandon the statement and skip to the next semicolon, rule 2 would have to be modified:

```
2'   s: {r ';' => $4, EOF => $$}  IDENT  ASSIGN  e  ';'
```

An r is used instead of e to the right of ' { ' to indicate this is a resynchronization rather than a normal error specification. It states that when expanding s with this rule, if an error occurs at any point in the expansion and there is no governing special error recovery (from a "{e" specification), start reading tokens until either ';' or EOF is found. If ';' is found first, advance the sentential form pointer to match the fourth vocabulary symbol in the rule ($4). This causes the parser to behave as if it has seen all

	Input String	Sentential Form
1	`^x=)1;y:=+3;1+2;`	`^ss`
2	`^x=)1;y:=+3;1+2;`	`^s ss`
3	`^x=)1;y:=+3;1+2;`	`^IDENT ASSIGN e ; ss`
4	`x^=)1;y:=+3;1+2;` (invoke error recovery after ASSIGN in rule 2.1)	`x ^ASSIGN e ; ss`
5	`x^:=)1;y:=+3;1+2;`	`x ^ASSIGN e ; ss`
6	`x:=^)1;y:=+3;1+2;` (invoke default error recovery, skipping ")" in input)	`x ASSIGN ^e ; ss`
7	`x:=)^1;y:=+3;1+2;`	`x ASSIGN ^e ; ss`
8	`x:=)^1;y:=+3;1+2;`	`x ASSIGN ^t es ; ss`
9	`x:=)^1;y:=+3;1+2;`	`... ^f ts es ; ss`
10	`x:=)^1;y:=+3;1+2;`	`... ^p ts es ; ss`
11	`x:=)^1;y:=+3;1+2;`	`... INTEGER ts es ; ss`
12	`x:=)1^;y:=+3;1+2;` `...`	`... 1 ^ts es ; ss`
13	`x:=)1;^y:=+3;1+2;` `...`	`... 1 ; ^ss`
14	`x:=)1;y:=^+3;1+2;` (invoke error recovery after e in rule 3)	`... y ASSIGN ^e ss`
15	`x:=)1;y:=^-3;1+2;` `...`	`... y ASSIGN ^e ss`
16	`x:=)1;y:=-3;^1+2;` (invoke error recovery to right of ss in rule 1)	`... 3 ; ^ss`
17	`x:=)1;y:=-3;1+2;^`	`... 3 ; ^ss`
18	`x:=)1;y:=-3;1+2;^`	`... 3 ; ^`

Figure 6-17. Error Recovery Demonstrated.

of the statement except the semicolon. If EOF is found first, advance the sentential form pointer to indicate that all of rule 2 has been expanded and matched ($$). The parser then behaves as if it had seen all of an assignment statement including the semicolon. *ss* then becomes the current symbol and the parse terminates normally.

With resynchronization plus the other strategies described earlier, *marli* can provide extremely intelligent error recovery. The implementation of these strategies is left as an exercise.

EXERCISES

1. Trace the execution of program *ll-express* on:

    (a) `(1)`
    (b) `(-1+2)*(3/4)`
    (c) `12*-2+4/6`

2. Given the following grammar:

```
1 bexp: NOT bexp | rexp
2 rexp: aexp rop aexp | aexp
```

```
⌐  ]  rop:  =  ¦  <˙
   4  aop:  +  ¦  OR
   5  aterm:  aterm  mop  afact  ¦  afact
    b  mop:  AND  ¦  DIV  ¦  *
   7  afact:  (  bexp  )  ¦  INTEGER
   8  aexp:  aexp  aop  aterm  ¦  aterm
```

where uppercase identifiers are named tokens with the obvious interpretation.

(a) List all operators in decreasing order of precedence.

(b) Rewrite the grammar so that the operators have the following precedence with ( ) highest and OR lowest:

```
( )
DIV  *
+
=  <
NOT
AND
OR
```

3. Given grammar:

```
1  s:  s  X  u  ¦  X  u
2  t:  s  ¦  C
3  u:  t  Y
```

(a) Compute the selection set of each production using the matrix multiplication algorithm from Section 6.2.

(b) Compute the selection set using the graph search algorithm.

(c) Convert the grammar into an LL(1) grammar. Compute the selection set of your revised grammar using both methods.

(d) Implement a parser for your new grammar.

4. The following grammar defines regular expressions.

```
1  e:  e  '¦'  t  ¦  t
2  t:  t  f  ¦  f
3  f:  p  *  ¦  p  +  ¦  p
4  p:  (  e  )  ¦  OPERAND
```

(a) Convert it to an equivalent LL(1) grammar.

(b) Prove your conversion is correct by computing the selection set of each production using the matrix multiplication algorithm.

(c) Repeat (b) but using the graph search algorithm.

5. Implement Algorithm 6-3 in either Pascal or *C*.

6. Prove that no LL(1) grammar is ambiguous.

7. Complete the implementaton of *marli*.

8. Extend *marli* to include error recovery strategies

(a) skip token
(b) replace token
(c) insert token

9. Add *resynchronization* to *marli*'s error recovery strategies.

10. Prove that a left-recursive grammar without useless productions is not LL(1).

Chapter 7
LR(1) PARSING

7.1. BOTTOM-UP PARSING

LL(1) parsing is called *top-down* because the derivation tree is constructed from the root and continues down to the frontier. The obvious alternative is to build the tree from the frontier elements up to the root. Parsers that behave in this way are, appropriately enough, called *bottom-up*. A number of different bottom-up parsing algorithms have been used throughout the past 20 years including simple, operator, and mixed precedence parsers, bounded context parsers, and LR parsers. This chapter concentrates only on the LR method, which has largely replaced other bottom-up techniques in recent years.

In many respects LR is the most general bottom-up parsing method. It subsumes all other common parsing methods in power. Originally defined by Donald Knuth [Knuth 65], LR parsing is also more complex than LL, and is much less intuitive in its operation, which is why LL parsing was introduced first in this text. However, LR parsing has one major advantage over LL parsers which has made it widely adopted. Although LR parsers also require grammars to be in a special form, many more "common" grammars fit this form than fit the form required for LL parsers. For example, with only trivial modification grammar *unambig-express* is an LR grammar, even though it is far from being LL. In general, left recursion causes no problem for LR parsers. Furthermore, there are several natural extensions to the LR parsing method which enhance their practical utility even more. Some of these extensions are studied in Chapter 8 where *yacc* is examined, since they have been cleanly incorporated into that translator-writing system.

Like LL parsers, LR parsers have the viable prefix property. An LR parser will never scan further into a string than its longest viable prefix. This facilitates error processing because the parser will not waste time scanning past the point where the error occurs.

Recall that LL parsers are classified by the length of the lookahead strings found in their selection sets. There are LL(1), LL(2), . . ., LL(k) parsers, although the last chapter only examined LL(1) parsers. LR parsers also use a lookahead string. Depending on the length of that string, there are LR(1), LR(2), . . ., LR(k) parsers. This text only explores LR(1) parsers and simpler models based on the LR(1) scheme.

Right-most Derivations

The letters *LR* are an abbreviation for how the parser operates; that is, scanning the input **L**eft to right, generating the inverse **R**ightmost derivation. Recall that a leftmost derivation is one in which the leftmost nonterminal is expanded at each step; similarly, a rightmost derivation is one in which the rightmost nonterminal is expanded.

Example 7-1. The rightmost derivation of "1+20*-2" with respect to *unambig-express* is in Fig. 7-1. Quotes around terminals have been omitted to avoid clutter. The inverse of that derivation is in Fig. 7-2. Figure 7-3 shows the stepwise construction of the tree corresponding to this inverse derivation. An LR(1) parser for *unambig-express* would perform this stepwise construction.
◆

108

```
1    e
2    e   ao   t
3    e   ao   t   mo   f
4    e   ao   t   mo   -   2
5    e   ao   t   *    -   2
6    e   ao   f   *    -   2
7    e   ao   20  *    -   2
8    e   +    20  *    -   2
9    t   +    20  *    -   2
10   f   +    20  *    -   2
11   1   +    20  *    -   2
```

Figure 7-1. Rightmost Derivation of `"1+20*-2"`.

```
1    1   +    20   *   -   2
2    f   +    20   *   -   2
3    t   +    20   *   -   2
4    e   +    20   *   -   2
5    e   ao   20   *   -   2
6    e   ao   f    *   -   2
7    e   ao   t    *   -   2
8    e   ao   t    mo  -   2
9    e   ao   t    mo  f
10   e   ao   t
11   e
```

Figure 7-2. Inverse Rightmost Derivation of `"1+20*-2"`.

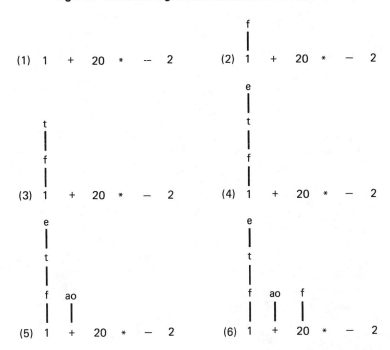

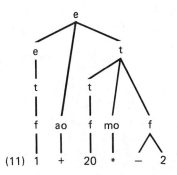

Figure 7-3. Step-wise Construction of Tree for Inverse Derivation.

109

Reductions

When parsing top-down, nonterminals are expanded. A nonterminal is replaced by the right-hand side of one of its alternative rules. When parsing bottom-up, a string in the sentential form corresponding to the right-hand side of a production is replaced by the nonterminal corresponding to the left-hand side. Such a replacement is called a *reduction*. When parsing top-down using the LL(1) parsing algorithm, there is never any doubt which nonterminal to expand next—it is always the leftmost one. When parsing bottom-up, it is not immediately clear where in the derivation to reduce. For example, in step 8 of the inverse rightmost derivation of `"1+20*-2"`, if the leftmost possible reduction had been performed instead of reducing token `"*"`, the resulting sentential form would have been

```
e    *    -    2
```

This reduction would have been incorrect and would have made it impossible to reduce back to e without backtracking, something that is clearly to be avoided. The tricky part, of course, is making the parser smart enough to know which substring in the sentential form to reduce. The correct substring is called the *handle*. Just as LL(1) parsers use previous analysis by computing the selection set in order to facilitate selecting the correct alternative rule, bottom-up parsers use previous analysis of the grammar to correctly determine the handle. The primary difference between the various bottom-up techniques lies in their varying abilities to locate the handle and, in cases where there are two rules

```
a:  w
b:  w
```

in their abilities to choose between them when the handle is w. This analysis is summarized in two tables for an LR parser: the *parsing action* and the *goto* tables. The LR parsing algorithm performs simple decision making based on the contents of those tables.

Variations on the Basic Algorithm

As originally conceived by Knuth in 1965, the tables produced by grammatical analysis were impractically large for real programming languages. It was not until several years later that DeRemer showed that in many cases the tables could be compacted by merging some of the rows, while still maintaining the correctness of the parser [DeRemer 71]. These reductions in table size were substantial enough to make LR parsing practical. Since then, still other reductions in table size have been proposed and there are many variations on the basic LR parser generation scheme. It is important to recognize that the parsing algorithm used by DeRemer is the same as Knuth's. Only the table construction algorithms were modified to reduce table size. DeRemer described what are called *simple* LR grammars (SLR) and the *look-ahead* LR grammars (LALR). *yacc*, the parser generator on Unix, produces LALR(1) parsers. A language that has an LR(k), SLR(k), or LALR(k) grammar is said to be an LR(k), SLR(k), or LALR(k) language, respectively.

Not every LR(k) grammar is LALR(k), and not every LALR(k) grammar is SLR(k), although the converse is true. In that sense LR(k) parsing is more powerful than LALR(k) parsing which in turn is more powerful than SLR(k). However, this difference does not extend to languages. For any k, the set of LR(k), LALR(k), and SLR(k) languages are equal. Furthermore, these languages do not form a true hierarchy. For any k and $j \geq 1$, the LR(k) languages are the same set as the LR(j) languages; similarly, for LALR and SLR languages. Contrast this with the LL languages, for which the LL(k) languages are a proper subset of the LL($k+1$) languages for any $k \geq 1$. In practice, the only grammars used are SLR(1) and LALR(1) because the tables are too large for $k > 1$.

7.2. LR(1) PARSING ALGORITHM

Figure 7-4 depicts an LR parser. It has an input string with endmarker EOF, push-down stack of parser states, a *parsing action* table, acttab, and a *goto* table, gotab. The input is read from left to right, one token at a time. A state symbol summarizes the information contained in the stack below it and serves to direct the parser's action.

Each step of the parse begins by examining the next input token in variable token and state stack[top] currently on top of the stack. acttab has one row for each state of the parser, one column for each token type. The parser selects table entry acttab[stack[top],token]. The entry can have one of four values:

1. shift *S*
2. reduce *B:z*
3. accept
4. error

The last two actions are the easiest to explain. If the action is *accept*, the parser halts and accepts the string; it is a sentence of the grammar's language. Alternatively, if the table entry is *error*, the parser rejects the string (or takes a more elegant approach to error recovery—but elegance is discussed later); it is not a sentence. Options 1 and 2 are only slightly more complex. If the action is *shift S*, the parser gets the next token and pushes state *S* onto the stack. Finally, if the action is *reduce B:z*, then several events occur: first, the top *r* states are popped off the top of the stack, where *r* is the length of *z*. Second, the parser looks up an entry in gotab, which has rows labeled by the states, columns labeled by the nonterminals, and states as entries. It pushes gotab[stack[m],B] onto the stack, where stack[m] is the new top of stack. The current token is not touched.

These few steps are the heart of the LR parsing algorithm. Initially, the parser begins with a designated start state on the stack and token equal to the first token of the candidate string. The LR, SLR, and LALR parsers all use this one parsing algorithm; only the methods of constructing the parsing action and goto tables differ.

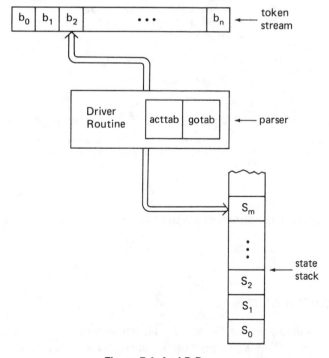

Figure 7-4. An LR Parser.

It would be convenient if a reduction to the grammar axiom always coincided with recognizing the input string. Ordinarily this is not possible; for example, axiom *e* of *unambig-express* can occur at an arbitrary number of points in a derivation tree. To force axiom *ax* to appear only at the root of a parse tree, the grammar is *augmented* by adding a new axiom *ax'* and a new rule

```
ax': ax
```

This rather trivial change to the grammar to support LR parsing has only the most modest cosmetic effect on the form of parse trees when compared to the radical surgery performed on grammars to eliminate left recursion for LL parsing. This is typically the extent to which grammars are modified to make them LR parsable.

C pseudocode for an LR parser follows. The code assumes that the tables and other data structures are initialized before parsing begins. The algorithms to analyze the grammar to determine the values of those data structures are presented in subsequent sections of this chapter. Not until the table construction methods are presented will it become clear why the LR parsing algorithm works.

Algorithm 7-1. LR parser.

```
1    state     curstate;          /* current state of parser */
2    actentry  curaction;         /* current action to be taken by parser */
3    int       token;
4
5    push start state onto stack;
6    curstate = start state;
7    token = yylex ();
8
9    while (!ateof) {    /* cycle til end of stream or error */
10       curaction = acttab [curstate, token];
11       switch (kind of curaction) {
12          case ACCEPT:
13             done - candidate is a sentence;
14          case REDUCE:   /* pop off rhs of handle rule; push new */
15             pop m states where m is the size of right-hand
16                 side of production in curaction;
17             push gotab[top, k] where k is left-hand side
18                 of production in curaction;
19             break;
20          case SHIFT:   /* read next token; push state onto stack */
21             token = yylex ();
22             push state in curaction;
23             break;
24          case ERROR:
25             error ("input is not a sentence.", appropriate);
26             break;
27          default:  /* internal error if this is ever reached */
28             error ("internal error: bad parsing action table.",
29                  PANIC);
30       }
31    }
```

Error processing in LR parsers is not discussed until Section 7.7, hence the vagueness in line 25.
♦

7.3. SLR(1) TABLE CONSTRUCTION

The previous section explained how the LR parsing algorithm works once the parsing action and goto tables have been constructed. This section gives the most rudimentary common method for building those tables, *Simple LR* (SLR) table construction.

Augmentation

The first step in generating SLR(1) tables is to augment the grammar as described earlier so that there is a new axiom, `ax'`, constructed from old axiom `ax` and one new rule, `ax':ax`.

Collection of LR(0) Items

After augmentation the collection of LR(0) *items* is constructed. Intuitively, these are the states of a finite-state machine that accepts the prefixes of all sentential forms of the grammar. Note this is *not* the same as accepting the sentences of the grammar. Recall that in general context-free grammars generate languages that cannot be accepted by any finite-state machine. From the collection of items the tables can be directly constructed. The reason why these are LR *zero* items will become clear in the next section where general LR(1) items are constructed.

An *item* is represented by a rule of the grammar with a dot at some position on the right-hand side. To help visually distinguish items from rules, the former are surrounded by square brackets; for example, the following are all possible items constructed from rule 1.2 of *unambig-express*':

```
1   [e: • e ao t]
2   [e: e • ao t]
3   [e: e ao • t]
4   [e: e ao t •]
```

Null rule, *B*:, generates only one item:

```
[B: •]
```

Intuitively, an item represents how much of a rule's right-hand side has been seen during the parse in a situation where that right-hand side might be the handle. For example, the first item above shows that none of the rule has yet been seen because the dot is at the beginning of the right-hand side. The second item implies that e has been seen, but not yet ao. The third shows that both e and ao have been shifted, and finally, the last item indicates that all three right-hand side components have been found. An item whose dot is at the far right side is said to be *completed* because it signals the parser that this right-hand side is the handle and a reduction is in order using the rule on which the item is based. Item 4 constructed from rule 1.2 above is completed. An item produced from the null rule is always completed.

Items are grouped into collections; each collection represents a state of a finite-state machine that accepts viable prefixes. The generation of each collection is called *closure*, which is illustrated on the singleton set of items SI, formed from rule 0 of *unambig-express*':

```
{ [e': • e] }
```

Closure(SI) is the set containing nine items:

```
1   [e': • e]
2   [e: • t]
3   [e: • e ao t]
4   [t: • f]
5   [t: • t mo f]
6   [f: • ( e )]
7   [f: • INTEGER]
8   [f: • - INTEGER]
9   [f: • - ( e )]
```

Intuitively, the closure operation formalizes the notion that since eventually the parser will be looking for a handle that is the right-hand side of rule `e' : e` (in order to reduce that handle), it must first look for the handles based on those strings that are derived from e (and reduce them); in this case, there are two such sentential forms: t and e ao t. Extending this reasoning, in seeking t it should look for f and t mo f. This finally leads us to add the last four items.

Algorithm 7-2. Closure.
Purpose: Compute closure on set of items *IT*.
Steps

1. Every item in *IT* is in closure(*IT*).
2. If [*B*: *w*●*Cz*] is in closure(*IT*) and *C*: *v* is a rule, then add [*C*: ●*v*] to closure(*IT*). Apply step (2) until it can no longer be applied.

◆

The closure operation produces the states of the machine. The machine's transition function is generated from the goto operation. The definition of goto requires that the term *valid* item first be explained. Item [*B*: *w*●y] is said to be *valid* for viable prefix *vw* if there is a rightmost derivation

```
ax'
    ...
v B z
    ...
v w y z
```

A valid item indicates whether to shift or reduce the LR parser's stack. If *vw* has been seen so far and *y* is not null, then the entire handle *wy* has not yet been seen and more tokens need to be shifted onto the stack. On the other hand, if *y* is null, then *w* is the handle, and a reduction via rule *B*: *w* is required. If *IT* is a set of items and *x* is a vocabulary symbol, then *goto(IT,x)* is simply the closure of the set of all items [*C*: *vx*●*z*] where [*C*: *v*●*xz*] is in *IT*. Intuitively, if *IT* is the set of items that are valid for viable prefix *y*, then goto(*IT,x*) is the set of items valid for *yx*. goto(closure(*IT*),e) is:

```
1   [e': e ●]
2   [e: e ● ao t]
3   [ao: ● +]
4   [ao: ● -]
```

The first item in the set comes directly from [*e'*: ●*e*] by moving ● to the right of *e*. Similarly, the second item comes from advancing ● in [*e*:●*e ao t*]. The last two items in the set come from applying the closure operation on the second item. Applying closure to the first, third, and fourth items has no effect.

The algorithms to compute both the states and the transition function having been presented, the following algorithm to compute *CSI*, the collection of set of LR(0) items of an augmented grammar, puts it all together.

Algorithm 7-3. Collection of set of LR(0) items.
Steps

1. *CSI* = closure([*ax'*:●*ax*]).
2. For each set *IT* of items in *CSI* and each vocabulary symbol *x* such that goto(*IT,x*) is not empty and not in *CSI*, add goto(*IT,x*) to *CSI*.
3. Repeat step (2) until nothing more can be added to *CSI*.

◆

Example 7-2. The collection of sets of items for *unambig-express'* are numbered consecutively from 0. To the right of each set is the operation that generated it and the viable prefix the state represents. The computation of duplicate sets is also shown:

```
IT0:   [e': ● e]              closure ([e':e])
       [e: ● t]               NULL
       [e: ● e ao t]
       [t: ● f]
       [t: ● t mo f]
```

```
        [f: • ( e )]
        [f: • INTEGER]
        [f: • - INTEGER]
        [f: • - ( e )]

IT1:    [e': e •]                       closure (goto (IT0, e))
        [e: e • ao t]                   e
        [ao: • +]
        [ao: • -]

IT2:    [e: t •]                        closure (goto (IT0, t))
        [t: t • mo f]                   t
        [mo: • *]
        [mo: • /]

IT3:    [t: f •]                        closure (goto (IT0, f))
                                        f

IT4:    [f: ( • e )]                    closure (goto (IT0, '('))
        [e: • e ao t]                   (
        [e: • t]
        [t: • f]
        [t: • t mo f]
        [f: • ( e )]
        [f: • INTEGER]
        [f: • - INTEGER]
        [f: • - ( e )]

IT5:    [f: INTEGER •]                  closure (goto (IT0, INTEGER))
                                        INTEGER

IT6:    [f: - • INTEGER]                closure (goto (IT0, '-'))
        [f: - • ( e )]                  -

IT7:    [e: e ao • t]                   closure (goto (IT1, ao))
        [t: • f]                        e ao
        [t: • t mo f]
        [f: • ( e )]
        [f: • INTEGER]
        [f: • - INTEGER]
        [f: • - ( e )]

IT8:    [ao: + •]                       closure (goto (IT1, '+'))
                                        e +

IT9:    [ao: - •]                       closure (goto (IT1, '-'))
                                        e -

IT10:   [t: t mo • f]                   closure (goto (IT2, mo))
        [f: • ( e )]                    t mo
        [f: • INTEGER]
        [f: • - ( e )]
        [f: • - INTEGER]

IT11:   [mo: * •]                       closure (goto (IT2, '*'))
                                        t *

IT12:   [mo: / •]                       closure (goto (IT2, '/'))
                                        t /

IT13:   [f: ( e • )]                    closure (goto (IT4, e))
        [e: e • ao t]                   ( e
        [ao: • +]
        [ao: • -]

IT14: closure (goto (IT4, f)) = IT3

IT15:   [t: t • mo f]                   closure (goto (IT4, t))
        [e: t •]                        ( t
        [mo: • *]
        [mo: • /]

IT16: closure (goto (IT4, '(')) = IT4
```

```
IT17: closure (goto (IT4, INTEGER)) = IT5

IT18: closure (goto (IT4, '-')) = IT6

IT19: [f: - INTEGER •]                    closure (goto (IT6, INTEGER))
                                          - INTEGER

IT20: [f: - ( • e )]                      closure (goto (IT6, '('))
      [e: • e ao t]                       - (
      [e: • t]
      [t: • f]
      [t: • t mo f]
      [f: • ( e )]
      [f: • INTEGER]
      [f: • - INTEGER]
      [f: • - ( INTEGER]

IT21: [e: e ao t •]                       closure (goto (IT7, t))
                                          e ao t

IT22: closure (goto (IT7, f)) = IT3

IT23: closure (goto (IT7, t)) = IT15

IT24: closure (goto (IT7, '(')) = IT4

IT25: closure (goto (IT7, INTEGER)) = IT19

IT26: closure (goto (IT7, '-')) = IT6

IT27: [t: t mo f •]                       closure (goto (IT10, f))
                                          t mo f

IT28: closure (goto (IT10, '(')) = IT4

IT29: closure (goto (IT10, INTEGER)) = IT5

IT30: closure (goto (IT10, '-')) = IT6

IT31: [f: ( e ) •]                        closure (goto (IT13, ')'))
                                          ( e )

IT32: closure (goto (IT13, ao)) = IT7

IT33: closure (goto (IT13, '+')) = IT8

IT34: closure (goto (IT13, '-')) = IT9

IT35: closure (goto (IT15, mo)) = IT10

IT36: closure (goto (IT15, '*')) = IT11

IT37: closure (goto (IT15, '/')) = IT12

IT38: [f: - ( e • )]                      closure (goto (IT20, e))
      [e: e • ao t]                       - ( e
      [ao: • +]
      [ao: • -]

IT39: closure (goto (IT20, t)) = IT2

IT40: closure (goto (IT20, f)) = IT14

IT41: closure (goto (IT20, '(')) = IT4

IT42: closure (goto (IT20, INTEGER)) = IT5

IT43: closure (goto (IT20, '-')) = IT6

IT44: [f: - ( e ) •]                      closure (goto (IT38, ')'))
                                          - ( e )

IT45: closure (goto (IT38, ao)) = IT7
```

```
IT46: closure (goto (IT38, '+')) = IT8

IT47: closure (goto (IT38, '-')) = IT9
```

There are 22 new and 26 duplicate sets. The deterministic finite-state machine that accepts the viable prefixes of the sentential forms of *unambig-express*' is determined by the `closure(goto())` entries in the computation above.

♦

Tables

The SLR(1) parsing action table for *unambig-express*' is shown in Fig. 7-5. States label the rows, terminals label the columns. There are three types of entries indicating whether to shift, accept, or reduce. A blank entry indicates error. *Sj* means shift and enter state *j*. Entry *Rj* means reduce using rule *j*. `gotab` is in Fig. 7-6. Only the states that have entries are shown. The algorithm for constructing this table uses the `goto` function and the `follow` set of each nonterminal. The algorithm for computing the `follow` set of each nonterminal was presented in the last chapter in the discussion of LL(1) grammars. Suppose COLL = { $IT0$, $IT1$, . . ., ITn } is the collection of sets of items. The numbers of these states label the rows of action. The columns are labeled only by tokens. This represents the fact that the next symbol is always a token in a left to right scan of a string.

1. For terminal b, if [$B: w \bullet b z$] is in ITi and `goto(`ITi`,b) = `ITj, then `acttab[`i`,b] = `Sj.
2. If [$B: w \bullet$] is in ITi, then `acttab[`i`,b] = `Rn for all b in `follow(`B`)`, where n is the rule number of $B: w$.
3. If [$ax': ax \bullet$] is in ITi, where ax' is the augmented grammar's axiom, then `acttab[`i`,EOF] = ` `accept`.

Example 7-3. Figure 7-7 shows the sequence of transitions taken by this parser on the string "1+20*-2". Figure 7-8 shows the transitions on the nonsentence "1+*20". Note that the parser rejects "1+*20" before scanning past the erroneously placed '*'.

♦

State	Terminal							
	INTEGER	+	−	*	/	(	)	EOF
0	S5		S6			S4		
1		S8	S9					accept
2		R1.1	R1.1	S11	S12			
3		R2.1	R2.1	R2.1	R2.1		R2.1	R2.1
4	S5		S6			S4		
5		R3.2	R3.2	R3.2	R3.2		R3.2	R3.2
6	S19					S20		
7	S19		S6			S4		
8	R4.1						R4.1	
9	R4.2						R4.2	
10	S5		S6			S4		
11	R5.1		R5.1				R5.1	
12	R5.2		R5.2				R5.2	
13		S8	S9				S31	
15		R1.1	R1.1	S11	S12			
19		R3.3	R3.3	R3.3	R3.3		R3.3	R3.3
20	S5		S6			S4		
21		R1.2	R1.2	R1.2	R1.2		R1.2	R1.2
27		R2.2	R2.2	R2.2	R2.2		R2.2	R2.2
31		R3.1	R3.1	R3.1	R3.1		R3.1	R3.1
38		S8	S9				S44	
44		R3.4	R3.4	R3.4	R3.4		R3.4	R3.4

Figure 7-5. `acttab` **Parsing Action Table for *unambig-express*'.**

State	Nonterminal				
	e	t	ao	f	mo
0	1	2		3	
1			7		
2					10
4	13	15			
7		21			
10				27	
20	38				

Figure 7-6. gotab **Goto Table for** *unambig-express'.*

Stack	Input String	Action	Resulting Sentential Form
0	^1+20*-2	S5	1
0 5	1^+20*-2	R3.2	f
0 3	1^+20*-2	R2.1	t
0 2	1^+20*-2	R1.1	e
0 1	1^+20*-2	S8	e +
0 1 8	1+^20*-2	R4.1	e ao
0 1 7	1+^20*-2	S5	e ao 20
0 1 7 5	1+20^*-2	R3.2	e ao f
0 1 7 3	1+20^*-2	R2.1	e ao t
0 1 7 2	1+20^*-2	S11	e ao t *
0 1 7 2 11	1+20*^-2	R5.1	e ao t mo
0 1 7 2 10	1+20*^-2	S6	e ao t mo −
0 1 7 2 10 6	1+20*-^2	S19	e ao t mo − 2
0 1 7 2 10 6 19	1+20*-2^	R3.3	e ao t mo f
0 1 7 2 10 27	1+20*-2^	R2.2	e ao t
0 1 7 21	1+20*-2^	R1.2	e
0 1	1+20*-2^	accept	

Figure 7-7. Accepting "1+20*-2".

Stack	Input String	Action	Resulting Sentential Form
0	^1+*20	S5	1
0 5	1^+*20	R3.2	f
0 3	1^+*20	R2.1	t
0 2	1^+*20	R1.1	e
0 1	1^+*20	S8	e +
0 1 8	1+^*20	error	

Figure 7-8. Rejecting "1+*20".

Conflict Resolution

Two types of conflicts can occur when constructing the SLR(1) parsing action table:

1. shift/reduce
2. reduce/reduce

Shift/reduce conflicts arise when a state has two items

```
[B: w • b v ]
[C: z •]
```

where terminal b is in follow(C). The first item forces a shift when b is seen, while the second forces a reduction using rule C:z. Reduce/reduce conflicts occur when a state has two items:

```
[B: w •]
[C: w •]
```

Both completed items indicate a reduction is necessary, but via two distinct rules. There are three ways to resolve the conflict:

1. Use a more powerful LR table construction method.
2. Force a choice.
3. Modify the grammar.

The first option would probably mean choosing either the LALR(1) or LR(1) table construction methods. Because LR(1) tables tend to be so much larger, LALR(1) construction would likely be tried first. These two methods, by doing more thorough analyses of the grammar, may increase the number of rows in acttab, creating a sparser matrix. In some cases, this may eliminate an entry that is the source of conflict.

The second option is often quite satisfactory. Simply force the parser to choose one way or the other by erasing a conflicting entry in the parsing action table. *yacc*, studied in the next chapter, has a default tie-breaking strategy which guarantees that for any context-free grammar, it will produce a conflict-free parsing action table. Of course, the conflicts must be settled in a satisfactory way if the parser is to be useful. Having the ability to break ties often enables the translator writer to simplify the grammar.

Example 7-4. Ambiguous grammar *gram-express*, defined in Section 5.1 has the following sets of collections of items:

```
IT0:  [e': • e]              closure ([e':e])
      [e: • e o e]           NULL
      [e: • ( e )]
      [e: • INTEGER]
      [e: • - INTEGER]
      [e: • - ( INTEGER]

IT1:  [e': e •]              closure (goto (IT0, e))
      [e: e • o e]           e
      [o: • +]
      [o: • -]
      [o: • *]
      [o: • /]

IT2:  [e: ( • e )]           closure (goto (IT0, '('))
      [e: • e o e]           (
      [e: • ( e )]
      [e: • INTEGER]
      [e: • - INTEGER]
      [e: • - ( INTEGER]
```

```
IT3:  [e: INTEGER •]              closure (goto (IT0, INTEGER))
                                  INTEGER

IT4:  [e: - • INTEGER]            closure (goto (IT0, '-'))
      [e: - • (' INTEGER]         -

IT5:  [e: e o • e]                closure (goto (IT1, o))
      [e: • e o e]                e o
      [e: • ( e )]
      [e: • INTEGER]
      [e: • - INTEGER]
      [e: • - ( INTEGER]

IT6:  [o: + •]                    closure (goto (IT1, '+'))
                                  e +

IT7:  [o: - •]                    closure (goto (IT1, '-'))
                                  e -

IT8:  [o: * •]                    closure (goto (IT1, '*'))
                                  e *

IT9:  [o: / •]                    closure (goto (IT1, '/'))
                                  e /

IT10: [e: ( e • )]                closure (goto (IT2, e))
      [e: e • o e]                ( e
      [o: • +]
      [o: • -]
      [o: • *]
      [o: • /]

IT11: closure (goto (IT2, '(')): IT2

IT12: closure (goto (IT2, INTEGER)) = IT3

IT13: closure (goto (IT2, '-')) = IT4

IT14: [e: - INTEGER •]            closure (goto (IT4, INTEGER))
                                  - INTEGER

IT15: closure (goto (IT4, '(')) = IT2

IT16: [e: e o e •]                closure (goto (IT5, e))
      [e: e • o e]                e o e
      [o: • +]
      [o: • -]
      [o: • *]
      [o: • /]

IT17: closure (goto (IT5, '(')) = IT2

IT18: closure (goto (IT5, INTEGER)) = IT3

IT19: closure (goto (IT5, '-')) = IT4

IT20: [e: ( e ) •]                closure (goto (IT10, ')'))
                                  ( e )

IT21: closure (goto (IT10, o)) = IT5

IT22: closure (goto (IT10, '+')) = IT6

IT23: closure (goto (IT10, '-')) = IT7

IT24: closure (goto (IT10, '*')) = IT8

IT25: closure (goto (IT10, '/')) = IT9

IT26: closure (goto (IT16, o)) = IT5

IT27: closure (goto (IT16, '+')) = IT6
```

State	Terminal							
	INTEGER	+	−	*	/	(	)	EOF
0	S3		S4			S2		
1		S6	S7	S8	S9			accept
2	S3		S4			S2		
3		R1.3	R1.3	R1.3	R1.3		R1.3	R1.3
4	S14					S2		
5	S3		S4			S2		
6	R2.1					R2.1		
7	R2.2					R2.2		
8	R2.3					R2.3		
9	R2.4					R2.4		
10		S6	S7	S8	S9		S20	
14		R1.4	R1.4	R1.4	R1.4		R1.4	
16		R1.1	R1.1	R1.1	R1.1		R1.1	
		S6	S7	S8	S9			
20		R1.2	R1.2	R1.2	R1.2		R1.2	

Figure 7-9. *acttab* Parsing Action Table for *gram-express'*.

```
IT28: closure (goto (IT16, '-')) = IT7

IT29: closure (goto (IT16, '*')) = IT8

IT30: closure (goto (IT16, '/')) = IT9
```

This leads to the parsing action table in Fig. 7-9. Conflicts arise in state 16, which represents viable prefix `"eoe"`. It is precisely at this point that the ambiguity arises. Reduction mimics left to right evaluation of the expression, while shifting mimics right to left evaluation. Striking out the shift entries will force left to right evaluation. Note that this will not force multiplication and division to have a higher precedence than addition and subtraction.

♦

The third option to resolve conflicts, that is, change the grammar, is not necessary nearly as often for LR based parsers as it is for LL based ones. It will not be discussed further.

7.4. GENERAL LR(1) TABLE CONSTRUCTION

The last section showed how occasionally a conflict will arise in the parsing action table built using the SLR(1) table construction algorithm. The LR(1) table construction algorithm is more powerful in that through more thorough analysis of the context-free grammar defining the language, some of those conflicts may be eliminated. This section presents the LR(1) table construction algorithm, concentrating on the differences between it and the SLR(1) approach.

The SLR(1) table construction algorithm assumes that a reduction on completed item $[B:w\bullet]$ should be done whenever the next terminal is in the `follow` set of B. However, there are sentential forms for which terminal c cannot in fact follow B.

Example 7-5. Consider grammar *assign*:

```
1   s:  v  =  e
2   e:  f  ¦  e  +  f
3   f:  v  ¦  INTEGER  ¦  ( e )
4   v:  IDENT
```

which generates simple assignment statements. The set of LR(0) items for augmented grammar *assign'* is:

IT0: [*s'*: • *s*]   closure ([*s'*:*s*])
      [*s*: • *v* = *e*]   NULL
      [*v*: • IDENT]

IT1: [*s'*: *s* •]   closure (goto (IT0, *s*))
                                       s

IT2: [*s*: *v* • = *e*]   closure (goto (IT0, *v*))
                                       v

IT3: [*v*: IDENT •]   closure (goto (IT0, IDENT))
                                       IDENT

IT4: [*s*: *v* = • *e*]   closure (goto (IT2, '='))
      [*e*: • *f*]   *v* =
      [*e*: • *e* + *f*]
      [*f*: • *v*]
      [*f*: • INTEGER]
      [*f*: • (*e*)]
      [*v*: • IDENT]

IT5: [*s*: *v* = *e* •]   closure (goto (IT4, *e*))
      [*e*: *e* • + *f*]   *v* = *e*

IT6: [*e*: *f* •]   closure (goto (IT4, *f*))
                                       v = *f*

IT7: [*f*: *v* •]   closure (goto (IT4, *v*))
                                       v = *v*

IT8: [*f*: INTEGER •]   closure (goto (IT4, INTEGER))
                                       v = INTEGER

IT9: [*f*: (• *e*)]   closure (goto (IT4, '('))
      [*e*: • *f*]   *v* = (
      [*e*: • *e* + *f*]
      [*f*: • *v*]
      [*f*: • INTEGER]
      [*f*: • (*e*)]
      [*v*: • IDENT]

IT10: closure (goto (IT4, IDENT)) = IT3

IT11: [*e*: *e* + • *f*]   closure (goto (IT5, '+'))
      [*f*: • *v*]   *v* = *e* +
      [*f*: • INTEGER]
      [*f*: • (*e*)]
      [*v*: • IDENT]

IT12: [*f*: (*e* •)]   closure (goto (IT9, *e*))
      [*e*: *e* • + *f*]   *v* = (*e*

IT13: closure (goto (IT9, *f*)) = IT6

IT14: closure (goto (IT9, *v*)) = IT7

IT15: closure (goto (IT9, '(')) = IT9

IT16: closure (goto (IT9, INTEGER)) = IT8

IT17: closure (goto (IT9, IDENT)) = IT3

IT18: [*e*: *e* + *f* •]   closure (goto (IT11, *f*))
                                       v = *e* + *f*

IT19: closure (goto (IT11, *v*)) = IT7

IT20: closure (goto (IT11, INTEGER)) = IT8

IT21: closure (goto (IT11, '(')) = IT9

IT22: closure (goto (IT11, IDENT)) = IT3

```
IT23: [f: ( e ) •]                        closure (goto (IT12, ')'))
                                          v = ( e )

IT24: closure (goto (IT12, '+')) = IT11
```

which leads to the parsing action table in Fig. 7-10. The row labeled by state 3 shows that the reduction for rule v: IDENT is to be used whenever any member of the `follow` set of v; i.e., '+', ')', EOF, or '=' is the next token. However, state 3 actually represents two different situations. First, it represents the state of the parse when an identifier is seen on the right-hand side of the assignment operator. Under those circumstances '=' cannot be a legitimate next character. These three entries are in the columns labeled by '+', ')', and EOF. Second, it represents the state of the parse when the identifier is on the left-hand side of the assignment operator. This is the entry in the column labeled by '='.

♦

It is possible to do additional analysis of the grammar so that there are two different states for these different circumstances with entries for reductions only appearing in the appropriate columns where the indicated token really can follow. This analysis leads to sparser matrices, reducing the chances of shift/ reduce and reduce/reduce conflicts and is the difference between the SLR(1) and LR(1) table construction methods.

The LR(1) table construction algorithm uses a more general form of item which has two parts, a *core* rule as before plus a new *lookahead symbol*

```
[B: w, b]
```

where b is a terminal symbol that can follow B in the state that item represents. For example *assign*' this would mean items

```
[v: IDENT •, +]
[v: IDENT •, )]
[v: IDENT •, EOF]
```

in the state representing the reduction via rule 4 on the right-hand side of an assignment, and

```
[v: IDENT •, =]
```

in the state representing the same reduction on the left-hand side. The trailing token is not significant in building table entries for the shift operation. For completed item $[B: w•, b]$, however, instead of

State	Terminal						
	INTEGER	IDENT	+	(	)	=	EOF
0		S3					
1							accept
2						S4	
3			R4		R4	R4	R4
4	S8	S3		S9			
5			S11				R1
6			R2.1		R2.1		R2.1
7			R3.1		R3.1	R3.1	R3.1
8			R3.2		R3.2		R3.2
9	S8	S3		S9			
11	S8	S3	S18	S9			
12			S11		S23		
18			R2.2		R2.2		R2.2
23			R3.2		R3.2		R3.2

Figure 7-10. `acttab` SLR(1) Parsing Action Table for *assign*'.

marking entries in all columns labeled by elements in follow(*B*), only the column labeled by b is marked. Such items are called LR(1) to reflect the fact that the context in which the next character appears affects the table construction, unlike the LR(0) items of the last section. The latter used the follow set of the left-hand side of the reduction rule, ignoring the context in which the reduction was made. Obviously, the lookahead can be extended arbitrarily long, leading to LR(2) grammars, LR(3) grammars, and so on. From a practical view, LR(1) grammars normally lead to very large tables, so that longer lookaheads are never really used.

The algorithm to compute the set of LR(1) items is a slight generalization of the ones presented for LR(0) items. The closure and goto operations take into account the one-character lookahead.

Algorithm 7-4. LR(1) closure algorithm.
Steps

1. Every item in *IT* is in closure(*IT*).
2. If [*B*: *w*●*Cz*, b] is in closure(*IT*) and *C*: *v* is a rule, and terminal c is in first(*zb*) such that [*C*:●*v*, c] is not in *IT*, add [*C*:●*v*, c].
3. Repeat step (2) until it can no longer be applied.
◆

The goto operation is an even simpler extension of the original LR(0) version.

Algorithm 7-5. LR(1) goto algorithm.
Steps: If *IT* is a set of items and *x* is a vocabulary symbol, then goto(*IT*, *x*) is simply the closure of the set of all items [*C*: *vx*●*z*, b] where [*C*: *v*●*xz*, b] is in *IT*.
◆

Within the same set, two items that have the same core but different lookahead symbols

```
[B: w ● z, b]
[B: w ● z, c]
```

can be abbreviated by

```
[B: w ● z, b c]
```

Example 7-6. The revised closure and goto algorithms are demonstrated on *assign*':

```
IT0: [s': ● s, EOF]              closure([s':s,EOF])
     [s:  ● v = e, EOF]          NULL
     [v:  ● IDENT, =]

IT1: [s': s ●, EOF]              closure(goto(IT0,s))
                                 s

IT2: [s: v ● = e, EOF]           closure(goto(IT0,v))
                                 v

IT3: [v: IDENT ●, =]             closure(goto(IT0,IDENT))
                                 IDENT

IT4: [s: v = ● e, EOF]           closure(goto(IT2,'='))
     [e: ● f, EOF +]             v =
     [e: ● e + f, EOF +]
     [f: ● v, EOF +]
     [f: ● INTEGER, EOF +]
     [f: ● ( e ), EOF +]
     [v: ● IDENT, EOF +]

IT5: [s: v = e ●, EOF]           closure(goto(IT4,e))
     [e: e ● + f, EOF +]         v = e

IT6: [e: f ●, EOF +]             closure(goto(IT4,f))
                                 v = f
```

IT7: [f: v •, EOF +]   closure(goto(IT4,v))
                                         v = v

IT8: [f: INTEGER •, EOF +]   closure(goto(IT4,INTEGER))
                                         v = INTEGER

IT9: [f: (• e), EOF +]   closure(goto(IT4,'('))
      [e: • f,) +]   v = (
      [e: • e + f,) +]
      [f: • v,) +]
      [f: • INTEGER,) +]
      [f: • (e),) +]
      [v: • IDENT,) +]

IT10: [v: IDENT •, EOF +]   closure(goto(IT4,IDENT))
                                         v = v

IT11: [e: e + • f, EOF +]   closure(goto(IT5,'+'))
      [f: • v, EOF +]   v = e +
      [f: •(e), EOF +]
      [v: • IDENT, EOF +]

IT12: [f: (e •), EOF +]   closure(goto(IT9,e))
      [e: e • + f,) +]   v = (e

IT13: [e: f •,) +]   closure(goto(IT9,f))
                                         v = (f

IT14: [f: v •,) +]   closure(goto(IT9,v))
                                         v = (v

IT15: [f: INTEGER •,) +]   closure(goto(IT9,INTEGER))
                                         v = (INTEGER

IT16: [f: (• e),) +]   closure(goto(IT9,'('))
      [e: • f,) +]   v = ((
      [e: • e + f,) +]
      [f: • v,) +]
      [f: • INTEGER,) +]
      [f: • (e),) +]
      [v: • IDENT,) +]

IT17: [v: IDENT •,) +]   closure(goto(IT9,IDENT))
                                         v = (IDENT

IT18: [e: e + f •, EOF +]   closure(goto(IT11,f))
                                         v = e + f

IT19: closure(goto(IT11,v)) = IT7

IT20: closure(goto(IT11,'(')) = IT9

IT21: closure(goto(IT11,IDENT)) = IT10

IT22: [f: (e) •, EOF +]   closure(goto(IT12,')'))
                                         v = (e)

IT23: [e: e + • f,) +]   closure(goto(IT12,'+'))
      [f: • v,) +]   v = (e +
      [f: • (e),) +]
      [v: • IDENT,) +]

IT24: [f: (e •),) +]   closure(goto(IT16,e))
      [e: e • + f,) +]   v = ((e

IT25: closure(goto(IT16,f)) = IT13

IT26: closure(goto(IT16,v)) = IT14

IT27: closure(goto(IT16,INTEGER)) = IT15

IT28: closure(goto(IT16,'(')) = IT16

State	Terminal						
	INTEGER	IDENT	+	(	)	=	EOF
0		S3					
1							accept
2						S4	
3						R4	
4	S8	S10		S9			
5			S11				R1
6			R2.1				R2.1
7			R3.1				R3.1
8			R3.2				R3.2
9	S15	S17		S16			
10			R4				R4
11		S10		S9			
12			S23		S22		
13			R2.1		R2.1		
14			R3.1		R3.1		
15			R3.2		R3.2		
16	S15	S17		S16			
17			R4		R4		
18			R2.2				R2.2
22			R3.3				R3.3
23		S17		S16			
24			S23		S34		
30			R2.2		R2.2		
34			R3.3		R3.3		

Figure 7-11. `acttab` **LR(1) Parsing Action Table for** *assign'*.

```
IT29: closure(goto(IT16,IDENT)) = IT17

IT30: [e: e + f •, ) +]                closure(goto(IT23,f))
                                       v = ( e + f

IT31: closure(goto(IT23,v)) = IT14

IT32: closure(goto(IT23,'(')) = IT16

IT33: closure(goto(IT23,IDENT)) = IT17

IT34: [f: ( e ) •, ) +]                closure(goto(IT24,')'))
                                       v = ( ( e )

IT35: closure(goto(IT24,'+')) = IT23
```

which leads to the parsing action table in Fig. 7-11. This table has 24 states compared to the 14 in the corresponding SLR(1) table. States 3, 10, and 17 in the LR(1) table refine state 3 of the SLR(1) table. They correspond to the difference between when a variable is seen on the left- (state 3) or right-hand side of an assignment operator (state 10) and when the variable is nested inside a left parenthesis and therefore cannot be followed by EOF (state 17). States 7 and 14 similarly differentiate the case where nonterminal v is the handle inside a parenthesized expression from one where it is not. Similar differentiations account for state pairs 8 and 15, 9 and 16, 11 and 23, 12 and 24, 6 and 13, 18 and 30, 22 and 34, and states 18 and 30.

♦

7.5. LALR(1) TABLE CONSTRUCTION

Intermediate in power and complexity between the SLR(1) and LR(1) table construction algorithms is one that builds LALR(1) parsing tables. LALR and SLR parsers have the same number of states, but the LALR table is sometimes sparser than its SLR counterpart. On the other hand, a full LR parser for a

State	Terminal						
	INTEGER	IDENT	+	(	)	=	EOF
0		S3/10/17					
1							accept
2						S4	
3/10/17			R4		R4	R4	R4
4	S8/15	S3/10/17		S9/16			
5			S11/23				R1
6/13			R2.1		R2.1		R2.1
7/14			R3.1		R3.1		R3.1
8/15			R3.2		R3.2		R3.2
9/16	S8/15	S3/10/17		S9/16			
11/23	S3/10/17		S18/30	S9/16			
12/24			S11/23		S22/34		
18/30			R2.2		R2.2		R2.2
22/34			R3.3		R3.3		R3.3

Figure 7-12. `acttab` **LALR(1) Parsing Action Table for** *assign*'.

reasonable size language would normally have between 2 and 10 times as many states, depending on the constructs in the language. Hence, the storage economy in using LALR table construction is quite significant and in practice, most real programming language constructs fit the LALR model.

The LR table construction model distinguishes between two states if their lookahead symbols are different, but the cores are identical. The LALR model merges such states so that states in the table have distinct cores.

Example 7-7. Merging states with the same core, the LR(1) parsing action table of the last figure becomes Fig. 7-12. The states that were distinguished in the LR(1) table have been merged back together in the LALR(1) version.

♦

Merging cores can never produce a shift/reduce conflict that was not present in the original LR(1) table. Suppose in the union of two states from the LR(1) table there is an item $[A:w\bullet,b]$ forcing a reduction on b and item $[B:u\bullet bz,c]$ forcing a shift on b. Then some set IT of items from which the union was formed has item $[A:w\bullet,b]$. Since the cores of items are the same in the sets from which the union is formed, then IT must also contain an item $[B:u\bullet bz,d]$ for some possibly different terminal d. These two items, present in the original LR(1) table, force a shift/reduce conflict in IT.

A reduce/reduce conflict can be caused by merging states.

Example 7-8. Consider the following augmented grammar:

```
1   S': S
2   S:  a B c | b C c | a C d | b B d
3   B:  e
4   C:  e
```

The set of items for this grammar is:

```
ITO:    [S': • S, EOF]                 closure([S:S])
        [S: • a B c, EOF]              NULL
        [S: • b C c, EOF]
        [S: • a C d, EOF]
        [S: • b B d, EOF]

IT1:    [S': S •, EOF]                 closure(goto(ITO,S))
                                       S

IT2:    [S: a • B c, EOF]              closure(goto(ITO,'a'))
```

```
              [S: a • C d, EOF]                     a
              [B: • e, c]
              [C: • e, d]

      IT3:    [S: b • C c, EOF]          closure(goto(IT0,'b'))
              [S: b • B d, EOF]          b
              [C: • e, c]
              [B: • e, d]

      IT4:    [S: a B • c, EOF]          closure(goto(IT2,B))
                                         a B

      IT5:    [S: a C • d, EOF]          closure(goto(IT2,C))
                                         a C

      IT6:    [B: e •, c]                closure(goto(IT2,'e'))
              [C: e •, d]                a e

      IT7:    [S: b C • c, EOF]          closure(goto(IT3,C))
                                         b C

      IT8:    [S: b B • d, EOF]          closure(goto(IT3,B))
                                         b B

      IT9:    [C: e •, c]                closure(goto(IT3,'e'))
              [B: e •, d]                b e

      IT10:   [S: a B c •, EOF]          closure(goto(IT4,'c'))
                                         a B c

      IT11:   [S: a C d •, EOF]          closure(goto(IT5,'d'))
                                         a C d

      IT12:   [S: b C c •, EOF]          closure(goto(IT7,'c'))
                                         b C c

      IT13:   [S: b B d •, EOF]          closure(goto(IT8,'d'))
                                         b B d
```

This produces a conflict-free LR(1) parsing action table. When states IT6 and IT9 are merged, however, new state IT6/9 has items

```
      IT6/9:  [B: e •, c d]
              [C: e •, c d]
```

which demand the reduction via both rules 3 and 4 when the next token is either 'c' or 'd'.
◆

The difference between LALR(1) and SLR(1) may not be clear since the two tables always have the same set of states. After all, the LALR(1) and SLR(1) parsing action tables for *assign*' are identical isomorphic to the names of the states. The following example shows a grammar that is LALR(1), but not SLR(1).

Example 7-9. An LALR(1) grammar that is not SLR(1).

```
1    S': S
2    S:  B b b
3    S:  a a b
4    S:  b B a
5    B:  a
```

follow(S) = follow(S') = {EOF} and follow(B) = {a,b}. LR(1) table construction for this grammar produces:

```
      IT0:    [S': • S, EOF]             closure(|S':S|)
              [S: • B b b, EOF]          NULL
```

```
            [S: • a a b, EOF]
            [S: • b B a, EOF]
            [B: • a, b]

    IT1:    [S': S •, EOF]                        closure(goto(IT1,S))
                                                  S

    IT2:    [S: B • b b, EOF]                     closure(goto(IT0,B))
                                                  B

    IT3:    [S: a • a b, EOF]                     closure(goto(IT0,'a'))
            [B: a •, b]                           a

    IT4:    [S: b • B a, EOF]                     closure(goto(IT0,'b'))
            [B: • a, a]                           b

    IT5:    [S: B b • b, EOF]                     closure(goto(IT2,'b'))
                                                  B b

    IT6:    [S: a a • b, EOF]                     closure(goto(IT3,'a'))
                                                  a a

    IT7:    [S: b B • a, EOF]                     closure(goto(IT4,B))
                                                  b B

    IT8:    [B: a •, a]                           closure(goto(IT4,'a'))
                                                  b a

    IT9:    [S: B b b •, EOF]                     closure(goto(IT5,'b'))
                                                  B b b

    IT10:   [S: a a b a, EOF]                     closure(goto(IT6,'b'))
                                                  a a b

    IT11:   [S: b B a •, EOF]                     closure(goto(IT7,'a'))
                                                  b B a
```

The SLR(1) parsing action table for this grammar forces a shift in state 3 when 'a' is seen as well as a reduction via production 5 when either 'a' or 'b' is next. It has a shift/reduce conflict. The LALR(1) table, on the other hand, forces a similar shift in state 3, but only forces a reduction when 'b' is seen. There is no conflict. The trees in Fig. 7-13 reveal why the LALR(1) table is sparser, avoiding the conflict. The LALR(1) table distinguishes between viable prefixes "a" and "ba" when deciding under which conditions to reduce from 'a' to B. The SLR(1) does not.

◆

Example 7-10. Grammar

```
1    S': S
2    S:  B  c  B  b
3    S:  C  e
4    B:  d
5    C:  d
```

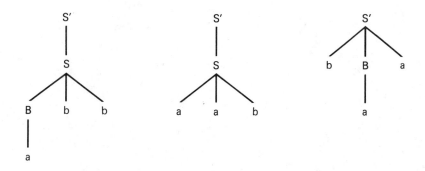

Figure 7-13. Parse Trees for LALR(1) Grammar Which Is Not SLR(1).

State	Terminal				
	a	b	c	e	EOF
0	S4	S4			
1					accept
2			S5		
3				S6	
4		R4	R4	R5	
5	S8				
6					R3
7		S9			
8		R4	R4		
9					R2

Figure 7-14. SLR(1) Parsing Action Table Distinct from LALR(1) Table.

is both SLR(1) and LALR(1), but has distinct parsing action tables. The reductions shown in entry (4,'b') and (8,'c') in Fig. 7-14 appear in the SLR(1) version only. In the LALR(1) table they are absent. In either case, there is no conflict.

◆

This section concludes by looking at a few interesting grammars.

Example 7-11. The following simple right recursive grammar shown with selection sets is SLR(1) but not LL(k) for any k. The decision as to whether to use rule 2.1 or 2.2 must be made at the second step in the derivation of a string when parsing top-down. However, the token needed to make that decision is always the rightmost one in the input string. A bottom-up parser, on the other hand, can make that decision at the very end. This is shown in Fig. 7-15.

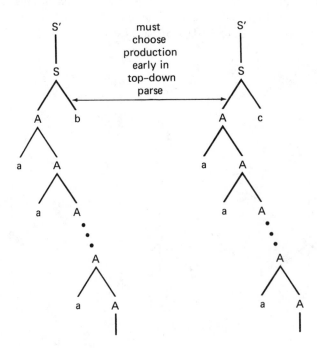

Figure 7-15. SLR(1) Grammar which is not LL(*k*).

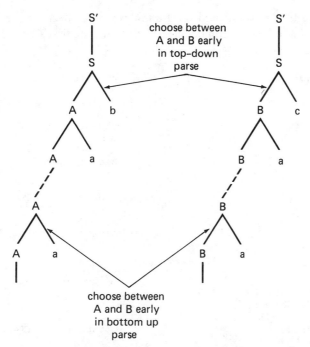

Figure 7-16. Grammar Which is not LR(k) but Language is.

```
1   S': S          [ a b c ]
2   S:  A b         [ a b ]
      : A c         [ a c ]
3   A:  a A         [ a ]
4   A:             [ b c ]
```

◆

Example 7-12. The following grammar is not LR(k) for any k, but the language is (via another grammar):

```
1   S': S
2   S:  A b : B c
3   A:  A a :
4   B:  B a :
```

Figure 7-16 shows why this grammar is not LR(k).
◆

7.6. EFFICIENT LALR(1) TABLE CONSTRUCTION

Building an LALR(1) action table by first producing the LR(1) table and then merging states with the same core has the strong disadvantage of requiring the voluminous storage of the LR(1) method during table construction. Table construction is also slowed enormously by having to generate and process all those extra states which are subsequently discarded anyhow. For these reasons, a more efficient algorithm for generating LALR(1) tables is needed.

The simplest storage efficient method is to merge sets of items at each step in the derivation of the collection of sets of items. Sets of states are constructed as in the LR(1) table construction method, but at each point where a new set is spawned it may be merged with an existing set. When new set S is created, all other states are checked to see if one with the same core exists. If not, S is kept; otherwise, it is merged with the previously existing set T with the same core to form set ST. The merged set is assigned a new set number and the original set T is deleted. Otherwise the generation process is the same.

Example 7-13. This algorithm is illustrated on grammar *assign'* used in the last section to illustrate LALR(1) table construction. Construction begins as before for the first 10 sets, all of which have unique cores:

```
IT0:  [s':  • s, EOF]                    closure([s':s,EOF])
      [s:  • v = e, EOF]                 NULL
      [v:  • IDENT, =]

IT1:  [s':  s •, EOF]                    closure(goto(IT0,s))
                                         s

IT2:  [s:  v • = e, EOF]                 closure(goto(IT0,v))
                                         v

IT3:  [v:  IDENT •, =]                   closure(goto(IT0,IDENT))
                                         IDENT

IT4:  [s:  v = • e, EOF]                 closure(goto(IT2,'='))
      [e:  • f, EOF +]                   v =
      [e:  • e + f, EOF +]
      [f:  • v, EOF +]
      [f:  • INTEGER, EOF +]
      [f:  • ( e ), EOF +]
      [v:  • IDENT, EOF +]

IT5:  [s:  v = e •, EOF]                 closure(goto(IT4,e))
      [e:  e • + f, EOF +]               v = e

IT6:  [e:  f •, EOF +]                   closure(goto(IT4,f))
                                         v = f

IT7:  [f:  v •, EOF +]                   closure(goto(IT4,v))
                                         v = v

IT8:  [f:  INTEGER •, EOF +]             closure(goto(IT4,INTEGER))
                                         v = INTEGER

IT9:  [f:  ( • e ), EOF +]               closure(goto(IT4,'('))
      [e:  • f, ) +]                     v = (
      [e:  • e + f, ) +]
      [f:  • v, ) +]
      [f:  • INTEGER, ) +]
      [f:  • ( e ), ) +]
      [v:  • IDENT, ) +]
```

IT10 has the same core as IT3:

```
IT10:  [v:  IDENT •, EOF +]              closure(goto(IT4,IDENT))
                                         v = v
```

This forces an immediate merger of IT3 and IT10 to form IT3/10:

```
IT3/10:  {v:  IDENT •, EOF + =}          closure(goto(IT4&0,IDENT))
                                         v = v
```

The closure operation on the right indicates the set comes from applying the goto operation on both IT4 and IT10. The states are reordered so that IT3/10 is last and a hole is left where IT3 previously existed:

```
 IT0:  IT1:  IT2:  IT4:  IT5:  IT6:  IT7:  IT8:  IT9:  IT3/10:
```

IT11 and IT12 have unique cores, but IT13 has the same core as IT6, forcing the creation of IT6/13:

```
 IT0:  IT1:  IT2:  IT4:  IT5:  IT7:  IT8:  IT9:  IT3/10:

IT11:  [e:  e + • f, EOF +]              closure(goto(IT5,'+'))
       [f:  • v, EOF +]                  v = e +
       [f:  • ( e ), EOF +]
       [v:  • IDENT, EOF +]
```

```
IT12:  [f: ( e • ), EOF +]                        closure(goto(IT9,e))
       [e: e • + f, ) +]                          v = ( e

IT6/13:  [e: f •, EOF ) +]                         closure(goto(IT4&9,f))
                                                   v = ( f
```

IT14 and IT7 have the same core as do pair IT15 and IT8. After the construction of IT7/14 and IT8/15, the collection of sets of items consists of

```
ITO:  IT1:  IT2:  IT3:  IT4:  IT5:  IT9:  IT3/10:  IT11:  IT12:
IT6/13:  IT7/14:  IT8/15:
```

All of the merged sets so far have consisted only of completed items. IT16, which is merged with IT9 is not completed, implying it will subsequently be used to generate new states via the goto operation.

```
IT9/16:  [f: ( • e ), EOF ) +]                    closure(goto(IT4&9,'('))
         [e: • f, ) EOF +]                         v = (
         [e: • e + f, ) EOF +]
         [f: • v, ) EOF +]
         [f: • INTEGER, ) EOF +]
         [f: • ( e ), ) EOF +]
         [v: • IDENT, ) EOF +]
```

The new collection of sets is

```
ITO:  IT1:  IT2:  IT3:  IT4:  IT5:  IT3/10:  IT11:  IT12:  IT6/13:
IT7/14:  IT8/15:  IT9/16:
```

The pointer into the sets of items was at IT9 prior to this operation; that is, IT16 = closure(goto(IT9,'(')). After the merger of IT9 and IT16, however, IT9 no longer exists. Generation continues with the next set, IT3/10. Since IT9/16 is now the last state, it will eventually be visited so that no set will be overlooked which would have been generated had IT9 not been removed. When generation continues, the order of set creation differs from that during LR(1) table construction because IT9 was removed before the goto operation was applied to all items in it:

```
ITO:  IT1:  IT2:  IT4:  IT5:  IT3/10:  IT11:  IT12:  IT6/13:
IT7/14:  IT8/15:  IT9/16:

IT17:  [e: e + f •, EOF +]                        closure(goto(IT11,f))
                                                   v = e + f

IT18:  closure(goto(IT11,v)) = IT7/14

IT19:  closure(goto(IT11,'(')) = IT9/16

IT20:  closure(goto(IT11,IDENT)) = IT3/10

IT21:  [f: ( e ) •, EOF +]                        closure(goto(IT12,')'))
                                                   v = ( e )
```

At this point IT22

```
IT22:  [e: e + • f, ) +]                          closure(goto(IT12,+))
       [f: • v, ) +]                              v = ( e +
       [f: • ( e ), ) +]
       [v: • IDENT, ) +]
```

is merged with IT11

```
IT11/22:  [e: e + • f, ) EOF +]                   closure(goto(IT11&22,+))
          [f: • v, ) EOF +]                        v = e +
          [f: • ( e ), ) EOF +]
          [v: • IDENT, ) EOF +]
```

Generation continues:

```
        ITD:  IT1:  IT2:  IT4:  IT5:  IT3/10:  IT12:  IT6/13:  IT7/14:
        IT8/15:  IT9/16:  IT17:  IT21:  IT11/22:
```

IT23: [f: e •), EOF) +]   closure(goto(IT9/16,e))
                                                    v = (e

IT23 has the same core as IT12 so they are merged and generation continues:

```
        ITD:  IT1:  IT2:  IT4:  IT5:  IT3/10:  IT6/13:  IT7/14:
        IT8/15:  IT9/16:  IT17:  IT21:  IT11/22:  IT12/23:
```

IT24: closure(goto(IT9/16,f)) = IT6/13

IT25: closure(goto(IT9/16,v)) = IT7/14

IT26: closure(goto(IT9/16,INTEGER)) = IT8/15

IT27: closure(goto(IT9/16,'(') = IT9/16

Set IT28 is

IT28: [v: IDENT •,) EOF +]   closure(goto(IT9/16,IDENT))
                                                    v = (IDENT

which has the same core as IT3/10. It is merged and generation continues:

```
        ITD:  IT1:  IT2:  IT4:  IT5:  IT6/13:  IT7/14:  IT8/15:
        IT9/16:  IT17:  IT21:  IT11/22:  IT12/23:  IT3/10/28:
```

IT29: [e: e + f •,) EOF +]   closure(goto(IT11/22,f))
                                                    v = (e + f

IT29 is merged with IT17. Generation continues:

```
        ITD:  IT1:  IT2:  IT4:  IT5:  IT6/13:  IT7/14:  IT8/15:
        IT9/16:  IT21:  IT11/22:  IT12/23:  IT3/10/28:  IT17/29:
```

IT30: [f: (e) •, EOF (+]   closure(goto(IT12/23,')'))
                                                    v = (e)

is merged with IT21:

```
        ITD:  IT1:  IT2:  IT4:  IT5:  IT6/13:  IT7/14:  IT8/15:
        IT9/16:  IT11/22:  IT12/23:  IT3/10/28:  IT17/29:  IT21/30:
```

State	Terminal						
	INTEGER	IDENT	+	(	)	=	EOF
0		S3/10/28					
1							accept
2						S4	
3/10/28			R4		R4	R4	R4
4	S8/15	S3/10/28		S9/16			
5			S11/22				R1
6/13			R2.1		R2.1		R2.1
7/14			R3.1		R3.1		R3.1
8/15			R3.2		R3.2		R3.2
9/16	S8/15	S3/10/28		S9/16			
11/22	S3/10/28		S17/29	S9/16			
12/23			S11/22		S21/30		
17/29			R2.2		R2.2		R2.2
21/30			R3.3		R3.3		R3.3

Figure 7-17. Efficiently Constructed LALR(1) Table for _assign_'.

No more sets can be generated. The parsing action table for this collection of sets of items is in Fig. 7-17. It is isomorphic to the LALR(1) table shown in Fig. 7-12 modulo the set numbers.

◆

There are still more efficient algorithms for generating LALR(1) tables; for example, the graph search approach adopted to the construction of LL(1) selection sets in the last chapter can likewise be adopted to the construction of LALR(1) tables [DeRemer and Pennello 82]. The one presented here has the advantage of being relatively intuitive and straightforward to implement.

7.7. ERROR RECOVERY

The default error recovery assumed so far is to simply panic and terminate the parse. The table-driven LR method lends itself well to elegant error recovery. It is not possible to reference a hole in the goto table (why not?), but referencing an empty spot in the parsing action table implies an illegal token has been found in the input stream. The blank entries can be replaced by references to error recovery actions which modify the parser stack and input stream. States can be popped off or pushed onto the stack and tokens can be inserted, replaced, or skipped in the input stream. To illustrate this, the SLR(1) parsing action table originally in Fig. 7-10 is repeated in Fig. 7-18 with several error entries, Ei, where i indicates the recovery action to be taken. A recovery action can easily be tailored to the state in which the error is found. For example, state 0 represents the NULL viable prefix when parsing has just begun. An IDENT is expected. If an INTEGER is found instead, a reasonable strategy is to skip tokens until '=', IDENT, or EOF is reached. If EOF is reached, the parser can just terminate gracefully. If IDENT is found first, it should simply act as if that were the beginning of the input string, ignoring all earlier tokens. Finally, if '=' is found, perhaps that is the assignment operator with the left-hand side missing. Insert a manufactured IDENT in front of it and act as if that is the beginning of the input string. This recovery strategy is captured in E1.

E1: State 0 represents the beginning of the parse when the variable on the left-hand side of the assignment should be found. Skip tokens until EOF, IDENT, or '=' is found. If EOF is reached first, use recovery E3. If IDENT is found, print "Identifier expected. Skipping until %s" substituting the identifier found in the message. State 0 is left on top of the stack. Finally, if '=' is found first, use recovery E2.

E2: Insert a manufactured IDENT before the '=', print "Identifier expected. Skipping until '='. Assuming it is assignment operator.", and resume the parse with IDENT as the current input. State 0 is still on top of the stack.

E3: EOF has been reached prematurely. Might as well just terminate the parse. Print the message "Null input. Parse terminated." and quit.

State	Terminal						
	INTEGER	IDENT	+	(	)	=	EOF
0	E1	S3	E1	E1	E1	E2	E3
1							accept
2	E4	E4				S4	
3			R4		R4	R4	R4
4	S8	S3		S9			
5			S11				R1
6			R2.1		R2.1		R2.1
7			R3.1		R3.1	R3.1	R3.1
8			R3.2		R3.2		R3.2
9	S8	S3		S9	E5		
11	S8	S3	S18	S9			
12			S11		S23		
18			R2.2		R2.2		R2.2
23			R3.2		R3.2		R3.2

Figure 7-18. SLR(1) Table for *assign'* with Error Entries.

E4: State 2 represents the situation where the variable on the left-hand side of the assignment statement has been found and reduced to v. The next symbol should be '='. If an INTEGER or IDENT is found, assume the '=' was forgotten and insert it into the input stream, printing the message "'=' expected, but not found. Inserted into input."; otherwise, skip tokens until an INTEGER or IDENT is found and then insert '=', printing the message "'=' expected, but not found. Skipping input until %s and then inserting '='." where %s is replaced by the integer or identifier eventually found. If EOF is found first, print message "'=' expected, but end of file reached instead. Parse terminated." and quit.

E5: State 9 represents the viable prefix "$v=($". If a ')' is found without an intervening expression, push state 12 onto the stack without advancing the input pointer. This has the effect of making the parser behave as if it saw an expression before encountering ')'. Print the message "Expression expected after '('.".

Obviously many more error entries could be made, the specification of which is left as an exercise. *yacc*, studied in Chapter 8, offers a way to specify such recovery methods through grammar augmentations much as resynchronization was specified for *marli*.

EXERCISES

1. For each of the following strings:

    (i) −2*3
    (ii) (−1+4)/((2*5)
    (iii) −1−−2/4*−3

  (a) Construct the rightmost derivation relative to *unambig-express*.
  (b) Construct the inverse rightmost derivation.
  (c) Trace the execution of the SLR(1) parser based on the tables in Figs. 7-6 and 7-7.

2. Trace the execution of the SLR(1) parser for *assign'* based on the table in Fig. 7-11 on the strings:

  (a) x = 3
  (b) y = (3+4)
  (c) z = (3+4)+(5+6)

3. For the grammar in Exercise 4 of Chapter 6:

  (a) Construct an SLR(1) parsing table.
  (b) Construct an LALR(1) parsing table.
  (c) Construct an LR(1) parsing table.
  (d) Modify each of the tables to add "reasonable" error recovery.

4. Prove that no LR(1) grammar is ambiguous.

5. Prove that if a grammar is ambiguous, its LR parsing table will have at least one conflict.

6. Prove that the FSM represented by Fig. 7-6 accepts all the viable prefixes of *unambig-express'*.

7. Can removing a shift/reduce conflict in an LR parsing table affect the language accepted? Prove it.

8. Can removing a reduce/reduce conflict in an LR parsing table affect the language accepted? Prove it.

Chapter 8
SYNTAX-DIRECTED TRANSLATION

A parser-writing system such as *marli* generates programs that recognize whether a string is in a particular language. It is a relatively small step to a more general program that translates the string as it parses. Such a program is often called a *syntax-directed translator* (SDT) because the flow of control of the translator is guided by the act of parsing the input stream. Other names for such programs are *compiler-compilers* and *translator-writing systems*. Both the LL and LR parsing methods can be extended to support SDT. This text shows how to extend *marli* to support LL based SDT and discusses the approach taken in *yacc* to support LR based SDT.

The fundamental approach to SDT was already revealed in the study of *lex* in Chapter 4 where C action code was associated with each pattern matching rule. That code was executed each time a pattern was selected. Furthermore, special predefined variables such as yytext (matched string) and yyleng (length of yytext) were assigned values during pattern matching which could be referenced in the action code. The same strategy can be applied in a parser specification so that action code is executed with the selection and expansion of a rule in a top-down parser and with the reduction of the handle in a bottom-up parser. As the parse proceeds, a symbol table can be filled, data structures manipulated, and object code produced. When the parser component of an SDT finishes its analysis of the entire input stream, the translation of that input is complete.

8.1. TOP-DOWN SYNTAX-DIRECTED TRANSLATION

Top-down SDT is illustrated by adding action code to *ll-express* producing a translator that evaluates arithmetic expressions (the translation is its value); for example, the magical expression

```
(2+1)*2*(223-1)/2
```

will be translated into 666 by executing that action code during the parse.

ll-express is repeated here without selection sets but with embedded action code that is patterned heavily after that used in *cecilia*. A grammar that has action code is said to be *attributed*:

```
1.  e:  t  es

2.  es:  ao  t  {rhs=popopand();
                 lhs=popopand();
                 switch (popoptor()) {
                    case _PLUS:   pushopand(lhs+rhs); break;
                    case _MINUS:  pushopand(lhs-rhs); break;
                    default: error ("illegal stack", PANIC);
                    }
                 }
            es  ;

3.  t:  f  ts

4.  ts:  mo  f  {rhs=popopand();
                 lhs=popopand();
```

137

```
                    switch (popoptor()) {
                      case _ASTERISK: pushopand(lhs*rhs); break;
                      case _SLASH:    pushopand(lhs/rhs); break;
                      default: error ("illegal stack", PANIC);
                      }
                    }

              ts  ¦

5.   f:   p  ¦  -  p   {pushopand (-popopand());}

6.   ao:  +  {pushoptor(_PLUS);}   ¦
          -  {pushoptor(_MINUS);}

7.   mo:  *  {pushoptor(_ASTERISK);}  ¦
          /  {pushoptor(_SLASH);}

8.   p:  ( e )  ¦  INTEGER  {pushopand($1);}
```

Action code specifies how to perform the translation. Each action code segment appears within curly brackets at arbitrary places on the right-hand side of a production just as did error recovery code in Section 6.4. The code itself is a series of *C* statements, except for special identifiers beginning with "$" whose purpose will be explained shortly. An embedded action code segment can reference separately defined constants, variables, and functions. Here they primarily define and manipulate optorstk, a stack of operators, and opandstk, a stack of operands. The parse of a string proceeds as before expanding nonterminals and matching terminals in the sentential form against tokens in the input stream, except that when embedded action code is encountered on the right-hand side of a rule it is executed. Since LL(1) parsers never backtrack, it is never necessary to undo such actions. The separately defined action code is:

```
1     #include "global.h"
2
3     #define  MAXOPAND 100
4     #define  MAXOPTOR 100
5
6     int opandstk[MAXOPAND], optorstk[MAXOPTOR];
7     int opandptr, optorptr;
8     int _attribute;
9
10    pushopand (t)  int t;
11    {
12        if (++opandptr == MAXOPAND)
13            error ("internal stack overflow.", PANIC);
14        opandstk[opandptr] = t;
15    }
16
17    popopand ()
18    {
19        if (opandptr < 0)
20            error ("internal stack underflow.", PANIC);
21        return (opandstk[opandptr--]);
22    }
23
24    pushoptor (t)  int t;
25    {
26        if (++optorptr == MAXOPTOR)
27            error ("internal stack overflow.", PANIC);
28        optorstk[optorptr] = t;
29    }
30
31    popoptor ()
32    {
33        if (optorptr < 0)
34            error ("internal stack underflow.", PANIC);
35        return (optorstk[optorptr--]);
36    }
37
38    preparse()
39    {
40        opandptr = optorptr = -1;
41    }
42
```

```
43    postparse()
44    {
45        printf ("%d\n", popopand());
46    }
```

Two special routines `preparse` and `postparse` will automatically be invoked at the beginning and end of the translation, respectively. These allow for any initialization and cleanup activities. In the example the two variables that indicate the size of the stacks are set to-1when `preparse` is called, and the final expression value is printed by `postparse` at the end.

Each symbol in the parse tree, both terminal and nonterminal, has associated with it variable `_attribute`, whose type will vary with each translator. `_attribute` holds information about that symbol which can be referenced in action code. In addition to returning the type of token such as `_ASTERISK` or `_INTEGER`, scanner `yylex` should assign a value to `_attribute` when it returns control to the parser. The parser will automatically associate that attribute value with the sentential form symbol representing the token. Attribute variables can be set and referenced using the `"$"` notation in action code. `$1` is the name of the attribute variable of the first vocabulary symbol on the right-hand side of a production, `$2` is the name of the attribute of the second symbol, and so on. `$$` stands for the attribute of the nonterminal on the left-hand side of the rule. The attribute variable of terminals is assigned by the scanner and referenced in action code, while the attribute variable of nonterminals must be explicitly assigned as well as referenced in action code.

In rule 8.2, `$1` refers to the attribute of `INTEGER`, the first vocabulary symbol on the right-hand of that rule. The declaration of `_attribute` on line 8 of the separate action code indicates that for this translator an attribute is of type **int**. In general, however, it could be any type including a **struct**, which would effectively allow many individual attributes to be associated with each node by making each a field of `_attribute`. `_attribute` is assigned the integer value of an `INTEGER` token by the scanner (which is not explicitly shown here). This value is pushed onto the operand stack for later reference after the rest of the expression has been parsed. The parser rather than the scanner needs to push the integer value because the parser, not the scanner, understands the context in which the integer appears. In a more complex example, integers could appear in several places, requiring actions for each.

Example 8-1. Figure 8-1 shows some of the steps the SDT based on the example grammar and action code would take on `"(2+1)*2*(223-1)/2"`.

◆

Input Symbol	Rule	Sentential Form	opandstk	optorstk
(2+1)*2...		e		
(2+1)*2...	1	t es		
(2+1)*2...	3	f ts es		
(2+1)*2...	5	p ts es		
(2+1)*2...	8.1	(e) ts es		
(2+1)*2...	'('	e) ts es		
2+1)*...	1	t es) ts es		
2+1)*...	3	f ts es) ts es		
2+1)*...	5	p ts es) ts es		
2+1)*...	8.2	2 {..} ts es) ts es		
2+1)*2...	'2'	{..} ts es) ts es		
+1)*2...	{..}	ts es) ts es	2	
+1)*2...	4.2	es) ts es	2	
+1)*2...	2.1	ao t {..} es es) ts es	2	
+1)*2...	6.1	+ {..} t {..} es es) ts es	2	
+1)*2...	'+'	{..} t {..} es es) ts es	2	
1)*2...	{..}	t {..} es es) ts es	2	_PLUS
1)*2...	3	f ts {..} es es) ts es	2	_PLUS
1)*2...	5	p ts {..} es es) ts es	2	_PLUS
1)*2...	8.2	1 {..} ts {..} es es) ts es	2	_PLUS
1)*2...	'1'	{..} ts {..} es es) ts es	2	_PLUS
)*2*(223...	{..}	ts {..} es es) ts es	2 1	_PLUS
)*2*(223...	4.2	{..} es es) ts es	2 1	_PLUS
)*2*(223...	{..}	es es) ts es	3	
...				

Figure 8-1. Translating `"(2+1)*2*(223-1)/2"`.

A more interesting example makes extensive use of attributes. By slightly revising grammar *ll-express* into *ll-express'* so there is a unique root and by revising the action code appropriately, the function of the two stacks `opandstk` and `optorstk` can be subsumed by `_attribute` of each node of the parse tree. `_attribute` now holds the partial value of the expression based on the state of the parse.

```
0.  e':  e  {printf("%d\n", $1);}

1.  e:  t  es  {$$.opand = eval($1.opand,$2.optor,$2.opand);
                $$.optor = _NULL;}

2.  es:  ao  t  es  {$$.optor = $1.optor;
                     $$.opand = eval($2.opand,$3.optor,$3.opand);}

         ¦  {$$.optor = _NULL; $$.opand = 0;}

3.  t:  f  ts  {$$.opand = eval($1.opand,$2.optor,$2.opand);}

4.  ts:  mo  f  ts  {$$.optor = $1.optor;
                     $$.opand = eval($2.opand,$3.optor,$3.opand);}

         ¦  {$$.optor = _NULL; $opand = 0;}

5.  f:  p  {$$ = $1;}

         ¦  -  p  {$$.opand = -$2.opand;}

6.  ao:  +  {$$.optor = _PLUS; }
         ¦  -  {$$.optor = _MINUS;}

7.  mo:  *  {$$.optor = _ASTERISK;}
         ¦  /  {$$.optor = _SLASH;}

8.  p:  ( e )  {$$ = $2;}
        ¦  INTEGER  {$$.opand = $1.opand;}
```

The separate action code is:

```
1    struct _attribute { int  optor, opand; };
2
3    eval (lhs, op, rhs)  int lhs, op, rhs;
4    {
5        switch (op) {
6            case _PLUS:  return (lhs+rhs);
7            case _MINUS: return (lhs-rhs);
8            case _SLASH: return (lhs/rhs);
9            case _ASTERISK: return (lhs*rhs);
10           case _NULL: return (lhs);
11       }
12   }
```

Example 8-2. Figure 8-2 shows the parse tree for "(2+1)*2*(223-1)/2" augmented with the value of `_attribute` on each node.

◆

`_attribute` of the root of the *attributed parse tree* is the value of the translation. Hence, the entire attributed parse tree must be saved as the parse is performed. This contrasts quite sharply with parsing alone where the top of the tree is never needed after it is expanded. If there are assignments to $$ in the action code, then information is being passed up the tree. References to $$ pass information down the tree. In the worst case this forces the entire parse tree to be saved since the value of the attribute of any node can, in general, depend on the value of the attribute of any other node in the tree. Moreover, it is not trivial to determine the correct order in which to evaluate assignments involving attributes so that the value of an attribute is always defined when referenced. It is usually cheaper to use auxiliary data structures, such as `optorstk` and `opandstk`, rather than maintain large parse trees. Restrictions on

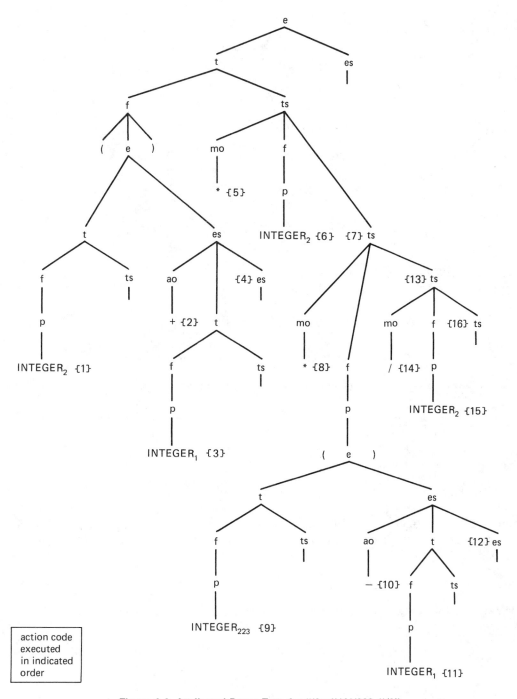

Figure 8-2. Attributed Parse Tree for "(2+1)*2*(223-1)/2".

the use of attributes can be defined so that a limited amount of the parse tree must be kept and the order of evaluation of attributes is trivial. For example, not allowing assignment to $$ ensures that only the sentential form needs to be saved and no ordering problems exist. Information can be maintained in auxiliary structures instead of attributes. Never allowing an action segment to reference an attribute to its right guarantees that information is only passed "up and toward the right" in the tree, allowing subtrees down and on the left to be discarded. Again, ordering is trivial. This is illustrated in Fig. 8-3.

Example 8-3. A simple attributed grammar whose attributes are so intertwined that the attribute of every node depends on every other attribute in the tree is

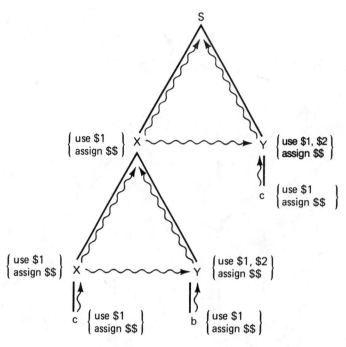

Figure 8-3. Passing Information Up and Towards the Right.

```
s:   e { $$.down = 0; $1.down = 1+$$.down; $$.up = 1+$1.up;}

e:   e { $$.up = 1+$1.up; $1.down = 1+$$.down;}

   ¦   0 {$1.up = 0; $$.up = 1+$1.up;  $1.down = 1+$$.down;}
```

where _attribute is defined by

```
        struct _attribute { int down,up; };
```

The value of _attribute.up at the root of the tree is its height as is the value of
_attribute.down at the frontier. Figure 8-4 shows the attributed parse tree with arrows indicating
the dependencies.

◆

Example 8-4. The following is a trivial grammar whose definition is circular:

```
s:   1   {$$ = $1; $1 = $$;}
```

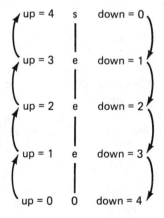

Figure 8-4. Interlaced Attribute Evaluation.

that is, the attributes have no well-defined values. It is usually possible to construct attributed grammars so that simple ordering rules can be used.

♦

8.2. BOTTOM-UP SYNTAX-DIRECTED TRANSLATION

Bottom-up SDT is defined in an analogous manner to top-down SDT except that actions are executed with each reduction. A single action segment is associated with a production, rather than allowing segments to be placed anywhere on the right-hand side. *unambig-express*' is rewritten with action code suitable for an LR based SDT. First using auxiliary stacks `opandstk` and `optorstk`:

```
0.  e':  e

1.  e:   t

    |  e ao t   {rhs=popopand();
                 lhs=popopand();
                 switch (popoptor()) {
                     case _PLUS:   pushopand(lhs+rhs); break;
                     case _MINUS:  pushopand(lhs-rhs); break;
                     default: error ("illegal stack", PANIC);
                 }
                }

2.  t:   f

    |  t mo f   {rhs=popopand();
                 lhs=popopand();
                 switch (popoptor()) {
                     case _ASTERISK:  pushopand(lhs*rhs); break;
                     case _SLASH:     pushopand(lhs/rhs); break;
                     default: error ("illegal stack", PANIC);
                 }
                }

3.  f:   ( e )  |  INTEGER  {pushopand($1);}
    |  - INTEGER   {pushopand(-$2);}
    |  - ( e )  {pushopand(-popopand());}

4.  ao:  +  {pushoptor(_PLUS);}
    |  -  {pushoptor(_MINUS);}

5.  mo:  *  {pushoptor(_ASTERISK);}
    |  /  {pushoptor(_SLASH);}
```

where the separate action code is as before. Using the attribute of each node to hold the partial value of the expression produces:

```
0.  e':  e  {printf ("%d\n", $1);}

1.  e:   t  {$$ = $1;}

    |  e ao t
           {switch ($2) {
                case _PLUS:  $$ = $1+$3; break;
                case _MINUS: $$ = $1-$3; break;
                default: error ("illegal stack", PANIC);
            }
           }

2.  t:   f  {$$ = $1;}

    |  t mo f
           {switch ($2) {
                case _ASTERISK: $$ = $1*$3; break;
                case _SLASH:    $$ = $1/$3; break;
                default: error ("illegal stack", PANIC);
            }
           }
```

```
3.  f:    (  e  )  {$$ = $2;}
     |    INTEGER  {$$ = $1;}
     |    -  INTEGER  {$$ = -$2;}
     |    -  (  e  )  {$$ = -$3;}

4.  ao:   +  {$$ = _PLUS;}
     |    -  {$$ = _MINUS;}

5.  mo:   *  {$$ = _ASTERISK;}
     |    /  {$$ = _SLASH;}
```

Because *unambig-express'* is a simpler more natural grammar than *ll-express'*, `_attribute` does not need to be a structure. It is just an integer. The action code is also much simpler, reflecting the fact that the right-hand side of a single production generates a whole expression, that is, an operand followed by an operator, followed by an operand.

As was true of top-down SDT, allowing arbitrary attribute expressions in action code of bottom-up SDT can, in the worst case, force the translator to save the entire parse tree. Not allowing attributes on the right-hand side of a production to be assigned a value in the action code forces information to only be passed up the tree. This guarantees that the bottom of the tree can be discarded as the tree is built and only the sentential form need be saved.

Top-down translators might appear more powerful because they allow action segments to appear anywhere on the right-hand side while bottom-up translators only allow one action segment per production. In fact, it is trivial to extend a bottom-up attributed grammar to allow action segments to be executed at arbitrary places in the recognition of the handle. To force code { . . } to be executed between the recognition of *c* and *d* in

```
b:   w c d z
```

replace this production by:

```
b:   w c e d z

e:   {..}
```

with new nonterminal *e*. When the null production *e:* is reduced, action code { . . } will be executed.

8.3. yacc: YET ANOTHER COMPILER-COMPILER

To complement *lex*, Unix offers *yacc*, which stands for "Yet Another Compiler-Compiler," a name modestly chosen by its Bell Labs author Stephen Johnson to reflect the fact that there were already a number of compiler-compilers when he released it. Because of the popularity of Unix, it is probably the most widely used translator-writing system today.

yacc is an LALR(1) based SDT with powerful extensions to make it easy for the grammar writer to express operator precedence and associativity. Like most of the tools studied here, *yacc* has a skeletal component which is fleshed out by processing user-supplied input which looks something like the bottom-up attributed grammar shown in the last section. The resulting function, `yyparse`, repeatedly invokes `yylex` to fetch tokens from the input stream, parses the string according to the underlying grammar, and calls action routines as appropriate with each rule reduction. `yyparse` eventually returns 0 if the input is correctly parsed and 1 otherwise.

An Expression Compiler

yacc is illustrated by developing a complete program, *express*, which implements the expression evaluator defined earlier in this chapter. There are a number of files that contribute to *express* as revealed by its *makefile* in Fig. 8-5. *express.y, express.l, main.c*, and *ER.c* are manually generated. The first is the *yacc* specification, the second is the input to *lex*, the third is the main program and supporting action routines, while the fourth is the familiar error-handling code. *lex.yy.c*, of course, is generated by *lex*, while the

```
1    express:  y.tab.h main.o lex.yy.o y.tab.o ER.o
2            cc -o express main.o lex.yy.o y.tab.o ER.o -ly -ll
3
4    y.tab.h: express.y
5            yacc -dv express.y
6
7    lex.yy.c: express.l
8            lex express.l
9
10   y.tab.c: y.tab.h express.h
11           yacc -dv express.y
12
13   main.c: express.h
```

Figure 8-5. *makefile* **for** *express.*

```
1    % make
2    yacc -dv express.y
3    cc  -c main.c
4    lex express.l
5    cc  -c lex.yy.c
6    cc  -c y.tab.c
7    cc  -c ER.c
8    cc -o express main.o lex.yy.o y.tab.o ER.o -ly -ll
```

Figure 8-6. Running *make* **to Generate** *express.*

other two source files, *y.tab.c* and *y.tab.h*, are produced by *yacc*. *y.tab.c* is the skeletal parser complete with the parsing action and goto tables produced from the grammar in *express.y*. *y.tab.h* is the vehicle for *yacc* to tell *lex* about certain defined constants it creates. Their use will become clear shortly. Note the reference to *-ly* in line 2 of the *makefile*. This is the *yacc* library analogous to the *lex* library invoked by the *-ll* flag. The output of *make* is shown in Fig. 8-6. Figure 8-7 shows how these files fit together to produce *express*. *yacc* expects its input to come from a file with a *.y* suffix. *express.y* is *unambig-express'* rewritten in correct *yacc* input form:

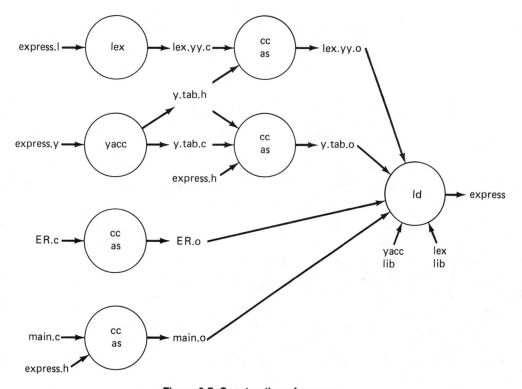

Figure 8-7. Construction of *express.*

```
 1    %token   INTEGER
 2    %{
 3    #include "express.h"
 4    %}
 5    %%
 6
 7    e:
 8            t
 9          ¦ e  ao  t
10                  {rhs=popopand();
11                   lhs=popopand();
12                   switch (popoptor()) {
13                      case _PLUS:   pushopand(lhs+rhs); break;
14                      case _MINUS:  pushopand(lhs-rhs); break;
15                      default: error ("illegal stack", PANIC);
16                   }
17                  } ;
18
19    t:
20            f
21          ¦ t  mo  f
22                  {rhs=popopand();
23                   lhs=popopand();
24                   switch (popoptor()) {
25                      case _ASTERISK:  pushopand(lhs*rhs); break;
26                      case _SLASH:     pushopand(lhs/rhs); break;
27                      default: error ("illegal stack", PANIC);
28                   }
29                  } ;
30
31    f:
32          '(' e ')'
33        ¦ INTEGER
34                {pushopand($1);}
35        ¦ '-' INTEGER
36                {pushopand(-$2);}
37        ¦ '-' '(' e ')'
38                {pushopand(-$3);} ;
39
40    ao:
41          '+'
42                {pushoptor(_PLUS);}
43        ¦ '-'
44                {pushoptor(_MINUS);} ;
45
46    mo:
47          '*'
48                {pushoptor(_ASTERISK);}
49        ¦ '/'
50                {pushoptor(_SLASH);} ;
51
```

It has three sections just like a *lex* specification: declarations, rules, and program text. `"%"` has a similar special role. `"%%"` separates sections; `"%{"` begins a *C* declaration segment and `"%}"` terminates it just as in *lex*. Line 1

```
 1    %token   INTEGER
```

tells *yacc* that `INTEGER` is a named token. Each named token must be declared in this manner.

Section 2 contains the productions. A colon `':'` as has been used in all of the previous examples separates the left- and right-hand sides of rules. The set of alternative productions is terminated by a semicolon `';'`. With a few more cosmetic differences, *yacc-express*' is the same as *unambig-express*'.

The main program appears in Fig. 8-8. It does the work of `preparse` and `postparse` explicitly before and after calling `yyparse`. The exit code of `yyparse` is 0 if all goes well, and 1 otherwise.

The *lex* specification for the scanner is:

```
 1    %{
 2    #include "y.tab.h"
```

```
1    #include "express.h"
2
3    main ()
4    {
5        opandptr = optorptr = -1;
6        if (!yyparse ())
7            printf ("%d\n", popopand());
8        else
9            error ("illegal expression", PANIC);
10   }
11
12   popopand ()
13   {
14       if (opandptr < 0)
15           error ("internal stack underflow.", PANIC);
16       return (opandstk[opandptr--]);
17   }
18
19   pushoptor (t)  int t;
20   {
21       if (++optorptr == MAXOPTOR)
22           error ("internal stack overflow.", PANIC);
23       optorstk[optorptr] = t;
24   }
25
26   popoptor ()
27   {
28       if (optorptr < 0)
29           error ("internal stack underflow.", PANIC);
30       return (optorstk[optorptr--]);
31   }
32
33   pushopand (t)  int t;
34   {
35       if (++opandptr == MAXOPAND)
36           error ("internal stack overflow.", PANIC);
37       opandstk[opandptr] = t;
38   }
```

Figure 8-8. Main Program for *express*.

```
3    extern int yylval;
4    %}
5    %%
6    [0-9]+        {yylval = atoi(yytext); return INTEGER;}
7    .             {return yytext[0];}
8    \n            ;
```

yylex simply returns the ASCII representation of most characters as seen in line 7. Newlines are ignored in line 8. The most interesting pattern, in line 6, assembles a sequence of digits into an integer. yylval is the name *yacc* uses for the attribute of tokens (rather than _attribute). It is set in the action code in line 6 to the actual integer value the token string represents and can be referenced in an attributed grammar using the "$" notation discussed earlier. The action code in line 6 also returns the value INTEGER, which is the name of the token group found in the *yacc* grammar. In fact *yacc* maps the name INTEGER, which appeared in:

```
1    %token   INTEGER
```

into some integer constant > 256. It expects yylex to tell it when a member of that group has been recognized by returning INTEGER. *lex* will be told into what value *yacc* mapped INTEGER:

```
1    #define INTEGER 257
```

through file *y.tab.h* which is generated by *yacc* and included in line 2 of the *lex* specification. Note the value of each token group is chosen to be greater than the representation of any legal ASCII character.

```
% echo 3 ¦ express
3
% echo 3+4 ¦ express
7
% echo '(2+1)*2*(223-1)/2' ¦ express
666
% echo '3+()' ¦ express
syntax error
illegal expression
% echo '+1' ¦ express
syntax error
llegal expression
% echo 3--1 ¦ express
4
```

Figure 8-9. Execution of express.

express uses the standard error recovery of *yacc*, which is to ungracefully announce a syntax error and terminate the parse.

Example 8-5. Figure 8-9 shows the output of *express* on several syntactically correct and incorrect strings.
♦

To aid in debugging the parser, *yacc* will optionally (with the -*v* option) produce the file *y.output* which summarizes the parsing action and goto tables. The output is too long to list completely, but a partial listing is:

```
 1
 2    state 0
 3             $accept : _e $end
 4
 5             INTEGER   shift 5
 6             (  shift 4
 7             -  shift 6
 8             .  error
 9
10             e   goto 1
11             t   goto 2
12             f   goto 3
13
14    state 1
15             $accept : e_$end
16             e : e_ao t
17
18             $end   accept
19             -  shift 9
20             +  shift 8
21             .  error
22
23             ao   goto 7
24
25    state 2
26             e : t_      (1)
27             t : t_mo f
28
29             *  shift 11
30             /  shift 12
31             .  reduce 1
32
33             mo   goto 10
34
35    state 3
36             t : f_      (3)
37
38             .  reduce 3
39
40
41    state 4
```

```
42              f :  (_e )
43
44              INTEGER  shift 5
45              (  shift 4
46              -  shift 6
47              .  error
48
49              e  goto 13
50              t  goto 2
51              f  goto 3
52
53   state 5
54              f :  INTEGER_      (6)
55
56              .  reduce 6
57
58
59   state 6
60              f :  -_INTEGER
61              f :  -_( e )
62
63              INTEGER  shift 14
64              (  shift 15
65              .  error
66
      ...
164  state 19
165             e :  e_ao t
166             f :  - ( e_)
167
168             )  shift 20
169             -  shift 9
170             +  shift 8
171             .  error
172
173             ao  goto 7
174
175  state 20
176             f :  - ( e )_      (8)
177
178             .  reduce 8
179
180
181  9/127 terminals, 5/300 nonterminals
182  13/600 grammar rules, 21/750 states
183  0 shift/reduce, 0 reduce/reduce conflicts reported
      ...
```

The underscore ' _ ' is equivalent to the bullet ' ● ' used in the last chapter to indicate how much of the right-hand side has been seen so far. *yacc* implicitly augments *yacc-express*' with rule

```
$accept:  e $end
```

where a reduction via this rule implies acceptance of the string. $end stands for end of file. State 0 represents the NULL viable prefix as shown by the underscore preceding *e*. Lines 5–7 indicate that the parser will shift to state 5 if an INTEGER is seen, shift to state 4 for a ' (', and shift to state 6 for a ' - '. The dot ' . ' in line 8 implies any other token is an error. State 2 represents the viable prefix " *t*" which contains a completed item in line 26. Line 31 indicates the parser will reduce via rule 1 if the lookahead token is not a ' * ' or ' / '. Line 33 shows the goto information. If the parser is in state 2 when the reduction occurs and the left-hand side of the rule just used in the reduction is *mo*, the parser goes to state 10.

Conflict Resolution

At the end of *y.output* is a summary of the actions taken by *yacc*. Of special interest is the number of shift/reduce and reduce/reduce conflicts that *yacc* resolved. Line 183 shows that there were none in this example, but in general *yacc* will resolve all conflicts using the default tie-breaking strategy:

1. In a shift/reduce conflict, do the shift.
2. In a reduce/reduce conflict, reduce by the earlier grammar rule.

Rule 1 defers reductions as long as possible and is quite often used. Reduce/reduce conflicts are rarer and often indicate problems elsewhere (perhaps a bug in the grammar). They are normally best avoided by understanding the source of the conflict and restructuring the grammar.

Example 8-6. The *dangling else* construct illustrates the use of default conflict resolution. The nested `if` statement:

```
if..then if..then stmt else stmt
```

has two "reasonable" parsings depending on whether the single `else` clause is attached to the first or second `if..then`. This is shown pictorially in Fig. 8-10. Most languages such as *C* and Pascal force the `else` to be attached to the nearest `if`. Curly brackets must be used in *C* and a `begin-end` pair in Pascal to force the far nesting. The problem, of course, is to make the parser understand the near nesting policy. Grammar *dangle* does so:

```
1    %token  IF..THEN  ELSE
2    %%
3    stmt:
4            IF..THEN  stmt
5          ; IF..THEN  stmt  ELSE  stmt
6          ; ';' ;
```

It produces *y.output*:

```
1
2    state 0
3
4            $accept : _stmt $end
5
6            IF..THEN  shift 2
7          ; shift 3
8          . error
9
10           stmt  goto 1
11   state 1
12
13           $accept :  stmt_$end
14
15           $end  accept
16         . error
17
18   state 2
19           stmt :  IF..THEN_stmt
20           stmt :  IF..THEN_stmt ELSE stmt
21
22           IF..THEN  shift 2
23         ; shift 3
24         . error
25
26           stmt  goto 4
27
28   state 3
```

```
        if..then              if..then
          if..then              if..then
            stmt                  stmt
          else                  else
            stmt                  stmt


        (a) Near Nesting        (b) Far Nesting
```

Figure 8-10. Ambiguity with Nested `if..then` Statements.

```
29           stmt :  ;_     (3)
30
31              .  reduce 3
32
33
34     4: shift/reduce conflict (shift 5, red'n 1) on ELSE
35     state 4
36           stmt :  IF..THEN stmt_     (1)
37           stmt :  IF..THEN stmt_ELSE stmt
38
39           ELSE  shift 5
40              .  reduce 1
41
42
43     state 5
44           stmt :  IF..THEN stmt ELSE_stmt
45
46           IF..THEN  shift 2
47           ;  shift 3
48              .  error
49
50           stmt  goto 6
51
52     state 6
53           stmt :  IF..THEN stmt ELSE stmt_     (2)
54
55              .  reduce 2
56
57
58     5/127 terminals, 1/300 nonterminals
59     4/600 grammar rules, 7/750 states
60     1 shift/reduce, 0 reduce/reduce conflicts reported
       ...
```

Line 60 indicates that there was one shift/reduce conflict resolved. Line 34 notes that conflict explicitly in state 4 where the `if..then` statement without the `else` clause is completed, but the variant with the `else` clause is still incomplete. *yacc* will shift rather than reduce, forcing the **ELSE** to be matched with the closest `if..then` as desired.

yacc allows the grammar writer to indicate his or her own conflict resolution at a high level in the declaration section of the specification by explicitly declaring operator associativity and precedence.

Example 8-7. Consider the highly ambiguous grammar, *ambig-express*:

```
1     %token  INTEGER
2     %%
3
4     e:
5             e '+' e
6           | e '-' e
7           | e '*' e
8           | e '/' e
9           | e '=' e
10          | '(' e ')'
11          | INTEGER ;
```

It lacks the desired operator precedence among the arithmetic and assignment operators, and does not enforce the left associativity of the arithmetic and the right associativity of the assignment operators. Passing this grammar through *yacc* produces:

```
1
2     state 0
3             $accept : _e $end
4
5             INTEGER  shift 3
6             (  shift 2
```

```
  7                 .  error
  8
  9             e  goto 1
         ...
104
105    10: shift/reduce conflict (shift 4, red'n 1) on +
106    10: shift/reduce conflict (shift 5, red'n 1) on -
107    10: shift/reduce conflict (shift 6, red'n 1) on *
108    10: shift/reduce conflict (shift 7, red'n 1) on /
109    10: shift/reduce conflict (shift 8, red'n 1) on =
110    state 10
111             e :  e_+ e
112             e :  e + e_      (1)
113             e :  e_- e
114             e :  e_* e
115             e :  e_/ e
116             e :  e_= e
117
118             +  shift 4
119             -  shift 5
120             *  shift 6
121             /  shift 7
122             =  shift 8
123             .  reduce 1
124
125
126    11: shift/reduce conflict (shift 4, red'n 2) on +
127    11: shift/reduce conflict (shift 5, red'n 2) on -
128    11: shift/reduce conflict (shift 6, red'n 2) on *
129    11: shift/reduce conflict (shift 7, red'n 2) on /
130    11: shift/reduce conflict (shift 8, red'n 2) on =
131    state 11
132             e :  e_+ e
133             e :  e_- e
134             e :  e - e_      (2)
135             e :  e_* e
136             e :  e_/ e
137             e :  e_= e
138
139             +  shift 4
140             -  shift 5
141             *  shift 6
142             /  shift 7
143             =  shift 8
144             .  reduce 2
145
146
147    12: shift/reduce conflict (shift 4, red'n 3) on +
148    12: shift/reduce conflict (shift 5, red'n 3) on -
149    12: shift/reduce conflict (shift 6, red'n 3) on *
150    12: shift/reduce conflict (shift 7, red'n 3) on /
151    12: shift/reduce conflict (shift 8, red'n 3) on =
152    state 12
153             e :  e_+ e
154             e :  e_- e
155             e :  e_* e
156             e :  e * e_      (3)
157             e :  e_/ e
158             e :  e_= e
159
160             +  shift 4
161             -  shift 5
162             *  shift 6
163             /  shift 7
164             =  shift 8
165             .  reduce 3
166
167
168    13: shift/reduce conflict (shift 4, red'n 4) on +
169    13: shift/reduce conflict (shift 5, red'n 4) on -
170    13: shift/reduce conflict (shift 6, red'n 4) on *
171    13: shift/reduce conflict (shift 7, red'n 4) on /
172    13: shift/reduce conflict (shift 8, red'n 4) on =
```

```
173    state 13
174            e :  e_+ e
175            e :  e_- e
176            e :  e_* e
177            e :  e_/ e
178            e :  e / e_    (4)
179            e :  e_= e
180
181            +  shift 4
182            -  shift 5
183            *  shift 6
184            /  shift 7
185            =  shift 8
186            .  reduce 4
187
188
189    14: shift/reduce conflict (shift 4, red'n 5) on +
190    14: shift/reduce conflict (shift 5, red'n 5) on -
191    14: shift/reduce conflict (shift 6, red'n 5) on *
192    14: shift/reduce conflict (shift 7, red'n 5) on /
193    14: shift/reduce conflict (shift 8, red'n 5) on =
194    state 14
195            e :  e_+ e
196            e :  e_- e
197            e :  e_* e
198            e :  e_/ e
199            e :  e_= e
200            e :  e = e_    (5)
201
202            +  shift 4
203            -  shift 5
204            *  shift 6
205            /  shift 7
206            =  shift 8
207            .  reduce 5
208
209
210    state 15
211            e :  ( e )_    (6)
212
213            .  reduce 6
214
215
216    10/127 terminals, 1/300 nonterminals
217    8/600 grammar rules, 16/750 states
218    25 shift/reduce, 0 reduce/reduce conflicts reported
           ...
```

The default resolution in states 10–14 make all of the operators right associative with equal precedence. The grammar writer can explicitly state associativity and precedence in the declaration section to overcome this:

```
1    %token  INTEGER
2    %right  '='
3    %left   '+'   '-'
4    %left   '*'   '/'
5    %%
     ...
```

This tells *yacc* that '=' is right associative, and that the four arithmetic operators are left associative. Furthermore, the order of the declarations states that '=' has lower precedence than '+' and '-', which in turn have lower precedence than '*' and '/'. With this change, *y.output* becomes:

```
1
2    state 0
3            $accept : _e $end
4
5            INTEGER  shift 3
6            (  shift 2
7            .  error
```

```
  8
  9               e   goto 1
        . . .
105    state 10
106            e  :   e_+ e
107            e  :   e + e_      (1)
108            e  :   e_- e
109            e  :   e_* e
110            e  :   e_/ e
111            e  :   e_= e
112
113            *   shift 6
114            /   shift 7
115            .   reduce 1
116
117
118    state 11
119            e  :   e_+ e
120            e  :   e_- e
121            e  :   e - e_      (2)
122            e  :   e_* e
123            e  :   e_/ e
124            e  :   e_= e
125
126            *   shift 6
127            /   shift 7
128            .   reduce 2
129
130
131    state 12
132            e  :   e_+ e
133            e  :   e_- e
134            e  :   e_* e
135            e  :   e * e_      (3)
136            e  :   e_/ e
137            e  :   e_= e
138
139            .   reduce 3
140
141
142    state 13
143            e  :   e_+ e
144            e  :   e_- e
145            e  :   e_* e
146            e  :   e_/ e
147            e  :   e / _e      (4)
148            e  :   e_= e
149
150            .   reduce 4
151
152
153    state 14
154            e  :   e_+ e
155            e  :   e_- e
156            e  :   e_* e
157            e  :   e_/ e
158            e  :   e_= e
159            e  :   e = e_      (5)
160
161            =   shift 8
162            +   shift 4
163            -   shift 5
164            *   shift 6
165            /   shift 7
166            .   reduce 5
167
168
169    state 15
170            e  :   ( e )_      (6)
171
172            .   reduce 6
173
174
```

```
175    10/127 terminals, 1/300 nonterminals
176    8/600 grammar rules, 16/750 states
177    0 shift/reduce, 0 reduce/reduce conflicts reported
       ...
```

The shift/reduce conflicts arising from ambiguity over operator associativity and precedence have been eliminated. For example, compare state 10 of the two parsers which represents the viable prefix "e+e". The first parser shifts for all operators. The second shifts only for the '*' and '/' operators which have higher precedence; otherwise it reduces (lines 113–115). This also forces left associativity since it reduces if the next symbol is '+'. Similar behavior is seen in states 11–14. State 14, which represents the viable prefix "e=e", shifts on a '=', an action appropriate for a right associative operator. Note that the two parsers have the same number of states. In general this is true. *yacc* does conflict resolution by changing the shift and reduce entries, but not by changing the number or meaning of the states.

◆

Error Handling

`yyparse` calls `yyerror` to handle parsing errors. The version supplied in the standard *yacc* library writes its single string argument to `stderr` and causes `yyparse` to return. The last chapter showed how to explicitly put error-handling routines into the parsing action table, but this method will not work here since the writer does not have direct access to the table. The interface is the grammar specification which must be augmented with error-handling information. *yacc* allows the user to include `error` tokens in the grammar rules to indicate where he or she wants special error handling to occur and what that handling is. When an error occurs, the parser pops its stack until it enters a state where the token `error` can legally occur. It then behaves as if `error` were the current lookahead token, and performs the action encountered. The lookahead symbol is then reset to the token that caused the error.

To prevent cascading error messages, the parser, after first detecting an error, remains in an error state until it has successfully read and shifted three tokens. If an error is detected while the parser is already in the error state, no message is written, and the input token provoking the error is quietly discarded. This can be overridden by executing action `yyerrok`. As mentioned earlier, the lookahead symbol is reset to the token that caused the error. If it is desired to flush that token instead, executing `yyclearin` will do the trick.

Example 8-8. User-defined error handling is illustrated with a full implementation of a subset of the expression evaluator defined earlier. Addition and division are dropped to reduce the size of the generated parser tables, keeping *y.output* manageable. Grammar *compact-express* is:

```
1    %{
2    #include "express.h"
3    %}
4
5    %token  INTEGER
6    %right  '='
7    %left   '-'
8    %left   '*'
9    %right  UMINUS
10   %%
11
12   e:
13           e '-' e
14                   {rhs=popopand(); lhs=popopand(); pushopand(lhs-rhs);}
15         | e '*' e
16                   {rhs=popopand(); lhs=popopand(); pushopand(lhs*rhs);}
17         | '(' e ')'
18
19         | '-' '(' e ')'  %prec UMINUS
20                   {pushopand(-popopand());}
21         | INTEGER
22                   {pushopand($1);}
23         | '-' INTEGER  %prec  UMINUS
24                   {pushopand(-$2);}  ;
```

The lexical analyzer is identical and the action code is trivially simplified for this version of *express*.

This grammar illustrates another feature of *yacc* to handle precedence. Token ' - ' is used as both a unary and a binary operator. The former has a higher precedence than either ' * ' or ' / '. The latter has an equal precedence with ' + '. To resolve this conflict, lines 19 and 23 contain an explicit %prec specification which is applicable only for the rule in which it appears. It states that ' - ' has the same precedence as the bogus operator UMINUS which was declared in line 9 just for the purpose of having a higher precedence than ' * '. UMINUS is not otherwise used.

The grammar is rewritten as *error-express* with one error-handling production added in line 25:

```
1    %{
2    #include "express.h"
3    %}
     ...
23         ¦   '-' INTEGER  %prec UMINUS
24                  {pushopand(-$2);} ;
25         ¦   error ;
```

y.output for *error-express* is:

```
1
2    state 0
3            $accept : _e $end
4
5            error  shift 5
6            INTEGER  shift 4
7            -  shift 3
8            (  shift 2
9            .  error
10
11           e  goto 1
12
13   state 1
14           $accept :  e_$end
15           e :   e_- e
16           e :   e_* e
17
18           $end   accept
19           -  shift 6
20           *  shift 7
21           .  error
22
23
24   state 2
25           e :  (_e )
26
27           error  shift 5
28           INTEGER  shift 4
29           -  shift 3
30           (  shift 2
31           .  error
32
33           e  goto 8
34
35   state 3
36           e :  -_( e )
37           e :  -_INTEGER
38
39           INTEGER  shift 10
40           (  shift 9
41           .  error
42
43
44   state 4
45           e :  INTEGER_    (5)
46
47           .  reduce 5
48
49
50   state 5
```

```
 51              e :   error_      (7)
 52
 53                 .  reduce 7
 54
 55
 56      state 6
 57              e :   e -_e
 58
 59              error  shift 5
 60              INTEGER  shift 4
 61              -  shift 3
 62              (  shift 2
 63              .  error
 64
 65              e  goto 11
 66
 67      state 7
 68              e :   e *_e
 69
 70              error  shift 5
 71              INTEGER  shift 4
 72              -  shift 3
 73              (  shift 2
 74              .  error
 75
 76              e  goto 12
 77
 78      state 8
 79              e :   e_- e
 80              e :   e_* e
 81              e :   ( e_)
 82
 83              -  shift 6
 84              *  shift 7
 85              )  shift 13
 86              .  error
 87
 88
 89      state 9
 90              e :   - (_e )
 91
 92              error  shift 5
 93              INTEGER  shift 4
 94              -  shift 3
 95              (  shift 2
 96              .  error
 97
 98              e  goto 14
 99
100      state 10
101              e :   - INTEGER_     (6)
102
103                 .  reduce 6
104
105
106      state 11
107              e :   e_- e
108              e :   e - e_     (1)
109              e :   e_* e
110
111              *  shift 7
112                 .  reduce 1
113
114
115      state 12
116              e :   e_- e
117              e :   e_* e
118              e :   e * e_     (2)
119
120                 .  reduce 2
121
122
123      state 13
```

```
124              e :  ( e )_      (3)
125
126              .  reduce 3
127
128
129    state 14
130              e :  e_- e
131              e :  e_* e
132              e :  - ( e_)
133
134              -  shift 6
135              *  shift 7
136              )  shift 15
137              .  error
138
139
140    state 15
141              e :  - ( e )_      (4)
142
143              .  reduce 4
       ...
```

Now there are explicit shift entries for the error token, such as in lines 5 and 27. Line 5 means that if an INTEGER, '-', or '(' is not seen, the parser should manufacture an error token, pretend it has seen it in the input, shift it, and goto state 5. State 5 has a completed item whose underlying rule is "e=error". Line 53 says to reduce via this rule no matter what the lookahead token is.

◆

Example 8-9. Suppose the input string is "+". Running *express* produces:

```
% echo '+' ¦ express
syntax error
illegal expression
```

The parser behavior leading to this output is in Fig. 8-11.

◆

Example 8-10. Consider input "+-3", which produces the same output as the last example, but has to work harder to do so as shown in Fig. 8-12. The effect of the encountering "+-" is twofold. First, the parser pretends it has seen error in the input stream where an expression was expected. Second, the '+' is discarded. The parser, in essence, behaves as if has seen the viable prefix "e-".

◆

Example 8-11. Input "3---)4" causes the parser to pop its stack and force an internal stack underflow within *express* as shown in Fig. 8-13. The problem with the error recovery strategy used in *error-express* is that there is an overlooked semantic implication when error is reduced to an e in rule 7. An integer

Stack	Lookahead	Action
0	+	error—create error token, write "syntax error" message, insert **error** into input stream, and shift to state 5.
0 5	+	reduce via rule 7 which tells parser to goto state 1.
0 1	+	have not shifted character since last error occurred so discard lookahead.
0 1	EOF	reached end of file still in error state. terminate yyparse.

Figure 8-11. Parsing Illegal String "+".

Stack	Lookahead	Action
0	+	error—create error token, write ''syntax error'' message, insert error into input stream, and shift to state 5.
0 5	+	reduce via rule 7 which tells parser to goto state 1.
0 1	+	have not shifted character since last error occurred so discard lookahead.
0 1	−	parser has resynchronized with a valid continuation and can shift to state 6. it is behaving as if it has seen "e-".
0 1 6	INTEGER	shift 4
0 1 6 4	EOF	reduce 5
0 1 6 11	EOF	reduce 1
0 1	EOF	terminate yyparse.

Figure 8-12. Parsing Illegal String "+-3".

Parser Stack	Remaining	Action	Opandstk
0	"3---)4"	shift 4	
0 4	"---)4"	reduce 5	3
0 1	"---)4"	shift 6	3
0 1 6	"--)4"	shift 3	3
0 1 6 3	"-)4"	error—with no prescribed action in state 3. print ''syntax error'' and pop state 3 from parser stack.	3
0 1 6	"-)4"	state 6 has an action when an error occurs. shift error token and goto state 5.	3
0 1 6 5	"-)4"	reduce 7	3
0 1 6 11	"-)4"	reduce 1	*underflow*

Figure 8-13. Parsing Illegal String "3---(4".

must be pushed onto opandstk in order to be consistent with all other reductions to e. Since it does not really matter which value is pushed onto opandstk, 0 is used in line 26 of *error-express'*:

```
1    %{
2    #include express.h"
3    %}
     ...
23        ¦  '-' INTEGER  %prec  UMINUS
24                {pushopand(-$2);} ;
25        ¦  error
26                {pushopand(0);} ;
```

There are many more subtleties of writing error-handling code with *yacc* which doing the exercises at the end of the chapter should help the reader master.

8.4. YACC PARSER FOR PASCAL

To more fully illustrate *yacc*'s use, a grammar for full Pascal is presented. Error handling is not graceful here. That is left as an important exercise. The scanner is virtually identical to the one that appeared in Section 4.6 and is not repeated here.

```
1    /* yacc grammar for Pascal based on ISO Standard */
2
3    /* keywords - lex uses BEGIN and stdio uses FILE internally
4        so fudge */
5
6    %token AND   ARRAY  _BEGIN  CASE  CONST  DIV  DO  DOWNTO  ELSE
7    %token END  _FILE  FOR  FORWARD  FUNCTION  GOTO  IF  IN  LABEL
```

```
 8     %token MOD  NIL  NOT  OF  OR  PACKED  PROCEDURE  PROGRAM  RECORD
 9     %token REPEAT SET  THEN  TO  TYPE  UNTIL  VAR  WHILE  WITH
10
11     /* token groups other than operators */
12
13     %token IDENT INT  REAL  STRING
14
15     /* multi-character operators */
16
17     %token ASSIGN    /* := */
18     %token NE        /* <> */
19     %token GE        /* >= */
20     %token LE        /* <= */
21     %token DOTDOT    /* .. */
22
23     /* precedence and associativity among operators */
24
25     %left  '='  '<'  '>'  NE  LE  GE  IN
26     %left  '+'  '-'  OR
27     %left  '*'  '/'  DIV  AND  MOD
28     %right NOT
29     %left  '.'
30     %right UNARY
31
32     %%
33
34     program:
35             PROGRAM  IDENT  '('  opt_identifier_list  ')'  ';'
36                 block  '.'  ;
37
38     opt_identifier_list:
39             identifier_list
40         ¦ ;
41
42     identifier_list:
43             IDENT
44         ¦ IDENT  ','  identifier_list  ;
45
46     block:
47             opt_labels  opt_constants  opt_types  opt_variables
48                 opt_procedure_or_function_heading_dcls  _BEGIN
49                 statements  END  ;
50
51     opt_labels:
52             LABEL  integer_list  ';'
53         ¦ ;
54
55     integer_list:
56             INT
57         ¦ INT  ','  integer_list  ;
58
59     opt_constants:
60             CONST  constant_dcls
61         ¦ ;
62
63     opt_types:
64             TYPE  type_dcls
65         ¦ ;
66
67     opt_variables:
68             VAR  variable_dcls
69         ¦ ;
70
71     opt_procedure_or_function_heading_dcls:
72             opt_procedure_or_function_heading_dcls
73                 procedure_or_function_heading  ';'
74                 block_directive  ';'
75         ¦ ;
76
77     block_directive:
78             block
79         ¦ directive ;
80
```

```
81    directive:
82            FORWARD ;
83
84    statements:
85            statement
86          ¦ statements ';'  statement  ;
87
88    constant_dcls:
89            IDENT  '='  constant  ';'
90          ¦ constant_dcls  IDENT  '='  constant  ';' ;
91
92    variable_dcls:
93            identifier_list  ':'  type  ';'
94          ¦ variable_dcls  identifier_list  ':'  type  ';'  ;
95
96    statement:
97            opt_label  unlabeled_statement  ;
98
99    opt_label:
100            INT  ':'
101          ¦ ;
102
103   unlabeled_statement:
104            variable  ASSIGN  expression
105          ¦ IDENT  opt_proc_parameter_list
106          ¦ _BEGIN  statements  END
107          ¦ IF  expression  THEN  statement
108          ¦ IF  expression  THEN  statement  ELSE  statement
109          ¦ WHILE  expression  DO  statement
110          ¦ CASE  expression  OF  case_body  END
111          ¦ REPEAT  statements  UNTIL  expression
112          ¦ FOR  IDENT  ASSIGN  expression  direction  expression
113                  DO  statement
114          ¦ WITH  variable_list  DO  statement
115          ¦ GOTO  INT
116          ¦ ;
117
118   variable_list:
119            variable
120          ¦ variable_list  ','  variable   ;
121
122   constant_list:
123            constant
124          ¦ constant_list  ','  constant  ;
125
126   case_body:
127            constant_list  ':'  statement  case_trailer  ;
128
129   case_trailer:
130            ';'
131          ¦ ';'  case_body
132          ¦ ;
133
134   direction:
135            DOWNTO
136          ¦ TO  ;
137
138   opt_proc_parameter_list:
139            '('  expression_opt_formats_list  ')'
140          ¦ ;
141
142   expression_opt_formats_list:
143            expression_opt_formats
144          ¦ expression_opt_formats_list  ','
145                  expression_opt_formats ;
146
147   expression_opt_formats:
148            expression  opt_formats  ;
149
150   opt_formats:
151            ':'  expression
152          ¦ ':'  expression  ':'  expression
153          ¦ ;
```

```
154
155    expression_list:
156            expression
157          ¦ expression_list  ','  expression ;
158
159    expression:
160            expression  binop  expression
161          ¦ '-'  expression   %prec UNARY
162          ¦ '+'  expression   %prec UNARY
163          ¦ NOT expression
164          ¦ primary ;
165
166    primary:
167            IDENT  variable_trailer_func_parm_list
168          ¦ '('  expression  ')'
169          ¦ unsigned_literal
170          ¦ '['  opt_elipsis_list  ']' ;
171
172    variable_trailer_func_parm_list:
173            variable_trailers
174          ¦ '('  expression_list  ')'  ;
175
176    opt_elipsis_list:
177            elipsis_list
178          ¦ ;
179
180    elipsis_list:
181            elipsis
182          ¦ elipsis_list  ','  elipsis ;
183
184    elipsis:
185            expression
186          ¦ expression  DOTDOT  expression ;
187
188    binop:
189            '+'  ¦  '-'  ¦  '*'  ¦  DIV  ¦  MOD  ¦  AND  ¦  OR
190          ¦ '>'  ¦  '<'  ¦  '='  ¦  NE   ¦  GE   ¦  LE   ¦  '.'
191          ¦ IN   ¦  '/' ;
192
193    variable:
194            IDENT  variable_trailers ;
195
196    variable_trailers:
197            '['  expression_list  ']'  variable_trailers
198          ¦ '.'  IDENT  variable_trailers
199          ¦ '^'  variable_trailers
200          ¦ ;
201
202    constant:
203            '+'  unsigned_constant  %prec UNARY
204          ¦ '-'  unsigned_constant %prec UNARY
205          ¦ unsigned_constant;
206
207    unsigned_literal:
208            REAL
209          ¦ INT
210          ¦ STRING
211          ¦ NIL ;
212
213    unsigned_constant:
214            IDENT
215          ¦ unsigned_literal ;
216
217    type:
218            '^'  IDENT
219          ¦ ordinal_type
220          ¦ opt_packed  packable_type ;
221
222    packable_type:
223            ARRAY  '['  ordinal_type_list  ']'  OF  type
224          ¦ RECORD  field_list  END
225          ¦ _FILE  OF  type
```

```
226              ¦ SET  OF  ordinal_type ;
227
228   ordinal_type_list:
229              ordinal_type
230              ¦ ordinal_type_list ',' ordinal_type;
231
232   ordinal_type:
233              IDENT
234              ¦ '(' identifier_list ')'
235              ¦ constant  DOTDOT  constant ;
236
237   field_list:
238              identifier_list ':'  type
239              ¦ identifier_list ':'  type ';'  field_list
240              ¦ CASE  tag  OF  cases
241              ¦ ;
242
243   tag:
244              IDENT  /* really type identifier */
245              ¦ IDENT  ':'  type ;
246
247   cases:
248              constant_list ':'  '('  field_list ')'
249                   cases_trailer ;
250
251   cases_trailer:
252              ';'  cases
253              ¦ ';'
254              ¦ ;
255
256   procedure_or_function_heading:
257              PROCEDURE  IDENT  opt_formal_parm_list
258              ¦ FUNCTION  IDENT  opt_formal_parm_list  opt_return ;
259
260   opt_formal_parm_list:
261              '('  formal_parms ')'
262              ¦ ;
263
264   formal_parms:
265              opt_var identifier_list  ':'  formal_parm_trailer
266              ¦ procedure_or_function_heading  proc_parm_trailer ;
267
268   opt_var:
269              VAR
270              ¦ ;
271
272   formal_parm_trailer:
273              IDENT  proc_parm_trailer
274              ¦ conformant_array_schema  proc_parm_trailer ;
275
276   proc_parm_trailer:
277              ';'  formal_parms
278              ¦ ;
279
280   conformant_array_schema:
281              opt_packed  '['  index_type_spec_list  ']'  OF  IDENT
282              ¦ opt_packed  '['  index_type_spec_list  ']'  OF  IDENT
283                   conformant_array_schema ;
284
285   opt_packed:
286              PACKED
287              ¦ ;
288
289   index_type_spec_list:
290              IDENT  DOTDOT  IDENT  ':'  IDENT ;
291
292   opt_return:
293              ':'  IDENT
294              ¦ ;
295
296   type_dcls:
297              IDENT  '='  type ';'
298              ¦ type_dcls IDENT  '='  type ';'  ;
```

EXERCISES

1. Using the SDT built from *ll-parse* in Section 8.2, draw the attributed parse trees for:

    (a) (3−4)
    (b) 1−(3+5/2)
    (c) ((−3−4/2*(4)))

2. Draw the parse tree for the Pascal program in Fig. 1-5 relative to the grammar in section 8.4.

3. Add the alternate form of comment "(*..*)" to the lexical analyzer for Pascal.

4. The Pascal grammar has productions that are left recursive; for example,

    ```
    statements:
                statement
            ¦ statements ';' statement ;
    ```

    (a) Even though *yacc* could correctly handle this production if it were right recursive instead, that would still present a problem in parsing some programs. Why? (Hint: think of how long the sentential form will grow.)
    (b) Modify all remaining right recursive productions in the grammar to become left recursive ones.

5. **(a)** Write a top-down SDT that maps arithmetic expressions into prefix expressions; for example,

    ```
    (3+4)*(5-6)
    ```

    becomes:

    ```
    *+34-56
    ```

    (b) Write a *yacc* program to do the same.

6. Pascal **if-then** and **if-then-else** statements can be translated into the simpler FORTRAN logical **if** statements.

    (a) Construct a top-down SDT that performs this mapping.
    (b) Write a *yacc* program to do the same.

7. The **while** construct of Pascal can be mapped into the more primitive loop formed from **if** and **goto** statements.

    (a) Construct a top-down SDT which performs this mapping.
    (b) Show the actions of your SDT on the statement:

    ```
    while x<0 do begin x := x+1; y := y*x end
    ```

    (c) Construct a *yacc* program that does the same.
    (d) Show the actions of the *yacc* program on the same statement.

8. You are given the following LL(1) grammar:

    ```
    1 dcl:
            IDENT ':' type ';'      [IDENT]

    2 type:
            INTEGER                 [INTEGER]
          ¦ RECORD ';' dcls END     [RECORD]

    3 dcls:
            dcl trailer             [IDENT]

    4 trailer:
            dcls                    [IDENT]
          ¦                         [END]
    ```

Each sentence generated by this grammar is a variable declaration. A variable may be declared to be an integer (a *simple* declaration):

(i) `x: INTEGER ;`

or a record:

(ii)
```
x: RECORD;
    y: INTEGER;
    z: RECORD;
        a: INTEGER;
        b: INTEGER;
        END;
    END;
```

Convert this grammar into a SDT that will:

(a) Emit a simple declaration unchanged.

(b) Translate a record declaration into a sequence of simple declarations for fully qualified names reflecting the structure of the record. For example, (i) is passed unchanged, but (ii) is mapped to:

```
x.y: INTEGER;
x.z.a: INTEGER;
x.z.b: INTEGER;
```

9. Extend the grammar in Section 8.4 to incorporate "reasonable" error handling.

10. Write a *yacc* program that removes redundant parentheses from infix arithmetic expressions; for example,

```
((3*4)-(5/6*4*(2+3)))
```

becomes:

```
3*4-5/6*4*(2+3)
```

11. Write a *yacc* program that translates an arithmetic expression into its parse tree.

12. Revise the Pascal grammar in Section 8.4 so that the operators have the more traditional precedence of *C*.

13. Turn the *yacc* grammar in Section 8.4 into a complete *C* program that prints "ok" if it recognizes the input string, and "whoops" if it does not.

14. Extend the *yacc* program from the last exercise to:

(a) Check whether an identifier is declared twice in the same block.

(b) Check whether the target of a `goto` exists with its scope.

(c) Check whether identifiers appearing in constant declarations are themselves either predefined or previously declared constants.

Chapter 9
RUN-TIME ENVIRONMENTS

9.1. SOURCE LANGUAGE FEATURES

So far the text has primarily focused on manipulating program text as a static entity. Run-time management, the topic of this chapter, centers on the semantics of a program when it is executing. "Cosmetic" differences between languages such as the symbol used for the assignment operator (" : =" in Pascal and "=" in C), the method of terminating statements (" , " and " . " in COBOL, " ; " in C), and how comments are bracketed ("−−" in Ada makes the rest of the line a comment, "/*..*/" in C, a "C" in column 1 in FORTRAN), are easily handled by the techniques studied in earlier chapters. Differences in the run-time semantics of programming languages have far more significant consequences to the compiler writer implementing a language and to the programmer applying a language to solve some problem.

Some areas where language semantics strongly influence compiler implementation strategies (and the choice of algorithms by the language user) are:

1. Are recursive calls supported?
2. What is the policy on scope of names?
3. What is the persistence of a name's value; for example, does a local variable lose its value on exit from the module in which it is declared?
4. How are parameters passed?
5. Is code modifiable at run-time?

Fortunately, there are several reasonably standard paradigms that language designers follow when answering these questions, making it possible to describe implementation strategies that are applicable across a broad range of languages.

Example 9-1. Program *treedoodle* randomly builds a binary tree and prints out its nodes in left-first order (visit left branch, then current node, then right branch):

```
1    /*  randomly construct a binary tree with argv[1] nodes and print
2         it in left subtree order
3    */
4
5    #include <stdio.h>
6
7    extern long random();
8    extern struct tree *newnode();
9
10   struct tree {
11       int value;
12       struct tree  *left, *right;
13   };
14
15   main (argc, argv) int argc; char *argv[];
16   {
17       struct tree *t;
18       int i;
19
```

```
20          t = newnode (0);
21          for (i=1; i<atoi(argv[1]); i++)
22              sprout (t);
23          treeprint (t);
24      }
25
26      sprout (t)  struct tree *t;
27      {
28              /* randomly walk to frontier and add node */
29
30          static int times = 1;
31
32          struct tree *n;
33
34          if (random()&01)  /* work on left leg */
35              if (t->left != NULL)
36                  sprout (t->left);
37              else
38                  t->left = newnode (times++);
39          else  /* work on right leg */
40              if (t->right != NULL)
41                  sprout (t->right);
42              else
43                  t->right = newnode (times++);
44      }
45
46      treeprint (t)  struct tree *t;
47      {
48          if (t != NULL) {
49              treeprint (t->left);
50              printf ("%d\n", t->value);
51              treeprint (t->right);
52          }
53      }
54
55      struct tree
56      *newnode (v)  int v;
57      {
58          struct tree *t;
59
60          t = (struct tree *)malloc (sizeof (struct tree));
61          t->left = t->right = NULL;
62          t->value = v;
63          return t;
64      }
```

Executing *treedoodle* with argument ''4'' leads to

```
% treedoodle  4
1
3
0
2
```

It has `atoi(argv[1])` nodes, each one a unique integer in the range `0..atoi(argv[1])-1`.
◆

Example 9-1 has features that demonstrate nearly all of the lessons of this chapter:

1. *treedoodle* has two nonrecursive functions: `main` and `newnode`.
2. *treedoodle* has both local and global data.
3. `newnode` returns a value, while `sprout` does not.
4. `sprout` is a recursive function.
5. `times` is a local `static` variable.
6. `newnode` explicitly allocates storage.

Declaration, Static Scope, and Block Structure

A name is *declared* at the point in a program where it first occurs. Line 17 of *treedoodle* declares variable t. Each declaration has a *scope* of statements in which it applies. t is known within the main block bounded by lines 16 and 24. A declaration normally also tells some of the properties of that name within its scope. t is a pointer to a tree structure. Some languages allow those properties to be specified in more than one place. FORTRAN allows a variable's properties to be declared in several statements; for example, the three statement sequence

```
COMMON    X
INTEGER   X(10)
DATA      X/10*0/
```

states that X is an integer array in the unnamed COMMON block, all of whose elements are initialized to 0.

Each language has its own policy on name scope, a policy that the compiler must carefully enforce. For example, each name in a *C* program is either *global*, that is, it can be referenced anywhere in the code, or it is local to a block which is itself global. The declaration of newnode in lines 55–56 states that it is a function with *global* scope; that is, newnode can be referenced anywhere in the program, even in other files that are separately compiled. It also states that newnode returns a pointer to a tree structure. Variable t in line 58 is local to global newnode. In fact there are four different declarations of t in *treedoodle*, each with a unique scope.

Pascal supports a more general *block-structure* policy than C allowing blocks to be nested arbitrarily deep. This is illustrated in Fig. 9-1. Variables i, j, and k declared in line 3 are local to block nesting, and will be denoted here by i.nesting, j.nesting, and k.nesting to indicate this. Procedure firstlevel is also local to nesting, but secondlevel is not because it occurs within a block inside nesting. Line 6 redeclares variables i and j local to firstlevel. The reference to i and j in line 13 are to i.firstlevel and j.firstlevel, since the closest physically enclosing declaration occurs in block firstlevel. These references are said to be *bound* to the declarations in line 6. The reference to k in line 14, however, is bound to k.nesting since it was not redeclared in firstlevel. secondlevel redeclares nothing. Consequently, the references to i and j in line 9 are bound to i.firstlevel and j.firstlevel, and the reference to k is bound to k.nesting.

```
1      program  nesting (input, output);
2          var
3              i,j,k: integer;
4          procedure firstlevel (m: integer);
5              var
6                  i,j: integer;
7              function secondlevel (n,r: integer): integer;
8              begin
9                  i := 0; j := 1; k := 2;
10                 secondlevel := n+r
11             end;
12         begin
13             i := 3; j := 4;
14             k := secondlevel (i,m)
15         end;
16         procedure anotherfirstlevel;
17             var
18                 k:  integer;
19         begin
20             i := 6; j:= 7; k := 8;
21             firstlevel (k)
22         end;
23     begin
24         i := 9; j := 10; k := 11;
25         firstlevel (i);
26         anotherfirstlevel
27     end.
```

Figure 9-1. nesting: General Block Structure.

```
1    first ()
2    {
3        int x;
4        third ();
5    }
6
7    second ()
8    {
9        int x;
10       third ();
11   }
12
13   third ()
14   {
15       x = 1;
16   }
```

Figure 9-2. Dynamic Binding of Names.

Dynamic Binding

A language uses *static* binding when the physical placement of a name uniquely determines the declaration to which it is bound. Most languages such as *C*, Pascal, and Ada use static binding. One notable exception is SNOBOL, which uses *dynamic* scoping. In SNOBOL the order of subprogram calls at runtime determines the binding of a name to a declaration. Dynamic binding is very powerful, but also extremely error prone. It is illustrated in *C*-like syntax in Fig. 9-2. Both first and second, which call function third, declare local variable x. When first calls third, x on line 15 is bound to the declaration in line 3, but when second calls third, x is bound to the declaration on line 9 instead. The binding changes as the program executes, making it much harder to understand the program's behavior and much easier to accidentally mangle data. Dynamic binding is usually a bad idea for classic third generation languages and must be introduced in a carefully controlled way in order to be effective.

Activation

A name becomes *active* during program execution when it becomes legal to use it. For variables this means it becomes legal to assign and reference its value, and for functions and procedures it becomes legal to call them. The act of making a name associated with a particular declaration active is also sometimes called *elaboration* of that declaration.

Activation may be implemented by allocating storage for a variable, but this is not necessary in all cases. Some languages, such as FORTRAN, are simple enough that all of the storage required during program execution can be completely determined during compilation and preallocated when the program is loaded into memory. Such *static* allocation is studied in the next section. *C*, as illustrated in *treedoodle*, has features which preclude static allocation. It requires *automatic* and *dynamic* allocation studied in Section 9.4.

By default in *C* and most other languages, a variable local to a function becomes *active* when that function is called and becomes *inactive* when the execution of that function terminates. When a variable becomes inactive it is no longer legal to reference its value. This may be implemented by deallocating the variable's storage with the obvious consequence that the next time the variable becomes active it will not have the same value it held just before it became inactive. Such a variable is said to be *automatic* because its storage is allocated and deallocated automatically on entry to and exit from the block in which it is declared. Variable n in line 32 of *treedoodle* is automatic. *C* also supports static variables, which become active and inactive on block entry and exit, but retain their values across activations. times in line 30 of *treedoodle* is static. This is normally implemented by placing storage for static variables in a separately managed pool from those that are automatic. Note that the issue of name scope is separated from storage persistence in *C*. Both n and times are local to sprout, but times retains its value across invocations while n does not.

Definition

An active variable is said to be *defined* if it has a legal value stored in it. Automatic variables have no value when they become active and become *undefined* when they become inactive. Static variables, on the other hand, once defined stay defined. Note that a variable could be defined but not active at some point in program execution, meaning that it has a value but there is no way to reference it at that time. Variable `times` has this property when `main` is executing after the first call to `sprout` has completed.

9.2. SYMBOL-TABLE MANAGEMENT

The simple model of a symbol table used in Chapter 2 is not adequate for "real" languages that support block structure, user-define datatypes, and other interesting features. This section looks at how a symbol table for languages with some of the characteristics of FORTRAN, *C*, and Pascal might be structured.

Simple Block-Structured Tables

A compiler for a language that only has a single block would never face the problem of resolving ambiguous references to names; there could be at most one legal declaration of a name. Real programming languages almost universally support some notion of limiting name scope so that the same name can be used again in a different context for a different purpose. *C* and FORTRAN blocks are never nested so that a name is either global or local to a block that is itself global. Figure 9-3 shows a FORTRAN program segment. One possible symbol table for this program appears in Fig. 9-4. It ignores any predefined lexicon, listing only user-defined names. INTEGERs and REALs are four bytes, BOOLEANs are one byte, and arrays are implemented as contiguous storage so that Z(10) in line 4 consumes 40 bytes. The actual symbol is augmented by the block to uniquely identify each name. The key is the actual symbol plus block. Since blocks are never nested, it is trivial to keep track of which block is current in order to assure the correct entry is referenced.

This table management scheme is quite storage expensive since entries are added but never deleted. Some compilers are organized so that they completely compile one module before beginning the compilation of the next. This is possible if the language does not allow forward references to names whose characteristics are not known until after the end of the module. FORTRAN is one such language.

```
1              PROGRAM   EXAMPLE
2              ...
3              INTEGER X
4              REAL Z(10)
5              BOOLEAN V
6              ...
7              CALL   A (X,1)
8              CALL   B (2.0,Z)
9              ...
10             STOP
11             END
12
13             SUBROUTINE A (Y,Z)
14             INTEGER Y,Z
15             REAL X(4)
16             ...
17             CALL   B (X,Z)
18             ...
19             END
20
21             FUNCTION B (X,Y)
22             REAL X
23             INTEGER Y, Z(3)
24             BOOLEAN W
25             ...
26             END
```

Figure 9-3. *samfort*: **Sample FORTRAN Program.**

Index	ACTUAL	BLOCK	TYPE	CLASS	LENGTH	...
1	X	_main	INTEGER	variable	4	
2	Z	_main	REAL	variable	40	
3	V	_main	BOOLEAN	variable	1	
4	A	_glob	SUBROUTINE			
5	1	_main	INTEGER	literal	4	
6	B	_glob	FUNCTION			
7	2.0	_main	REAL	literal	4	
8	Y	A	INTEGER	parameter	4	
9	Z	A	INTEGER	parameter	4	
10	X	A	REAL	variable	16	
11	X	B	REAL	parameter	4	
12	Y	B	INTEGER	parameter	4	
13	Z	B	INTEGER	variable	12	
14	W	B	BOOLEAN	variable	1	

Figure 9-4. Symbol Table for FORTRAN Program.

Assuming the compiler does its translation one module at a time, there is no point maintaining entries for variables X, Z, and V in the symbol table after line 11 and a significant storage savings from deleting them. Removing all local names once compilation of a block is complete assures that the symbol table will never grow larger than the amount of storage necessary to compile the biggest single module.

General Block-Structured Tables

Searching through a large linear symbol table such as the one in Fig. 9-4 is cumbersome even for a language as simple as FORTRAN, but becomes very cumbersome when arbitrary block nesting is allowed and even the block names can be ambiguous. A more elegant solution is to keep one symbol table per block and maintain a linked list of them to match the static block nesting. Figure 9-5 shows such a symbol table for nesting. In order to bind a name to its declaration the compiler first searches the table of the block it is currently compiling, then the table of the containing block, and so on, outward to the table representing the implicit global block. The first declaration of the name found is the one needed. If the name is not found in any table, there is no binding declaration and the compiler should initiate appropriate error handling.

This table organization implies that the number of searches per name may be as high as the nesting level of the program. Theoretically a program could be nested very deeply, which would force a large number of searches per name. In practice, however, programs rarely nest deeper than three levels,

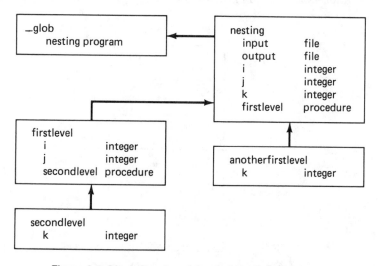

Figure 9-5. Block-Structured Symbol Table for *nesting*.

```
1    procedure q(i,j: real); forward;
2
3    procedure p(i: integer);
4        ...
5        q(a,b);
6        ...
7
8    procedure q;
9        ...
10       p(z);
11       ...
```

Figure 9-6. *forward* Declaration in Pascal.

making this table organization very efficient. Furthermore, search time within a single table is a function of table size, and each table is only as large as required for the number of entries within that single block.

Semantic Resolution

C and Pascal have been carefully defined so that all of the type attributes of an identifier are known when it is first encountered in a left to right scan of the source code. Even sticky situations such as forward references to a function are handled by explicit declarations such as the `forward` directive in Fig. 9-6 required to ensure that when the call to q is made in line 5, the compiler knows how many arguments are needed and what their types are.

Unfortunately for the compiler implementor, some languages (mostly older ones) such as PL/I offer the programmer enormous flexibility in the order of declarations. Identifiers can be declared after they are referenced, making it necessary to do two passes over the code in order to generate intermediate code. Lexical analysis and parsing can be done during the first pass, but intermediate code cannot be effectively generated until all of the attributes of the identifiers have been determined. By the time the first pass is complete, the attributes have been resolved and a subsequent pass can generate intermediate code that properly accounts for the data types of the operators and operands.

9.3. STATIC STORAGE ALLOCATION

Memory Management

A language in which all memory allocation can be anticipated at compile-time has the simplest run-time storage management scheme. Languages such as FORTRAN which do not support recursion or user-controlled storage allocation (such as `malloc` in C on Unix or `new` in Pascal) usually fall into this

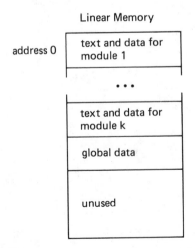

Figure 9-7. Static Storage Allocation in FORTRAN.

category. Figure 9-7 shows one possible storage map for FORTRAN which assumes a linear address space. Data and text for each module are mingled and there is one pool for global data such as a COMMON block.

Resolving local and global references is straightforward with this scheme, even if separate compilation is supported. Local data references are resolved at compile-time relative to some point in the combined text+data area. Global data is relative to the beginning of the global storage area, the address of which can be kept in a register.

A more sophisticated scheme separates text and data to support text sharing among concurrently executing processes (or within a single process in which there are recursive subprogram calls). This is possible if the text does not change during execution. Such programs are said to be *pure* or *reentrant*. Some languages such as LISP intentionally support self-modifying programs. If two or more processes wish to use the same pure text, the operating system can allocate just one copy of that text together with a separate data area for each process. This reduces the overall storage requirements for the simultaneous execution of multiple processes, with the advantage that this storage optimization is transparent to the programmer who writes the programs, to the compiler, and to the person executing the programs.

The Unix loader *ld* can be told to make a program pure through the *-n* flag or to mix text and data through the *-N* flag. The first word of an executable image produced by *ld* is a *magic number* that indicates whether or not the image can be shared. On System V and 4.2BSD Unix magic number 0407 means an image is not sharable, and 0410 means it is.

Depending on the machine architecture, it may be necessary to pad the text so that the subsequent data area begins on the start of a hardware segment or page boundary. Figure 9-8 shows a view of static allocation which supports shared text and assumes each text and data segment begins on a segment boundary. In a demand paged environment the text and data might occupy a large number of segments (one segment per hardware page). There are many methods to support memory protection and segmentation. A compiler is largely oblivious to all of these methods with the exception that it must separate

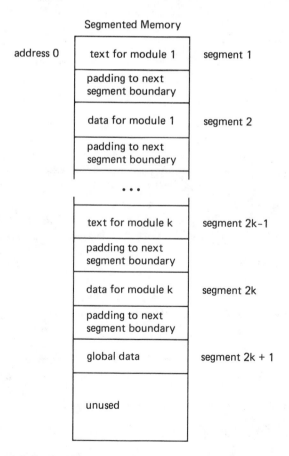

Figure 9-8. Static Allocation of Pure Code on Segment Boundaries.

text and data so that the loader can take advantage of pure code. It is the loader's job to worry about page and segment alignment.

Subprogram Calls

Two activations of the same pure process have separate main memory data areas but still share the single set of machine registers. When subprogram A calls B, care must be taken to ensure that when B returns control back to A the registers have the same values as when B was called. Module linkage conventions are established by the compiler to enforce this policy. One common convention in a static run-time environment is to have each module set aside storage to hold its register values. Assume each module has an area called SAVE in its data area large enough to hold the value of all registers whose values must be preserved across calls. Further assume the address of the global area is in register r, that the address of the data area of each module is accessible through the global pool, and that the address of the local data area for a module is in register s. Figure 9-9 shows the sequence of actions necessary when calling B from A.

Parameter Passing

There are several methods to pass parameters between subprograms including:

1. Call by value.
2. Call by reference.

A number of other schemes have been implemented, but these are the most common and together illustrate most of the aspects of the other methods. Several others are discussed in the exercises. An argument passed by value is unaffected by changes to its corresponding argument in the subprogram. *Call by value* is most useful where the caller simply wants to pass data to a subprogram without risking that data being modified. *Call by reference* allows a subprogram to modify the value of the argument.

Each language designer must choose among parameter passing schemes. Some languages such as C consistently use one scheme-call by value. Others give the programmer some control over the method used. Pascal allows the programmer to specify whether he or she wishes to use call by value or call by reference.

Example 9-2. The first parameter of procedure sample in Fig. 9-10 is passed by reference, while the second is passed by value. By default in Pascal a parameter is passed by value, but if it is preceded by the keyword var in the declaration, the parameter is passed by reference instead. Even this policy is not always uniform. Call by value is implemented by first copying the caller's argument, then passing the address of the copy to the called subprogram. Call by reference is implemented by simply passing the address of the caller's argument to the subprogram—no copy is made. For large data structures such as arrays, making copies with each call would be very expensive both in time and space. For efficiency

Calling Subroutine A:

1. Load the address of the next instruction into register t and branch to the address of A.

Called Subroutine B:

1. Save all registers except r and s in A's SAVE area, which is accessible through s.
2. Load register s with the address of B's data area, which is accessible through r.
3. B works its will . . .
4. Load register s with the address of A's data area, which is accessible through r.
5. Restore all registers except r and s from A's SAVE area, which is now accessible through s.
6. Branch to the address in register t, returning to A.

Figure 9-9. Calling Subprogram B from A.

```
1    procedure sample (var x: integer; y: integer);
2    begin
3        x := 3;
4        y := 4;
5        return
6    end;
```

Figure 9-10. Parameter Passing in Pascal.

Pascal mandates that arrays be passed by reference even if the **var** qualifier is omitted from the declaration.

♦

Call by Reference

The simplest parameter passing scheme is call by *reference* in which the binding between corresponding arguments of the called and calling subprogram makes them synonymous during the execution of the subprogram. The implementation of call by reference is illustrated on *samfort*, defined in Fig. 9-3. The compilation of line 17 causes the allocation of a two element array _arg[ ] in A's local data area. The compiler places the addresses of X.A and Z.A there.* This is shown in Fig. 9-11. As part of the sequence of instructions executed when A calls B at run-time, the address of _arg is loaded into register u. When execution of B begins, X.B is *bound* to X.A and Y.B is *bound* to Z.A. Any change to the value of X.B should immediately be reflected in X.A. Similarly, changing Y.B should immediately change Z.A. The address of X.A is $*u$ and the address of Z.A is $*u+1$. When B is compiled, a reference to the address of X.B is translated into $*u$, while the value of X.B is mapped into $**u$. The address of Y.B is compiled into $*u+1$, and its value into $*(*u+1)$. This establishes the necessary correspondence between the pairs of bound variables.

Call by Value

Call by value is implemented by first copying the caller's arguments and then passing the copy by reference. During compilation, storage is allocated in the local data area of the caller where copies can be made. The address of each copy is placed into _arg rather than the address of the original. At run-time when the call is made, a copy of the caller's arguments is made, then the call proceeds as if it were call by reference.

9.4. DYNAMIC STORAGE ALLOCATION

Static allocation does not work for a language that supports recursion such as *C* or Pascal. Separate local storage must be allocated for each active call to a recursive module. Since the number of simultaneously active calls cannot be bounded at compile-time, the run-time environment must do the allocation each time a call is made. Furthermore, most modern machine architectures such as the VAX,

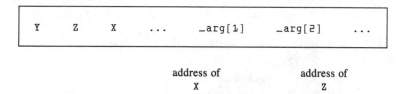

Figure 9-11. A's Data Area with _arg Allocated

---

* Actually, the compiler does not know the real addresses of X.A and Z.A since their relative position in the complete executable image is not known until all modules are linked. Instead it leaves a directive for the loader to supply the addresses when they are known.

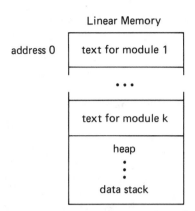

Figure 9-12. Dynamic Storage Allocation in Pascal.

Motorola 68000, and Intel 8086 families readily support a data stack that favors dynamic storage allocation even if static allocation is possible.

Figure 9-12 shows a simplified view of the memory organization a compiler might establish for a *C* or Pascal program. The text for all modules is clustered together at one end of memory followed by the heap where storage explicitly allocated by the program is kept. At the other end of memory is a stack where data are implicitly allocated by subprogram calls and deallocated by subprogram returns. Global data appear at the base of the stack. Each time a subprogram is called, local storage for it is allocated on the top of the stack in what is called an *activation record*. When the subprogram exits, the record is popped. Storage allocated in this manner is called *automatic* because its allocation and deallocation occurs automatically on subprogram call and return.

Automatic Storage Allocation

Automatic allocaton readily supports recursive subprograms. If there are *n* recursive calls, there are *n* activation records on the stack. Subprogram calls can be nested arbitrarily deep, limited only by the amount of memory by which the stack can grow.

The location of a subprogram's activation record on the stack cannot be predicted at compile-time; in fact, it will almost certainly vary during execution. Yet the compiler must establish at compile-time the addresses of identifiers in order to generate code. The solution to this dilemma is clever use of pointers to link activation records.

Activation Records for Static Block Structured Languages

Figure 9-13 shows the detailed structure of the stack at the point where `nesting` has called `anotherfirstlevel` in line 26, which has called `firstlevel` in line 21, which has called `secondlevel` in line 4.

The global data area contains all constants not embedded into the text (the integer literals could be stored either in the text since they will not change during execution or in a separate global area depending on the code generation scheme) and one activation record for each of the main and three active subprograms, stacked in the order in which the calls occurred. Constants cannot be kept in an activation record since it is deallocated and reallocated during execution.

At the bottom of each activation record is storage for parameters and a return value if any. Above that sits the area in which to save register values, store the return address the called subprogram must use to return control back to the caller, and keep any other status information that must be preserved across calls. This area is the same for all activation records since the information that must be preserved does not vary with the subprogram being called. Above this is the address of a pointer used to make nonlocal storage accesses. It will be explained shortly. Next comes the address of the caller's activation record; for example, `firstlevel`'s activation record contains the address of `nesting`'s activation record. This is needed to pop the stack when a called subprogram exits. Finally, at the top of the record is

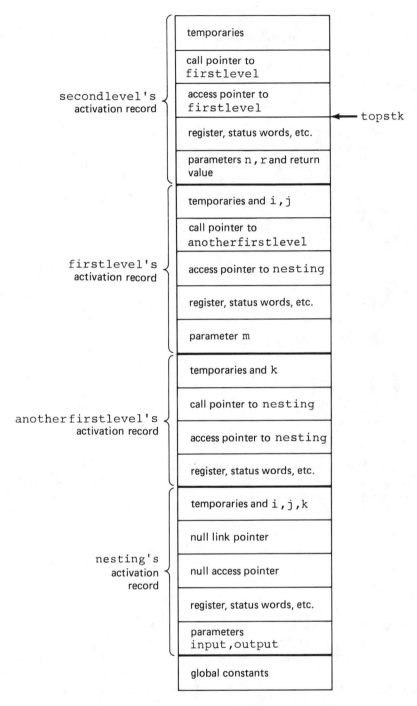

Figure 9-13. Activation Records for `nesting`.

storage for each local variable and compiler-defined temporary. The length of this area is different for each subprogram, but is constant for any particular subprogram across activations.

Accessing Local Storage

Local variables are referenced as offsets from variable `topstk`, which points to the top of the save area. *C* and Pascal are both defined so that the compiler can know as soon as the heading for a subprogram is compiled how many parameters it has and whether it returns a value. This tells the compiler the size of the parameter block in the activation record. The access and link pointers and the save areas have a fixed size for all subprograms. Hence, the compiler knows how far it is from `topstk` to the parameters, return value, temporaries, and local variables. References to this storage can be made relative to `topstk` with a known fixed offset.

Algorithm 9-1. Call a subprogram.
Caller

1. Evaluate value arguments if any.
2. Allocate part of the called's activation record including storage for the parameters and return value of the called, the save area, and the link and access pointers. Do not allocate room for called's local storage.
3. Store the old value of `topstk` into the called's link field, a return address into the called's save area, and initialize the called's parameter field.
4. Set `topstk` to the top of the called's link field.
5. Transfer control to called.

Called

1. Store registers and other status information in its save area.
2. Allocate rest of activation record for local storage.
3. Initialize local storage as required.
4. Begin execution.
♦

Algorithm 9-2. Return from a subprogram call.
Called

1. Store a return value if any in its activation record.
2. Using link field restore `topstk` to value it had when caller was active.
3. Using save field restore registers and other status information to values they had prior to call.
4. Branch to return address stored in save field.

Caller

1. If a return value is expected, it is in a known offset from `topstk`. Reference it as necessary.
♦

Subprograms with a variable number of arguments such as *C*'s `printf` are implemented correctly with this strategy, assuming the arguments are stored with the first one in the lowest memory location and the last argument in the highest location.* The first argument is always at the same offset from `topstk`, so that no matter how many arguments are actually passed, the called subprogram will be able to reliably access them. Of course, if the subprogram accesses more arguments than are actually passed, it will instead reference storage in the activation record of the calling subprogram with disastrous consequences.

Newer machine designs provide architectural support for many high-level language features such as subprogram calls. Virtually all newer machines support some sort of stack on which data and addresses can be placed. Some with sophisticated instruction sets such as Digital's VAX have atomic "call" and "return" machine instructions which directly implement the concept of an activation record.

Example 9-3. The Pascal statement

```
SORT (LIST,N)
```

---

* Recall that the stack is growing toward lower memory locations.

which calls procedure SORT to sort a series of N integers might be translated into

```
PUSHL   N
PUSHAL  LIST
CALLS   #2,SORT
```

in VAX-11 assembly language. This pushes the value of N and the address of LIST onto the machine stack, then calls SORT, indicating there are two arguments. The atomic CALLS instruction will save on the stack all registers, program counter, topstk pointer, and condition codes, and perform miscellaneous housekeeping. The RET instruction restores all of the registers and status codes, popping the stack.

◆

Dangling References

Silent allocation and deallocation of storage when subprograms are called and exited can get a careless programmer into trouble with a *dangling reference*, which occurs when a program points at storage that was previously deallocated.

Example 9-4. Consider the program in Fig. 9-14. Variable p in main points to automatic variable i which is allocated when dangle is called and deallocated when dangle is exited. The assignment of the address of i to p in line 6 is erroneous and is called a *dangling reference* to i because the reference exists after the storage to which it points has been freed. printf in line 7 will write out whatever value happens to be in the same address that was previously used to store i when dangle was called.

◆

Pascal does not allow a program to use the address of an automatic variable, making this scenario impossible. *C*, with its greater flexibility and power, presents additional opportunities for error.

Variable Length Automatic Storage

Some languages such as PL/I support variable length automatic storage; that is, storage which is allocated at block entry and deallocated at block exit, but whose size is not known at compile-time. For example, the PL/I declaration

```
DECLARE  A(N) FIXED;
```

declares A to be an array of fixed (integer) elements. The number of elements in the array varies depending on the value of variable N when this declaration is elaborated.

```
1    #include <stdio.h>
2
3    main ()
4    {
5        int  *p;
6        p = dangle ();
         ...
7        printf ("%d\n", *p);
8    }
9
10   int
11   *dangle ()
12   {
13       int  i;
14       i = 1;
15       return &i;
16   }
```

Figure 9-14. A Dangling Reference.

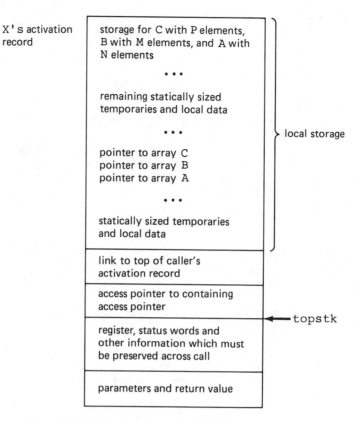

X's activation record

storage for C with P elements, B with M elements, and A with N elements
···
remaining statically sized temporaries and local data
···
pointer to array C pointer to array B pointer to array A
···
statically sized temporaries and local data

} local storage

link to top of caller's activation record
access pointer to containing access pointer

◄── topstk

register, status words and other information which must be preserved across call
parameters and return value

Figure 9-15. Addressing Dynamically Sized Data Structures.

Dynamically sized structures cannot be handled in quite the same way as those that are statically sized. Pushing a structure onto the stack whose size was not known at compile-time makes it impossible to know at compile-time the correct offset to any storage above it. A dynamically sized structure is properly addressed instead through a pointer. The pointer has a fixed length whose offset from topstk can be unambiguously determined at compile-time. The dynamically sized data structure itself can be placed at the top of the activation record as shown in Fig. 9-15 for subprogram X with dynamically sized arrays A(N), B(M), and C(P).

Access to Nonlocal Storage

In a static block structured language binding of names to declarations is based on the physical placement of blocks in the program text, not on the order of calls. There already is a pointer in each activation record back to topstk of the caller's record. An additional *access* pointer is defined which points to the activation record of the statically containing block. Suppose name n is in a block at nesting level i and its bound declaration is in a block at nesting level $j \leq i$. The values of i and j are known at compile-time. Assuming names must be declared prior to their use, a common restriction in most languages including C and Pascal, the offset o from topstk where the storage for n can be found can also be computed at compile-time.

Algorithm 9-3. Find a Nonlocal reference.

```
for (k=0; k<(i-j); k++)
    follow access field to next record;
n is o bytes offset from topstk of current record;
```
◆

Even though access to nonlocal storage still requires stepping through a series of pointers, Algorithm 9-3 is still relatively efficient. The number of steps is known at compile-time as is the offset from topstk.

Even greater efficiency in accessing nonlocal storage is possible through the use of a *display*, which is an array of pointers to the activation records of all containing blocks. When secondlevel is active in nesting, the display would contain pointers to the activation records of firstlevel and nesting. With this approach, it is never necessary to follow more than one pointer to the needed activation record for a nonlocal reference. Of course, each display is stored in the activation record to which it applies. Figure 9-16 shows the stack for nesting modified to include displays. The only difference occurs in the access pointer field for secondlevel's activation record where pointers to both firstlevel and nesting appear. The algorithm to compute a display is left as an exercise, but the algorithm to compute the access pointer for subprogram *B*, executed as part of *B*'s calling sequence, is next.

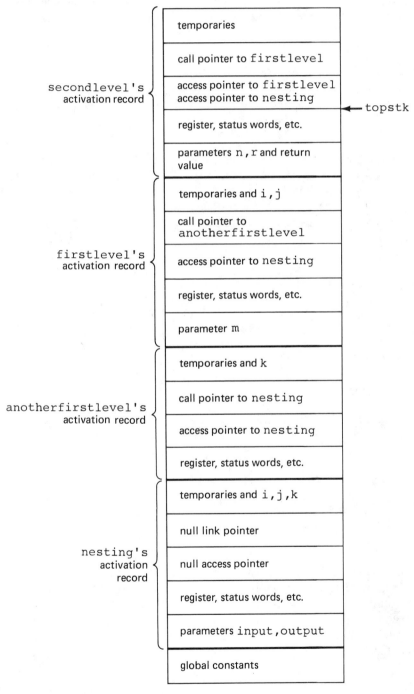

Figure 9-16. Activation Records for nesting with Displays.

Algorithm 9-4. Compute the access pointer for B.
Steps

Case 1: $i>j$.

> B is textually inside C. By scoping rules $i=j+1$. B's access field should point to C's access field which is in the activation record immediately below B's.

Case 2: $i<j$.

> C is textually inside B. B's access field should point to the access field of the block containing both B and C. Follow $j-i+1$ access pointers from C's access field. B's access field should point there.

Case 3: $i=j$.

> B and C are at the same nesting level. By scoping rules they must be surrounded by the same block or else C could not call B. B's access field should equal C's.

◆

Algorithm 9-4 assumes subprogram B is at nesting level i and C is at nesting level j. When `secondlevel` is called in line 14 of `nesting`, the access field for `secondlevel` must be computed. `secondlevel` is at nesting level 3 and `firstlevel`, the calling procedure is at nesting level 2. Case 1 applies with $i=3$ and $j=2$. `secondlevel`'s access field should point to `firstlevel`'s which is in the activation record immediately below `secondlevel`'s.

Nonlocal Storage in Dynamic Block Structured Languages

In a language with dynamic block structure the declaration to which a name is bound is determined by the run-time calling sequence. Activation records are stacked in the order in which calls were made, making it straightforward to find the correct storage.

Algorithm 9-5. Accessing nonlocal storage in dynamic block structure.

```
while (not at bottom of stack) {
    if (name is declared in subprogram corresponding to current
        activation record)
        this is needed record, use it and return;
    else
        follow link field down to next record;
}
error - name not bound to any active declaration;
```
◆

Algorithm 9-5 assumes that enough information has been kept at run-time and stored in the activation record to know whether any particular name is declared in the corresponding subprogram and how to find it. Much of the compiler's symbol table must be kept around at run-time and embedded into the activation record. In general the compiler cannot anticipate the offset from `topstk` where the storage for a particular name will be kept because the offset will be different for each declaration to which the name can be bound. Compare this to the algorithm for finding nonlocal storage in a static block structured language.

Because much of the symbol table must be retained and expensive searches conducted for each

```
electric ()                    clingfree ()
{                              {
    static int i;                  int i;
}                              }
```

Figure 9-17. Use of Static Variable.

reference, dynamic block structure is relatively inefficient. Very few languages use it, and the implementations of those that do are usually considered slow compared to languages using static block structure.

Local Static Storage

C allows a programmer to declare a local variable static, in which case its scope is determined by the same rules as automatic variables, but its value persists across calls to the subprogram where the variable is declared. times in line 30 of treedoodle is a static integer variable, initialized to 1 at compile-time and then incremented by 1 with each call to sprout, the function in which times is declared.

Storage for static variables cannot be placed on the stack since that would make it impossible to preserve that storage across calls. Instead the storage is allocated in the global area with a known offset.

Example 9-5. Figure 9-17 contains two trivial C programs which differ only in whether i is static or automatic. Figure 9-18 shows the output of one C compiler on these two programs. Lines 1–7 are prolog setting up the function calls. The key difference in line 7 of *electric.s* and *clingfree.s* is that .F1 in the former is 0 (line 17) and 4 in the latter (line 12). The moveml instruction sets up the size of the stack frame for local variables. *electric.s* reserves no room for local variables, *clingfree.s* saves four bytes. Lines 8–11 in *electric.s* set up four bytes in the global data area for i. There is no counterpart to this in *clingfree.s*.

◆

	electric.s		*clingfree.s*	
1		.data		.data
2		.text		.text
3		.globl _electri		.globl _clingfr
4	_electri:		_clingfr:	
5		link a6,#-.F1		link a6,#-.F1
6		tstb sp@(-.M1)		tstb sp@(-.M1)
7		moveml #.S1,a6@(-.F1)		moveml #.S1,a6@(-.F1)
8		.data		bra .L12
9		.even	.L12:	moveml a6@(-.F1),#0
10	.L13:			unlk a6
11		.space 4		rts
12		.text	.F1 = 4	
13		bra .L12	.S1 = 0x0	
14	.L12:	moveml a6@(-.F1),#0	.M1 = 132	
15		unlk a6	¦ end	
16		rts		.data
17	.F1 = 0			
18	.S1 = 0x0			
19	.M1 = 132			
20	¦ end			
21		.data		

Figure 9-18. M68000 Assembler Output Showing Effect of static.

EXERCISES

1. What is the value of *treedoodle* on input 8?

2. For the following Pascal program:

```
1       program convoluted (input,output);
2           var a,b: integer;
3           procedure x (var a: integer);
4               function y (b: integer): integer;
5               begin
6                   y := b+b;
7               end;
8           begin
9               a := y(b);
10          end;
11          procedure y (var a: integer);
12              function z (i: integer): integer;
13              begin
14                  x(i);
15                  z := i+a;
16              end;
17          begin
18              b := a+z(b);
19          end;
20      begin
21          readln (a,b);
22          x(a); y(b);
23          writeln (a,b);
24      end.
```

(a) What is the nesting level of each procedure and function?
(b) For each variable and subprogram parameter indicate to which declaration it is resolved.
(c) Draw the block-structured symbol table for this program.
(d) Show the run-time stack for this program if the value read for a=3 and b=2.

3. The following program implements Ackermann's highly recursive function. Show the run-time stack for this program at its deepest point when evaluating ackermann(4,2,2) = 16.

```
1       int
2       ackermann (n,x,y) int n,x,y;
3       {
4           if (n==0)
5               return x+1;
6           else if (n==1 && y==0)
7               return x;
8           else if (n==2 && y==0)
9               return 0;
10          else if (n==3 && y==0)
11              return 1;
12          else if (n>=4 && y==0)
13              return 2;
14          else if (n && y)
15              return ackermann(n-1,ackermann(n,x,y-1),x);
16          else {
17              fprintf (stderr, bad arguments\n");
18              exit (1);
19          }
20      }
```

4. Call by *value-result* is another parameter passing method in which the caller's actual argument a is considered to be passed by value to the called's formal argument f at the beginning of subprogram execution, but when the subprogram exits, the final value (result) of f is assigned to a.

(a) Describe an implementation strategy for call by value-result.
(b) Step through the series of steps in executing convoluted from Exercise 2 assuming procedure x in line 3 passes its argument by value-result.

5. Call by *result* is similar to call by value-result except that formal argument f is not initialized at all when subprogram B begins execution. When B terminates, the final value of f is assigned to its corresponding actual argument.

(a) Describe an implementation strategy for call by result.

(b) Step through the series of steps in executing `convoluted` from Exercise 2 assuming procedure x in line 3 passes its argument by result.

Chapter 10
DATA TYPES AND INTERMEDIATE CODE

10.1. INTERMEDIATE LANGUAGES

In the analysis–synthesis model of a compiler, the front-end translates the source program into an intermediate representation, while the back-end generates the target code. This model supports better object code optimization because the intermediate representations can be crafted specifically to facilitate optimization analysis; this model also facilitates the production of retargetable compilers by largely decoupling lexical analysis, parsing, symbol table manipulation, and semantic analysis from code generation. Virtually all production compilers built today first map the source program into some intermediate language along the way to producing object code. This is shown in Fig. 10-1. The earlier chapters on lexical analysis and syntax-directed methods focused on the analysis phase. The later chapters focus on the back-end synthesis phase.

Intermediate code is quite often stored in a treelike form based on the needs of optimizers and code generators, but a linear form called *three-address statements* is more suitable here.

Three-Address Statements

A program written in an intermediate language consists of a series of *three-address statements*. Intermediate code only contains instructions. Data are declared and represented implicitly in the symbol table.

The first two operators defined are `prolog` and `exit`. `prolog` appears at the beginning of a text segment and represents the start-up activities such as setting up the registers, and so on. `exit` is the analogous operator which is the last statement executed in a program. The simplest complete program is

```
prolog
exit      0
```

Additional instructions will be introduced as needed. The *C* segment

```
1    if (x≤y+1)
2        x = x-z;
3    z = f/z;
```

might be translated into the code in Fig. 10-2 where variables x, y, and z are integer valued and f is a floating point variable. The instructions are a mix of *C*, Pascal, and assembly language notations with fairly transparent meanings. The choice of instructions usually varies somewhat with the language being compiled and the target machine, although a large measure of language and machine independence is possible; for example, if the target machine supports an autoincrement instruction, then a similar instruction is likely to be found in the intermediate language.

Although there is no firm rule on what can and cannot be in an intermediate language, it is generally true that only one operation is allowed per statement. A complex source statement such as "z := (x+y)*(z-1)" would be mapped into separate statements to perform the addition, subtraction, and

186

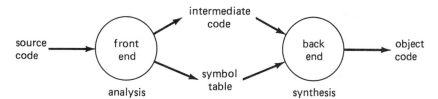

Figure 10-1. Role of Intermediate Code Generator.

```
1          T1 := y + 1
2          if x>T1 goto L0
3          T2 := x - z
4          x := T2
5    L0:   T3 := (float) z
6          T4 := f /F T3
7          T5 := (int) T4
8          z := T5
```

Figure 10-2. Translation of C Segment into Three-Address Code.

multiplication. This reflects the fact that underlying machine architectures invariably require such complex computation to be done in stages. Conditional and repetitive constructs are usually mapped into primitive conditional and unconditional branches. Arithmetic operations are normally typed; that is, there are distinct operators for floating and integer operands. In the example here, "−" is integer subtraction, while "/F" is floating point division. Conversions between types are usually explicit, shown here in a "cast" notation borrowed from C. if statements normally break down into conditional branches. The trade-off in selecting an intermediate language is that by making the language more machine independent, it becomes easier to write a single compiler front-end that can be used to produce compilers for a variety of machines, but it becomes harder to take advantage of architectural features of a machine to facilitate optimization. Most developers who reuse a compiler front-end customize the intermediate language slightly to reflect important machine features. The level of effort to tweek the front-end in this way is very modest compared to the task of writing a front-end from scratch.

A number of temporary variables are created to hold the results of the basic operations, none of which occurred in the original source program. One of the problems with three-address statements is that the large number of temporaries created clutters the symbol table, which must have an entry for each temporary. Also, these temporaries may eventually be mapped into physical storage locations during code generation, bloating code size. It is possible to reduce the number of distinct temporaries by reusing a temporary when its value is no longer needed; for example, after line 2, variable T1 is never used again. Instead of creating T2 in line 3, T1 could have been reused. A more clever allocation of temporaries is shown in Fig. 10-3 which carefully distinquishes between integer temporary T1 and floating point temporary T2. Complex schemes can be defined to determine when a temporary can be reused. For now it is adequate to observe that the value of a temporary is never needed beyond the scope of the source statement that spawned it. This means that the total number of temporaries of a given type needed will never exceed the maximum number needed for a single source statement.

```
1          T1 := y + 1
2          if x>T1 goto L0
3          T1 := x - z
4          x := T1
5    L0:   T2 := (float) z
6          T2 := f /F T2
7          T1 := (int) T2
8          z := T1
```

Figure 10-3. Clever Allocation of Temporaries.

Syntax-Directed Translation into Three-Address Code

Three-address statements are produced using the syntax-directed methods studied in Chapter 8.

Example 10-1. The following *yacc* specification maps simple assignment statements into three-address code:

```
1    %token  ASSIGN   IDENT   INTEGER
2    %left '+'
3    %left '*'
4    %right '-'
5    %%
6
7    S:
8            IDENT  ASSIGN  express
9                    { ICemit (ASSIGN,  $1, $3);};
10
11   express:
12           express '+'   express
13                   { ICemit (ADD, $$=newtemp(), $1, $3);};
14
15   express:
16           express '*'   express
17                   { ICemit (MULT, $$=newtemp(), $1, $3);};
18
19   express:
20           '-'  express
21                   { ICemit (UMINUS, $$=newtemp(), $2);};
22
23   express:
24           '(' express ')'
25                   { $$ = $2; } ;
26
27   express:
28           IDENT
29                   { $$ = $1;}
30         | INTEGER
31                   { $$ = $1;} ;
```

The action code calls function `ICemit` which takes up to four arguments. The first argument is the operator, whose arity determines the number of operands that follow; for example, `ASSIGN` has two operands, representing the three-address statement

```
op1 := op2
```

while `ADD` has three operands, representing

```
op1 := op2 + op3
```

Function `newtemp` is called when a new temporary name is needed. It creates a new temporary in the symbol table and returns the index into the table where that temporary can be found. The lexical analyzer, which is not shown, is presumed to assign `yylval` the integer index into the symbol table where each operand can be found.

Implementing Three-Address Statements Using Quadruples

The simplest implementation of three-address statements is *quadruples*. In this format the result of an operation is explicitly represented in the code, often as a temporary.

Example 10-2. Figure 10-4 shows quadruple representation for the code in Fig. 10-3. Only statement 2 is unusual in that label `L0:` has been replaced by a reference to state 5, which is where the statement labeled by `L0:` is kept.

	operator	operand₁	operand₂	result
1	+	y	1	T1
2	if>goto	x	T1	(5)
3	−	x	z	T1
4	:=	T1		x
5	(float)	z		T2
6	/F	f	T2	T2
7	(int)	T2		T1
8	:=	T1		z

Figure 10-4. Quadruple Representation of Code.

Triples

Quadruples require the entry of each temporary into the symbol table. To avoid this, *triple* notation is sometimes used in which the result of an operation is implicitly available through a reference to the tuple which computed that result.

Example 10-3. Figure 10-5 shows Fig. 10-4 rewritten as triples. The `if>goto` operator is special because it requires three operands, spilling over into the next tuple. For this example, changing from quadruples to triples increases the number of tuples by 1, but reduces overall storage requirements since the result field has been eliminated from all tuples.

◆

Indirect Triples

Optimization often moves tuples around to improve efficiency and also eliminates redundant tuples. In the triple notation, moving a tuple means modifying all of the tuples that reference it to show the new location. Eliminating a tuple affects the numbering of all tuples that follow. Such expensive renumbering is minimized through *indirect triples*. Instead of listing tuples directly, an array that contains pointers to them can be used to define the statement ordering.

Example 10-4. Figure 10-6 shows the intermediate code rewritten using indirect triples. For the sake of illustration this example assumes that there are physically eight previous statements that have been emitted (numbered 0–7) and that there are are 20 statements which logically precede them (numbered 0–19). Suppose an optimizer noticed that statements 11 and 12 could be replaced by the single statement

```
-=    x    z
```

where "−=" is the familiar *C* operator. This would only require creating a new statement and revising the index-pointer matrix—the actual statements themselves would be unaffected as shown in Fig. 10-7. Index 23 now points to newly constructed tuple 17. Indices 24–28 could have had their pointers all

	operator	operand₁	operand₂
1	+	y	1
2	if>goto	x	(1)
3		(6)	
4	−	x	z
5	:=	(4)	
6	(float)	z	
7	/F	f	(6)
8	(int)	(7)	
9	:=	(8)	

Figure 10-5. Triple Representation of Code.

Ordering			Actual Triples		
Index	Ptr		operator	op$_1$	op$_2$
20	8		8	+	y	1
21	9		9	if>goto	x	(8)
22	10		10		(13)	
23	11		11	−	x	z
24	12		12	:=	(11)	
25	13		13	(float)	z	
26	14		14	/F	f	(13)
27	15		15	(int)	(14)	
28	16		16	:=	(15)	

Figure 10-6. Indirect Triple Representation.

Ordering			Actual Triples		
Index	Ptr		operator	op$_1$	op$_2$
20	8		8	+	y	1
21	9		9	if>goto	x	(8)
22	10		10		(13)	
23	17		11	−	x	z
24			12	:=	(11)	
25	13		13	(float)	z	
26	14		14	/F	f	(13)
27	15		15	(int)	(14)	
28	16		16	:=	(15)	
			17	−=	x	z

Figure 10-7. Switching Statement Order for Indirect Triples.

reduced by 1, but for efficiency the pointer for index 24 is made null, indicating it no longer points to a valid statement.

♦

In the following examples, the underlying implementation of three-address statements will not be a concern.

10.2. SEMANTIC ANALYSIS OF ATOMIC TYPES

A compiler must uniquely infer the data type of each operator and operand. Most programming languages *overload* operators so a single symbol stands for more than one operation; for example, in *C*, '−' has many different meanings depending on the type of the operands and the context in which it is used as shown in Fig. 10-8. The picture is muddied still more by the implicit casting of one type to another; for example, "1−2.0" means convert integer 1 to floating point 1.0, then do a floating point subtraction of 2.0 from it.

Expression	Meaning
− f	floating point negation
− i	integer negation
f − f	floating point subtraction
i − i	integer subtraction
a − i	subtract integer from address
c − c	subtract integer representation of one character from another

Figure 10-8. Overloading '−' in C.

The arity of an operator is normally determined by the syntactic context in which it appears; that is, it is determined grammatically rather than semantically. Most languages are defined so that the type of an operand can be uniquely determined at compile-time in a single left to right scan of the source code. For example, C and Pascal generally require that identifiers be declared prior to reference. This assures that the compiler will be able to process the declaration and uniquely determine the data type of the identifier prior to reference. The syntax-directed translation of assignment statements defined in the last section becomes slightly more complex when the operands can be either integer or floating point:

```
1    %token ASSIGN  IDENT  INTEGER  REAL
2    %left '+'
3    %left '*'
4    %right '-'
5    %%
6
7    statement:
8          IDENT  ASSIGN  express
9              { if ($1.datatype == FLOAT) {
10                 if ($3.datatype) == FLOAT)
11                     ICemit (ASSIGNFLOAT, $1.place,
12                         $3.place);
13                 else {
14                     error ("casting int to float", CONTINUE);
15                     ICemit (CASTINTFLOAT, i=newtemp(FLOAT),
16                         $3.place);
17                     ICemit (ASSIGNINT, $1.place, i);
18                 }
19             }
20             else if ($3.datatype) == FLOAT) {
21                 error ("casting float to int", CONTINUE);
22                 ICemit (CASTFLOATINT, i=newtemp(FLOAT),
23                     $3.place);
24                 ICemit (ASSIGNFLOAT, $1.place, i);
25             }
26             else
27                 ICemit (ASSIGNINT, $1.place,
28                     $3.place);
29             } ;
30
31   express:
32         express  '+'  express
33             { if ($1.datatype == FLOAT) {
34                 $$.datatype = FLOAT;
35                 if ($3.datatype == FLOAT)
36                     ICemit (ADDFLOAT,
37                         $$.place=newtemp(FLOAT), $1.place,
38                         $3.place);
39                 else {
40                     error ("casting int to float", CONTINUE);
41                     ICemit (CASTINTFLOAT,
42                         i=newtemp(FLOAT), $3.place);
43                     ICemit (ADDFLOAT,
44                         $$.place=newtemp(FLOAT), $1.place,
45                         i);
46                 }
47             }
48             else if ($3.datatype == FLOAT) {
49                 $$.datatype = FLOAT;
50                 error ("casting int to float", CONTINUE);
51                 ICemit (CASTINTFLOAT, i=newtemp(FLOAT),
52                     $1.place);
53                 ICemit (ADDFLOAT, $$.place=newtemp(),
54                     i, $3.place);
55             }
56             else {
57                 $$.datatype = INT;
58                 ICemit (ADDINT, $$place=newtemp(INT),
59                     $1.place, $3.place);
60             }
61             } ;
62
```

```
63    express:
64            express '*' express
65                    { ... };
66
67    express:
68            '-' express
69                    { if ($2.datatype == FLOAT) {
70                            $$.datatype = FLOAT;
71                            ICemit (UMINUSFLOAT,
72                                $$.place=newtemp(FLOAT), $2.place);
73                        }
74                        else {
75                            $$.datatype = INT;
76                            ICemit (UMINUSINT, $$.place=newtemp(INT),
77                                $2.place);
78                        }
79                    } ;
80
81    express:
82            '(' express ')'
83                    { $$ = $2; };
84
85    express:
86            IDENT
87                    { $$ = $1;}
88          | INTEGER
89                    { $$ = $1;}
90          | REAL
91                    { $$ = $1;};
```

yacc's stack now holds a structure which contains the data type of the symbol if any and the place or index into the symbol table where information about that symbol is kept. The lexical analyzer is assumed to look up each identifier in the symbol table and if found, assign `yylval.datatype` and `yylval.place` the correct values. For integer and real constants, it likewise is assumed to assign `yylval` the correct value. `newtemp` now takes a single argument which is the data type of the temporary to be created. It returns the index into the symbol table where the newly created temporary can be found. The translator calls `error` to emit a warning whenever an implicit type casting occurs.

10.3. TYPE CONSTRUCTORS

Nearly all languages allow the user to define new types, but there is a wide range of support they extend in defining and using data types as entities. For example, a type may or may not have a unique name by which it can be referenced. In FORTRAN four predefined types are `INTEGER`, `REAL`, `LOGICAL`, and `DOUBLE PRECISION`. A variable can be assigned one of these types through a declaration

```
INTEGER    I, J
REAL       Z
DOUBLE PRECISION  D
LOGICAL    L
```

FORTRAN also allows a user to construct new *anonymous* types; that is, types that are not explicitly named:

```
INTEGER    IA(10), JA(20)
REAL       ZA(4,10)
DOUBLE PRECISION  DA(4,7,8)
LOGICAL    LA(5)
```

The notation used to declare that a variable is an array is called a *type constructor* because it is the vehicle for creating a new data type. The data type of variable `IA` is "array of integers with subscripts ranging from 1 through 10". `IA` inherits the array operation of subscripting by virtue of this declaration, but there is no name by which to refer to this type. Contrast this limited notion of data type with that of Pascal which treats types much more maturely:

```
type
    small = array [1..10] of integer;
    large = array [1..100] of integer;
var
    b,c: array [1..10] of integer;
    d: array [1..10] of integer;
    x,y: small;
    z,u: large;
```

small and large are the names of data types that can be referenced later in the program. Variables x and y are both declared to have type small, while z and u have type large. Data types small and large both inherit the array subscripting operation by virtue of being constructed using the **array** type constructor. This operation is similarly inherited by variables of those types.

Pascal also supports anonymous types. Variables b, c, and d are declared using the **array** type constructor rather than just referencing type small. A natural question arises over when two types are *synonymous*, that is, effectively are two different names for the same type. Clearly, variables x and y have the same type, as do z and u. But do variables b and c have the same type and more interesting, do they have the same type as variables d, x and y? In Pascal variables b and c would be said to have the same type because they both appear in the same declaration. Two variables that are declared in the same statement always have the same type. On the other hand, variables b, d, and x belong to three different types even though the underlying structure of those types is compatible. Two separate instances of "array [1..10] of integer" are considered distinct anonymous type declarations.

Languages that follow Pascal's policy are said to support *name* equivalence. A language that would treat all of b, c, d, x, and y as if they had the same type supports *structural* equivalence. Languages that support named types usually also support name equivalence or may do limited type checking. Having a compiler check for structural equivalence is rather difficult when complex type constructors such as arrays, structures, and pointers become involved.

Example 10-5. *C* predominantly uses name equivalence, although the **typedef** statement confuses matters somewhat. The program in Fig. 10-9 provokes the indicated error messages when run through *cc*. The left- and right-hand sides of the five assignments on line 13 have the same data type using name equivalence. The left- and right-hand sides of the assignment on line 14 are structurally equivalent, but it would be a significant amount of work to determine that fact, so the *C* compiler objects. Similar objections are raised for lines 15, 16, 18, and 19. Line 17 is unique in that the left-hand side has type

```
1     struct first {int left,right};
2     struct second {int left,right};
3     typedef struct first BOTH;
4
5     struct first   a,b;
6     struct second  c,d;
7     struct {int left, right;} e,f;
8     struct {int left, right;} g,h;
9     BOTH i,j;
10
11    main ()
12    {
13        a=b;   c=d;   e=f;   g=h;   i=j;
14        a=c;
15        a=e;
16        a=g;
17        a=i;
18        b=e;
19        e=g;
20    }

      "structequiv.c", line 14: assignment of different structures
      "structequiv.c", line 15: assignment of different structures
      "structequiv.c", line 16: assignment of different structures
      "structequiv.c", line 18: assignment of different structures
      "structequiv.c", line 19: assignment of different structures
```

Figure 10-9. Name and Structural Equivalence in C.

`struct` `first` while the right-hand side has type `BOTH` declared in line 3. The *C* compiler treats the `typedef` in line 3 as a fancy macro and substitutes `struct first` for `BOTH` in line 9 before resolving type equivalence. Hence, `a` and `i` really have the same type and the assignment in line 17 is legal.

When passing function arguments, many *C* compilers are more forgiving. *cc* does not check for equivalence between the data types of parameters of calling and called functions. *cc* does not object to passing a single floating point number to a function that has been declared as taking a `struct` or a `char` argument. Technically such passage is illegal but the law goes unenforced.

◆

The next four subsections examine the implementation of the

1. enumeration
2. set
3. array
4. structure

type constructors without regard to type equivalence.

Enumeration

Both *C* and Pascal support the *enumeration* type constructor:

```
enum  {green, blue, white}  color;      /* in C */
color:  (green, blue, white);           { in Pascal }
```

This allows a programmer to use symbolic names for constants and treat them in a more coherent fashion than merely using defined constants. A variable whose type is an enumeration is implemented using an integer representation. The first declaration is equivalent to

```
#define  green  0
#define  blue   1
#define  white  2
int  color;        /* only assign green, blue, and white */
```

and the second to

```
const
    green = 0; blue = 1; white = 2;
var
    color: integer;   {only assign green, blue, and white}
```

with the understanding that `color` should not be assigned any value other than 0, 1, or 2. Clearly the restriction on permissible values for `color` is far more transparent using an enumeration than having to read comments. With the enumeration notation the compiler can also enforce the restriction that only `green`, `blue`, and `white` be assigned to `color`, something that is not possible when `color` is an integer variable.

Example 10-6. When the program in Fig. 10-10 is run through *cc*, the message

```
"color.c", line 5: warning: enumeration type clash, operator =
```

is issued. However, the program still compiles and produces output "4" when executed, because `color` is otherwise treated as if it were an integer. Pascal is more restrictive. Figure 10-11 shows a program illegally assigning 4 to `color` and the partial output it provokes from the Pascal interpretor *pi* under 4.2BSD Unix. Enumerations in Pascal are also called *scalars*.

◆

```
1    main()
2    {
3        enum {green, blue, white} color;
4
5        color = 4;
6        printf ("%d\n", color);
7    }
```

Figure 10-10. Use of Enumeration in C.

A syntax-directed translation that processes the declaration of enumerations in *C* is:

```
1    %token  ENUM  IDENT
2    %{
3        int  t, enum_i;
4    %}
5
6    %%
7
8    enum_dcl:
9          ENUM
10                  {t = newtype(); enum_i=0;}
11          '{'  consts  '}'  vars  ';' ;
12
13   consts:
14         IDENT
15                  {insertconst ($1.place, t, enum_i++);}
16       | consts ',' IDENT
17                  {insertconst ($3.place, t, enum_i++);} ;
18
19   vars:
20         IDENT
21                  {insertvar ($1.place, t);}
22       | vars  ',' IDENT
23                  {insertvar ($3.place, t);} ;
24   %%
```

When ENUM is encountered, newtype is called, returning a unique integer that represents the anonymous type about to be created. Each member of the enumeration plus the variables declared to have that type are tagged with that integer in the table. As each identifier is encountered between curly brackets, the lexical analyzer enters it into the symbol table. Variable enum_i is also set to 0. It is the integer representation of the enumeration element currently being processed. It is incremented by 1 each time an identifier is inserted into the symbol table. insertconst inserts the identifier into the table with the correct type and representation value. When '}' is finally seen, each member of the enumeration has been entered into the symbol table. As each variable name is encountered, insertvars is called to update the symbol table appropriately.

The fact that nonterminal consts is left recursive is significant. It guarantees that the identifiers are reduced in the same order in which they appear in a left to right scan of the source program. This ensures that the correct integer constant is assigned to each identifer as shown in Fig. 10-12. A different scheme would need to be devised to preserve order if a right recursive grammar were used.

```
1    program color (output);
2    var
3        color: (green, blue, white);
4    begin
5        color := 4;
6        writeln (color);
7    end.


     E 5 - Type clash: integer is incompatible with scalar
        ... Type of expression clashed with type of variable in assignment
     w 6 - Writing scalars to text files is non-standard
```

Figure 10-11. Illegal Use of Enumeration in Pascal.

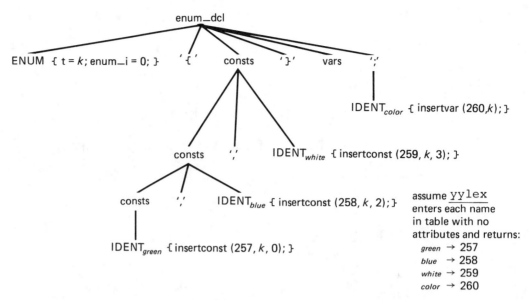

Figure 10-12. Attributed Parse Tree for Enumeration.

This SDT tracks which enumeration a constant is declared in so that a warning can be issued when enumerated elements are improperly mixed; for example, when a variable is assigned a constant from the wrong enumeration. The program in Fig. 10-13 defines two enumerations. The assignments to color in line 7 and to height in line 8 assign those variables values from the wrong enumerations. When this program is run through *cc* it produces

```
"sample.c", line 7: warning: enumeration type clash, operator =
"sample.c", line 8: warning: enumeration type clash, operator =
```

The translation of assignment statements from the last section is extended to allow for enumerated as well as floating and integer types:

```
1    %token ASSIGN IDENT INTEGER REAL
2    %left '+'
3    %left '*'
4    %right '-'
5    %%
6
7    statement:
8            IDENT ASSIGN express
9                    { switch ($1.datatype) {
10                     case FLOAT:
11                         switch ($3.datatype) {
12                         case FLOAT:
13                             ICemit (ASSIGNFLOAT, $1.place,
14                                     $3.place);
15                                 break;
16                         case ENUM:
```

```
1    main()
2    {
3        enum {green, blue, white} color;
4        enum {high, medium, low} height;
5
6        color = green;
7        color = low;
8        height = green;
9        height = low;
10       printf ("color: %d,  height: %d\n", color, height);
11   }
```

Figure 10-13. Tracking Elements Within Enumerations.

```
17                             error ("casting enum to floating", CONTINUE);
18                         case INT:
19                             ICemit (CASTINTFLOAT,
20                                 i=newtemp(FLOAT), $3.place);
21                             ICemit (ASSIGNINT, $1.place, i);
22                             break;
23                         }
24                     case INT:
25                         switch ($3.datatype) {
26                         case FLOAT:
27                             ICemit (CASTFLOATINT,
28                                 i=newtemp(FLOAT), $3.place);
29                             ICemit (ASSIGNINT, $1.place, i);
30                             break;
31                         case ENUM:
32                             error ("casting enum to int", CONTINUE);
33                         case INT:
34                             ICemit (ASSIGNINT, $1.place,
35                                 $3.place);
36                             break;
37                         }
38                     case ENUM:
39                         switch ($3.datatype) {
40                         case FLOAT:
41                             error ("casting float to enum", CONTINUE);
42                             ICemit (CASTFLOATINT,
43                                 i=newtemp(FLOAT), $3.place);
44                             ICemit (ASSIGNINT, $1.place, i);
45                             break;
46                         case INT:
47                             error ("casting int to enum", CONTINUE);
48                             ICemit (ASSIGNINT, $1.place,
49                                 $3.place);
50                             break;
51                         case ENUM:
52                             if (typeid($1.place) != typeid($3.place))
53                                 error ("enum types clash", CONTINUE);
54                             ICemit (ASSIGNINT, $1.place,
55                                 $3.place);
56                             break;
57                         }
58                     }
59                 } ;
60
61     express:
62             express '+' express
63                 { switch ($1.datatype) {
64                   case FLOAT:
65                     $$.datatype = FLOAT;
66                     switch ($3.datatype) {
67                     case FLOAT:
68                         ICemit (ADDFLOAT, $$.place=newtemp(),
69                             $1.place, $3.place);
70                         break;
71                     case ENUM:
72                         error ("casting enum to floating", CONTINUE);
73                     case INT:
74                         ICemit (CASTINTFLOAT,
75                             i=newtemp(FLOAT), $3.place);
76                         ICemit (ADDFLOAT, $$.place=newtemp(),
77                             $1.place, i);
78                         break;
79                     }
80                   case INT:
81                     switch ($3.datatype) {
82                     case FLOAT:
83                         $$.datatype = FLOAT;
84                         ICemit (CASTINTFLOAT,
85                             i=newtemp(FLOAT), $1.place);
86                         ICemit (ADDFLOAT, $$.place=newtemp(),
87                             i, $3.place);
88                         break;
```

```
89                                   case ENUM:
90                                       error ("casting enum to int", CONTINUE);
91                                   case INT:
92                                       $$.datatype = INT;
93                                       ICemit (ADDINT, $$.place=newtemp(),
94                                           $1.place, $3.place);
95                                       break;
96                                   }
97                           case ENUM:
98                               switch ($3.datatype) {
99                               case FLOAT:
100                                  $$.datatype = FLOAT;
101                                  error ("casting enum to float", CONTINUE);
102                                  ICemit (CASTINTFLOAT,
103                                      i=newtemp(FLOAT), $1.place);
104                                  ICemit (ADDFLOAT, $$.place=newtemp(),
105                                      i, $3.place);
106                                  break;
107                              case INT:
108                                  $$.datatype = INT;
109                                  error ("casting enum to int", CONTINUE);
110                                  ICemit (ASSIGNINT, $1.place,
111                                      $3.place);
112                                  break;
113                              case ENUM:
114                                  $$.datatype = ENUM;
115                                  ICemit (ASSIGNINT, $1.place,
116                                      $3.place);
117                                  break;
118                              }
119                          }
120                  } ;
121
122  express:
123          express '*' express
124                  { ... };
125
126  express:
127          '-'  express
128                  { switch ($2.datatype) {
129                    case FLOAT:
130                        $$.datatype = FLOAT;
131                        ICemit (UMINUSFLOAT,
132                            $$.place=newtemp(FLOAT), $2.place);
133                        break;
134                    case ENUM:
135                        error ("casting enum into int", CONTINUE);
136                    case INT:
137                        $$.datatype = INT;
138                        ICemit (UMINUSINT, $$.place=newtemp(INT),
139                            $2.place);
140                    }
141                  } ;
142
143  express:
144          '(' express ')'
145                  { $$ = $2; };
146
147  express:
148          IDENT
149                  { $$ = $1;}
150        | INTEGER
151                  { $$ = $1;}
152        | REAL
153                  { $$ = $1;};
```

The number of cases that must be handled grows exponentially with the number of types. This translation also assumes that types are cast implicitly as needed with an appropriate warning issued. The fact that enumerations are represented by integers is reflected wherever there is an implicit conversion from an **enum** to an **int** or an **enum** to a **float**. No intermediate code is actually emitted to perform the conversion from **enum** to **int**, and the operator CASTINTFLOAT is used to convert an **enum** to a

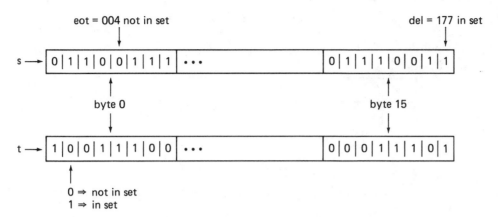

Figure 10-14. Implementation of Pascal Set Type.

float. `typeid` is called in line 52 to check whether the variable on the left-hand side of an assignment statement has the same underlying enumeration in its type as the right-hand side. That function looks up the needed information in the symbol table.

Sets

A Pascal set can be represented by a bit map. Operations on sets then become bit operations which are usually well supported in the hardware of most common computers. Assuming the underlying character set was ASCII, variables s and t in the declaration

```
s,t: set of char;
```

could each be represented by 128/8 = 16 bytes of storage as shown in Fig. 10-14. A 0 in the i-th bit would mean the i-th character was absent from s; a 1 would mean it was present. With this implementation, the union of s and t, denoted by s+t in Pascal, would simply be the bitwise "or" conducted on the 16 bytes for each variable. Intersection would be implemented by the bitwise "and" operation, and negation would be the bitwise complement of the operand.

It is clear why with this implementation Pascal compilers typically define a limit on how large a set they support. The seemingly innocent declaration

```
i: set of integer;
```

would consume millions of bytes of storage depending on the length of an integer.

Arrays

Arrays are usually implemented as a block of consecutive storage, a fact made readily apparent to C programmers who are exposed to the equivalence between an array subscript and an offset from the starting address of the array. Suppose one-dimensional array B has lower limit L and upper limit U, where each element is of type T. B[i] can be found at

```
&B + (i-L)*(sizeof T)
```

where &B is the address of the first element of storage. This is shown in Fig. 10-15. The expression to compute the address of B[i] can be partially evaluated at compile-time by rewriting it as

```
(&B-L*W) + i*W
```

where W is (**sizeof** T). L*W can be evaluated as soon as the declaration of B has been compiled. If the location of B is known at compile-time, then all of &B-L*W can be evaluated at compile-time. If B is

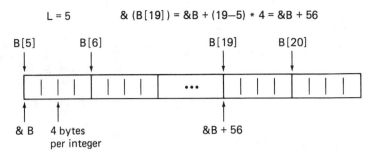

$$L = 5 \qquad \&(B[19]) = \&B + (19-5) * 4 = \&B + 56$$

B: array [5..20] of integer;

Figure 10-15. Implementation of 1-Dimensional Array B.

allocated on the stack at block entry, then L*W can be computed at compile-time and &B–L*W computed once at block-entry time. The temporary t where &B–L*W is stored can be saved in the symbol table for B, so that whenever the address of B[i] is needed, the computation t+i*W can be used.

Two-dimensional arrays can be stored either in row major or column major order as shown in Fig. 10-16. In row major order, the second subscript is varied most rapidly, so the elements are stored B[1,1], B[1,2], B[1,3], ..., B[n,1], B[n,2], ..., B[n,m]. The first subscript is varied most rapidly in column major order. FORTRAN uses column major order; Pascal and *C* use row major order. Assuming row major order, the location of B[i,j] for the declaration

    B: array [L₁..U₁, L₂..U₂] of T;

is

    &B + (i–L₁)*(U₂–L₂+1)*(sizeof T) + (j–L₂)*(sizeof T)

The expression (i–L₁)*(U₂–L₂+1)*(sizeof T) finds the storage for the i-th row, and (j–L₂)*(sizeof T) finds the correct column. This can be rearranged with a constant term at the beginning

    &B–L₁*(U₂–L₂+1)*(sizeof T)–L₂*(sizeof T) + (i*N₂+j)*W

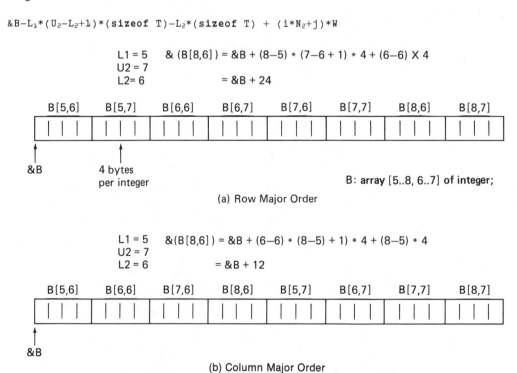

Figure 10-16. Row and Column Major Order for Two-Dimensional Arrays.

where $N_2=(U_2-L_2+1)$ and $W=(\texttt{sizeof } T)$. The first term can be precomputed at compile-time or block-entry time and used whenever the address of $B[i,j]$ is needed.

This analysis can be generalized to the *n*-dimensional case where $B[i_1,i_2,\ldots,i_k]$ can be found at

```
&B-(...(L₁*N₂+L₂)*N₃+L₃)...)*Nₖ+Lₖ)*W  +
        ((...((i₁*N₂+i₂)*N₃+i₃)...)*Nₖ+iₖ)*W
```

The first term can be computed at compile-time or block-entry time. The equivalent expression for column major order is left as an exercise.

If a language, such as PL/I, allows the dimensions of an array to be determined dynamically at block-entry time rather than at compile-time, the method for accessing an array element remains the same, except that the upper and lower bounds are not known and cannot be factored out as constants until block-entry.

An SDT to map array references to the correct expressions is

```
1    %token  ASSIGN  IDENT
2    %left '+'
3    %{
4        int ndimen, array_index, i;
5    %}
6    %%
7
8    S:
9            IDENT  ASSIGN  express
10                   { ICemit (ASSIGN, $1.place, $3.place);} ;
11
12   express:
13           express  '+'  express
14                   { ICemit (ADD, $$.place=newtemp(),
15                       $1.place, $3.place);} ;
16
17   express:
18           '(' express ')'
19                   { $$ = $2; } ;
20
21   express:
22           IDENT
23                   { $$ = $1;}
24         | IDENT '['
25                   { ndimen = 1; array_index = $1; }
26           subscripts ']'
27                   { ICemit (MULT, i=newtemp(),
28                       $3.place, STsize_base_type($1));
29                     ICemit (OFFSET, $$.place=newtemp(),
30                       $1.place, i);
31                     $$.datatype = $1.datatype;
32                   } ;
33
34   subscripts:
35           express
36                   { $$ = $1;}
37         | subscripts ','  express
38                   { ICemit (MULT, i=newtemp(),
39                       $1.place, STndimen(arrayindex, ndimen++));
40                     ICemit (ADD, $$.place=newtemp(),
41                       i, $3.place));
42                   } ;
```

These references appear in the context of assignment statements that have been simplified to only support integer operands and the '+' operation. Nonterminal express can either become a simple identifier or a subscripted identifier. The index into the symbol table of the array name is kept in global variable array_index because it would not otherwise be available when the subscripts are being parsed. ndimen indicates which array dimension is currently being scanned. It is incremented each time the translator steps to the next subscript. STndimen returns the size of the specified dimension. STsize_base_type returns the size of the base type of the array. Finally, OFFSET is the intermedi-

```
1    T1 := y * 9        -- lines 38-39
2    T2 := T1 + z       -- lines 40-41
3    T3 := T2 * 4       -- lines 27-28
4    T4 := B[T3]        -- lines 29-30
5    x := T4            -- line 10
```

Figure 10-17. Translation of "x:=B[y,z]".

ate code operation for referencing the subscripted element once the base and variable offset have been computed.

Example 10-7. To illustrate, suppose B is declared by

```
B: array [1..5][2..10] of integer;
```

where each integer is four bytes long. N_1 is $(5-1+1)=5$ and N_2 is $(10-2+1)=9$. The assignment "x:=B[y,z]" would be translated into the code in Fig. 10-17, assuming a simple algorithm for obtaining new temporary names. OFFSET has been represented by "[ ]" in line 4 for readability and implicitly subsumes the computation of the constant part of the subscript expression. The comments to the right of the code indicate the lines from the *yacc* specification which caused them to be emitted.
♦

Structures

A structure is an ordered collection of fields, each with a distinct name and type. In Pascal a structure is called a record, in C it is called a struct, and in PL/I it is actually called a "structure". Like an array, a structure is normally implemented as a contiguous block of storage. Each field occurs at a particular offset from the beginning of the structure. For most languages such as C and Pascal, the value of that offset can be computed at compile-time when the declaration of the structure is processed.

Sometimes machine architectures force field alignments leaving *holes* or *gaps* in a structure so that its size is larger than the sum of the size of its fields.

Example 10-8. The C structure in Fig. 10-18 is 76 bytes long on a VAX and 72 bytes on a Motorola 68000 because of differences in alignment. On a VAX each integer must be aligned on a four-byte word boundary forcing gaps at bytes 10–11 and 69–71. On a Motorola 68000 a two-byte short word boundary will do, forcing a single gap at byte 67. On both machines characters can be aligned on any byte boundary. The sum of all of the individual field lengths is 10+4+4+4+45+4=71 bytes.
♦

Having seen the details on implementing arrays, the mapping of structures to three-address code should be a straightforward exercise.

Symbol Table Representation of Types

Because the argument of one type constructor can typically be another constructed type, encoding of types in the symbol table has to be done carefully, but in a storage efficient manner.

Example 10-9. The Portable C compiler represents a type by an unsigned integer. The rightmost four bits holds one of the 13 basic types: int, char, short, long, their four unsigned analogs, plus float,

```
1    struct  personnel_data {      /* VAX        M68000  */
2        char name[10];            /* 0-9        0-9     */
3        int  age, height, weight; /* 12-23      10-21   */
4        char address[45];         /* 24-68      22-66   */
5        enum {male, female} sex;  /* 72-75      68-71   */
6    };
```

Figure 10-18. Alignment in Structures.

`double`, `struct`, `union`, and `enum`. The three type construction operators on base type *t* are: no-op (`NOP`), array of *t* (`ARY`), pointer to *t* (`PTR`), and function returning *t* (`FTN`). The operators appear as two-bit fields read right to left in the word until the `NOP` is found. Assuming the octal representation of these operators is `NOP=00`, `PTR=01`, `FTN=02`, and `ARY=03`, and that `DOUBLE` is represented by 7, then an array of pointers to functions returning doubles would be stored in binary as

```
00 00 00 10 01 11 01 11
```

on a machine with a 16-bit word size. It could be obtained by performing the bit shift operations

```
(ARY << 4) + (PTR << 6) + (FTN << 8) + DOUBLE
```

◆

Polymorphic Functions

A function is said to be *polymorphic* if its arguments can have more than one type. Such a function is also said to be *overloaded*. The ability to overload a function significantly impacts both a program's readability and the language's flexibility—and a compiler's complexity! Virtually all languages overload some of their predefined operators such as assignment, subtraction, addition, and equality over some set of predefined types. A handful of languages go further and allow a program to specify additional overloading of functions. (Some, like Smalltalk, go *much* further, allowing the data types of a function's arguments to be determined at run-time, greatly increasing the complexity of producing efficient code.) User-defined overloading increases the complexity of determining the data type of operands and operators.

Example 10-10. *C++* [Stroustrup 86] supports operator overloading which allows any operator to be overloaded with arbitrarily many meanings. The `"+"` operator could be extended so that x+y means mean "push x onto y" if the type of x is `int` and the type of y is `stack`, or perform `complex` addition if the type of x and y is `complex`:

```
1    typedef  struct  {float  real, imag;} COMPLEX;
2    COMPLEX x,y,z;
3
4    COMPLEX operator+ (op1, op2) COMPLEX op1, op2;
5    {
6        return (COMPLEX{op1.real+op2.real,op1.imag+op2.imag});
7    }
8
9    z = x+y;
```

A function declaration where the function name is the keyword `operator` followed by some operator ● tells the compiler to overload ●. In this example `"+"` is overloaded to support `COMPLEX` addition. A `struct` constructor is used here also. Note how the addition in line 9 looks very natural.

◆

The SDT in Section 10.2 decided what code to generate based on examining from among a predefined set of data types (just integer and floating point in the example). When a function can be overloaded arbitrarily many times, a different scheme is needed.

Example 10-11. In the symbol table an array is associated with each function name. Each element of the array contains the specification of one interpretation of *f* as shown in Fig. 10-19. Function f has three interpretations. First, it can be a binary function returning type k. The first argument has type w and the second has type u. Second, it can be another binary function returning type m. The first argument also has type w, but the second has type t. Finally, f can be a unary function returning type k, taking a single argument of type t. When f is encountered in the code, this array is consulted, an entry selected, and a call made to the indicated function pointed to in the `Emit Function` column. Each function understands one interpretation, emitting the correct intermediate code.

◆

Index	Arity	Return Type	Emit Function	Argument Types
1	2	k	*f1	w u
2	2	m	*f2	w t
3	1	k	*f3	t

Figure 10-19. Overloaded Function in Symbol Table.

10.4. FLOW OF CONTROL STATEMENTS

High-level flow of control statements can be mapped into more primitive three-address code statements that affect flow of control using unconditionally and conditional `goto` statements. This approach was briefly demonstrated in Section 10.1 when a *C* segment with an `if` statement was mapped into three-address code. Key to the translation is the correct mapping of Boolean expressions.

Evaluating Boolean Expressions

Boolean expressions are generated by the following grammar:

```
 1     %token  IDENT   TRUE    FALSE
 2     %left   OR
 3     %left   AND
 4     %left   EQ  NE
 5     %left   '>'  '<'  GE  LE
 6     %right  NOT
 7     %%
 8
 9     bexpress:
10             TRUE
11           ! FALSE
12           ! IDENT   rop   IDENT
13           ! '('  bexpress  ')'
14           ! NOT  bexpress
15           ! bexpress  bop   bexpress ;
16
17     bop:
18             OR  !  AND ;
19
20     rop:
21             '>'  !  '<'  !  EQ  !  NE  !  GE  !  LE ;
```

which intentionally allows complex Boolean expressions but only simple relational expressions.

Programming languages take different views on whether the binary Boolean operations `and` and `or` are commutative, and whether both operands have to be evaluated if the overall result of the expression can be determined from partial evaluation.

Example 10-12. The Pascal standard [ISO 82] specifically states that it is erroneous to assume anything about the order of evaluation of the operands in the expression "x and y" and whether both operands are actually evaluated. For example, one compiler could choose to evaluate y first, and if it were false, not evaluate x at all. Another equally valid compiler could evaluate x first and always evaluate y even if x were false. A Pascal program should not contain expressions such as

```
if (x<>0 and z/x>3) then ...
```

which assume that this is equivalent to the correct:

```
if x<> 0 then
   if z/x>3 then ...
```

Such a "trick" does work in *C* which explicitly specifies order of evaluation and defines when partial evaluation will be performed.

```
if (x!=0 && z/x>3) ...
```

is a proper *C* statement.

There are two primary methods for encoding a Boolean expression. The first, mapping false to 0 and true to 1 or some other nonzero value, causes each operation to be executed in a manner analogous to an arithmetic expression. This method is the simplest but yields relatively inefficient code.

The second method is by flow of control; that is, the value of the expression is determined by the location reached in the program. This method is well suited to the translation of expressions that support flow of control such as the conditional in an **if** or **while** statement. It also nicely supports partial evaluation of Boolean expressions.

Numerical Representation

Suppose true is represented by 1 and false by 0. The expression

```
NOT (a OR b) AND  NOT c
```

would be translated into

```
t1 := a or b
t2 := not t1
t3 := not c
t4 := t2 and t3
```

The relational expression

```
a < b
```

is equivalent to the conditional

```
if (a<b) then 1 else 0
```

which can be mapped into

```
1    if a<b goto 4
2    t := 0
3    goto 5
4    t := 1
5
```

The following SDT generates three-address code for Boolean expressions:

```
1    %token  IDENT   TRUE    FALSE
2    %left   OR
3    %left   AND
4    %left   EQ  NE
5    %left   '>'  '<'  GE  LE
6    %right  NOT
7    %{
8         int  i, curstmt;
9    %}
10   %%
11
12   bexpress:
13           TRUE
14                     { $$=$1; }
```

```
15          ¦ FALSE
16                  { $$=$1; }
17          ¦ IDENT  '<'  IDENT
18                  { ICemit (IFLTGOTO, $1.place, $3.place, curstmt+3);
19                    ICemit (ASSIGN, i=newtemp(), 0);
20                    ICemit (GOTO, curstmt+2);
21                    ICemit (ASSIGN, i, 1);
22                    ICemit (NULL);
23                    $$.place = i;
24                  }
25          ...
26
27          ¦ IDENT  EQ  IDENT
28                  { ICemit (IFEQGOTO, $1.place, $3.place, curstmt+3);
29                    ICemit (ASSIGN, i=newtemp(), 0);
30                    ICemit (GOTO, curstmt+2);
31                    ICemit (ASSIGN, i, 1);
32                    ICemit (NULL);
33                    $$.place = i;
34                  }
35          ¦ '('  bexpress  ')'
36                  { $$=$2; }
37          ¦ NOT  bexpress
38                  { ICemit (NOT, $$.place=newtemp(), $2.place); }
39          ¦ bexpress  AND  bexpress
40                  { ICemit (AND, $$.place=newtemp(), $1.place,
41                        $3.place); }
42          ¦ bexpress  OR  bexpress
43                  { ICemit (OR, $$.place=newtemp(), $1.place,
44                        $3.place); } ;
```

This scheme assumes that integer variable `curstmt` holds the address of the current statement so that offsets relative to the current address can be used in lines 18, 20, 28, and 30.

Numeric Representation in Flow of Control Statements

The section continues by showing how to map the Pascal flow of control statements

```
1.   if then else
2.   while
3.   repeat until
```

assuming a numeric implementation of Boolean expressions. The grammar for these three statements is:

```
1    %token  IF  THEN  ELSE  WHILE  DO  REPEAT  UNTIL  STMT  BEGIN  END
2    %%
3
4    stmt:
5           STMT
6         ¦ IF  bexpress  THEN  stmt
7         ¦ IF  bexpress  THEN  stmt  ELSE  stmt
8         ¦ WHILE  bexpress  DO  stmt
9         ¦ REPEAT  stmts  UNTIL  bexpress
10        ¦ BEGIN  stmts  END
11        ¦ ;
12
13   stmts:
14          stmt
15        ¦ stmts  ';'  stmt ;
```

To simplify the example, each statement generated is either just the literal token `STMT` or the null statement. The form of Boolean expressions derived from `bexpress` is that discussed earlier in this chapter.

yacc detects a shift/reduce conflict with the optional **else** clause of the **if** statement, but it is properly resolved using *yacc*'s default tie-breaking strategy favoring the shift so that an **else** is always matched with the closest **if**. Figure 10-20 shows the proposed implementation of these flow of control statements. The SDT that implements this translation scheme is:

source code	three-address equivalent
IF bexpress_x THEN stmt_y	if=goto x 0 1 translation of stmt_y 1:

IF bexpress_x THEN
    stmt_y
ELSE
    stmt_z
	if=goto x 0 l1
	translation of stmt_y
	goto l2
	l1:
	translation of stmt_z
	l2:

WHILE bexpress_x DO stmt_y	l1: if=goto x 0 l2 translation of stmt_y goto l1 l2:
REPEAT stmts_x UNTIL bexpress_y	1: translation of stmts_x if!=goto y 0 1

Figure 10-20. Translation of Control Statements.

```
1   %token  IF  THEN  ELSE  WHILE  DO  REPEAT  UNTIL  STMT  BEGIN  END
2   %%
3
4   stmt:
5       STMT
6     ¦ IF  bexpress  THEN
7               { ICemit (IFEQGOTO, $2.place, 0, i=newlabel());
8                 pushlabel(i);
9               }
10      stmt
11              {ICemit (LABEL, i=poplabel()); backpatch(i);}
12    ¦ IF  bexpress  THEN
13              { ICemit (IFEQGOTO, $2.place, 0, i=newlabel());
14                pushlabel(i);
15              }
16      stmt  ELSE
17              { ICemit (GOTO, i=newlabel());
18                ICemit (LABEL, j=poplabel()); backpatch(j);
19                pushlabel(i);
20              }
21      stmt
22              { ICemit (LABEL, i=poplabel()); backpatch(i); }
23    ¦ WHILE
24              { ICemit (LABEL, i=newlabel());
25                pushlabel(i);
26              }
27      bexpress  DO
28              { ICemit (IFEQGOTO, $2.place, 0, i=newlabel());
29                pushlabel(i);
30              }
31      stmt
32              { i = poplabel();
33                ICemit (GOTO, poplabel());
34                ICemit (LABEL, i);  backpatch(i);
35              }
36    ¦ REPEAT
37              { ICemit (LABEL, i=newlabel());
38                pushlabel(i);
39              }
40      stmts  UNTIL  bexpress
41              { ICemit (IFNEGOTO, $4.place, 0, poplabel()); }
42    ¦ BEGIN  stmts  END
```

```
43              │ ;
44
45    stmts:
46              stmt
47              │ stmts ';'   stmt ;
```

The three-address code uses symbolic names for labels wherever a label is referenced before it is defined. There is also a stack of labels pushed and popped to guarantee access to the correct label when needed. Note that use of a simple global variable to hold a symbolic label name is inadequate because control statements can be nested arbitrarily deep. Alternatively, the labels could be passed as an attribute in the parse tree.

Symbolic labels must be used wherever there is a forward reference because unlike the scheme for generating code for relational operations, there can be arbitrarily many statements between the label reference and its definition. For example, the **else** clause must be skipped after the completion of the **then** clause of an **if-then-else**, but the **else** clause has not yet been scanned. There is no way to know which three-address statement is the correct branch target. When the label is subsequently defined, the symbolic name in earlier references to it are replaced by the correct value in a process called *backpatching*. One easy way to implement backpatching is to enter each symbolic label in the symbol table when it is first created by **newlabel**. A list of the location of each reference to a symbolic label is placed in the table as part of the execution of **ICemit**. When the label is finally defined, the symbol table contains the list of all three-address statements that need to be backpatched. A call to function **backpatch** does the job.

Note that not all generated labels require backpatching. For example, the label that heads a **repeat** statement is defined before any reference to it, obviating the need for backpatching.

Flow of Control Translation

Boolean expressions can be evaluated using flow of control, leading to more efficient overall code. The SDT for this scheme is

```
1     %token   TRUE  FALSE   IDENT
2     %left    OR
3     %left    AND
4     %left    EQ   NE
5     %left    '>'  '<'   GE   LE
6     %right   NOT
7     %{
8          int  i,j;
9     %}
10    %%
11
12    bexpress:
13              TRUE
14                      { initial($$.true,i=newlabel());
15                        initial($$.false,0);
16                        ICemit (GOTO, i);}
17              │ FALSE
18                      { initial($$.true,0);
19                        initial($$.false,i=newlabel());
20                        ICemit (GOTO, i);}
21              │ IDENT  '<'  IDENT
22                      { initial($$.true, i=newlabel());
23                        initial($$.false, j=newlabel());
24                        ICemit (IFLTGOTO, $1.place, $3.place, i);
25                        ICemit (GOTO, j);
26                      }
27                      ...
28              │ IDENT  EQ  IDENT
29                      { initial($$.true, i=newlabel());
30                        initial($$.false, j=newlabel());
31                        ICemit (IFEQGOTO, $1.place, $3.place, i);
32                        ICemit (GOTO, j);
33                      }
34              │ '(' bexpress ')'
```

```
35                      { $$=$2; }
36            ; NOT  bexpress
37                      { swap($$.true, $$.false); }
38            ; bexpress  AND
39                      { ICemitlabels ($1.true); }
40                bexpress
41                      { copy ($$.true, $3.true);
42                        copy ($$.false, $1.false);
43                        append ($$.false, $3.false);
44                      }
45            ; bexpress  OR
46                      { ICemitlabels ($1.false); }
47                bexpress
48                      { copy ($$.true, $1.true);
49                        append ($$.true, $3.true);
50                        copy ($$.false, $3.false);
51                      } ;
```

This scheme uses synthesized attributes true and false to indicate the instruction to branch to in case the expression is true and false, respectively. This attribute holds a list of labels. Functions initial, copy, and append manipulate these lists in the obvious ways. ICemitlabels(list) emits a label for each element in the list of labels. Figure 10-21 shows the attributed parse tree for

```
NOT (a<b) OR c<d AND FALSE
```

which translates into

```
    if a<b goto L0
    goto L1
L0: if c<d goto L2
    goto L3
L2: goto L4
```

At the end of the translation label L1 is the value of bexpress.true at the root of the parse tree and labels L3 and L4 are bexpress.false. They are used in the following SDT to implement flow of control for the IF, WHILE, and REPEAT statements:

```
1    %token  IF  THEN  ELSE  WHILE  DO  REPEAT  UNTIL  STMT  BEGIN  END
2    %%
3
4    stmt:
5          STMT
6        ; IF  bexpress  THEN
7                  { ICemitlabels ($2.true); }
8          stmt
9                  {ICemitlabels ($2.false); }
10       ; IF  bexpress  THEN
```

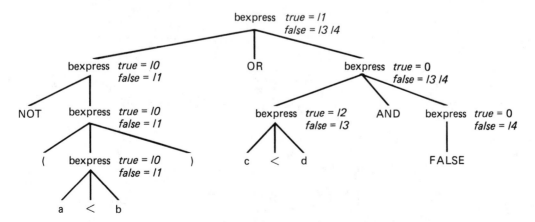

Figure 10-21. Attributed Parse Tree for "NOT (a<b) OR c<d AND FALSE".

```
11                          { ICemitlabels ($2.true); }
12          stmt    ELSE
13                          { ICemit (GOTO, i=newlabel());
14                            ICemitlabels ($2.false);
15                            pushlabel(i);
16                          }
17          stmt
18                          { ICemit (LABEL, poplabel()); }
19        : WHILE
20                          { ICemit (LABEL, i=newlabel());
21                            pushlabel(i);
22                          }
23          bexpress  DO
24                          { ICemitlabels ($2.true); }
25          stmt
26                          { ICemit (GOTO, poplabel());
27                            ICemitlabels ($2.false);
28                          }
29        : REPEAT
30                          { ICemit (LABEL, i=newlabel());
31                            pushlabel(i);
32                          }
33          stmts   UNTIL  bexpress
34                          { ICemitlabels ($4.false);
35                            ICemit (GOTO, poplabel());
36                            ICemitlabels ($4.true);
37        : BEGIN   stmts   END
38        : ;
39
40   stmts:
41          stmt
42        : stmts   ';'   stmt ;
```

Example 10-13. Figure 10-22 shows the attributed parse tree for

```
IF NOT (a<b) OR c<d AND FALSE THEN BEGIN
    STMT; STMT;
    END
ELSE BEGIN
    STMT; STMT;
    END
```

◆

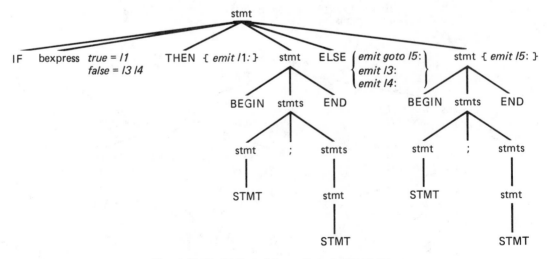

Figure 10-22. Attributed Parse Tree for IF..ELSE..

EXERCISES

1. Translate the arithmetic expression `"a*(b-c)+2"` into:

   (a) A parse tree.
   (b) Three-address statements.
   (c) Postfix notation.

2. Translate the expression `"-(x/2.0)+(4-y*2)"` into:

   (a) Three-address statements.
   (b) Quadruples.
   (c) Direct triples.
   (d) Indirect triples.

3. Translate the *C* program:

```
main ()
{
    int i=0, limit, a[100];
    char slimit[10];
    limit = atoi(gets (slimit));
    while (i<limit) {
            a[i++] = 0;
            printf ("another loop\n");
    }
}
```

   into:

   (a) A parse tree.
   (b) Three-address statements.

   Show the symbol table entries.

4. Suppose an implicit conversion were defined between strings and both integers and floating point numbers so that an expression such as

```
("31"+5)*(3+"2.0")
```

   evaluated to `(31+5)*(3+2.0)=180.0`. Extend the SDT of Section 10.3 to accommodate this.

5. Define a *yacc* SDT that translates:

   (a) FORTRAN EQUIVALENCE statements into three-address statements assuming only INTEGER and INTEGER array variable declarations.
   (b) References to equivalenced variables in FORTRAN assignment statements.

6. Write a *yacc* SDT that implements Pascal

   (a) Set declarations.
   (b) Set references including literals, the union operator `"+"`, the intersection operator `"*"`, the negation operator `"-"`, assignment `":="`, and tests for equality `"="` and inequality `"<>"`.

7. Extend your SDT for Pascal sets to also support the proper subset operation `"<"` and the improper subset operation `"<="`. These operations return Boolean `true` or `false`.

8. Write a *yacc* SDT that allows array literals in Pascal assignment statements; for example

```
array[1, 3, 7]
```

   is a one-dimensional array of three integers, while

```
array[1, 3, 7][2, 4, 6]
```

is a 2 by 3 array literal whose first row is [1, 3, 7] and whose second row is [2, 4, 6]. Your implementation should check that all elements of the array have the same type.

9. Extend Pascal assignment statements to support the concatenation operator from PL/I " ¦ ¦ "; for example,

```
'abc' ¦¦ 'def'
```

would be 'abcdef'.

10. Write a *yacc* SDT to translate the *C* for statement into three-address code

```
for (e₁; e₂; e₃) stmt;
```

which has the same meaning as

```
e₁;
while ( e₂ ) {
   stmt;
   e₃;
}
```

11. Write a *yacc* SDT to translate the Pascal **for** statement into three-address code

```
for v := initial to final do stmt
```

which has the same meaning as

```
begin
    t₁ := initial; t₂ := final;
    if t₁ <= t₂ then begin
        v := t₁;
        stmt;
        while v <> t₂ do begin
            v := succ(v);
            stmt
        end
    end
end
```

Note that in Pascal loop variable v always steps by a single unit, and that the loop bounds are evaluated only once at the beginning of loop execution. This contrasts dramatically with the *C* **for** loop in which the controlling expressions are evaluated each time through the loop and the loop variable may change by any value with each iteration.

12. Write a *yacc* SDT that maps the **switch** statement of the Unix *C* shell [Anderson-Anderson 86] into three-address statements.

13. Write a SDT that implements *C*'s **struct**.

14. Write a SDT that implements Pascal's **record**.

15. Write a SDT that extends *C* to support a literal **struct** constructor and maps expressions using them to three-address code:

```
1   typedef struct {float real,imag;} COMPLEX;
2   COMPLEX x,y,z;
3
4   x = COMPLEX{3.0, 4.0};
5   y = COMPLEX{-2.1, 5.6};
6   z = COMPLEX{x.real+y.real, x.imag+y.imag};
```

16. Assuming `char` is represented by 1 and `int` by 2, use the encoding defined in Section 10.3 to show the representation of:

```
(a) char   ***c;        /* pointer to pointer to pointer to char */
(b) int    *f();        /* function returning a pointer to an int */
(c) double (*f)();      /* pointer to a function returning a double */
```

Chapter 11
CODE OPTIMIZATION

No compiler produces truly optimal code, but nearly every commercial compiler makes at least some modest effort toward providing "improved" code over the most brute-force code generation techniques. The essence of optimization is to transform one program into another which is functionally equivalent but is better either in execution time or space than the original.

Parsing and lexical analysis are nicely supported by a small number of well-understood paradigms. Optimization, on the other hand, still retains a sizable measure of mysticism. Although there is much unifying literature that demonstrates the relationships among the various optimizing methods, and although there are actual catalogs of possible optimizations, this area has much the feel of art, not science. The compiler writer selects from among literally hundreds of possible optimizations depending on personal taste, the source language, the target machine, and quite often on the compiler development schedule.

Optimization techniques for relatively standard languages such as C and Pascal are reasonably well understood. As languages such as Smalltalk [Goldberg and Robson 80] have become more widely available and moved outside the laboratory, they have introduced new optimization problems [OOPSLA 86]. Much of the delay in making Ada a viable commerical language has centered around difficulties in generating efficient code compared to other available languages such as FORTRAN, Pascal, and C.

Some of the greatest sources of optimization are:

1. A better algorithm by the programmer.
2. Intelligent register allocation.
3. Tuning code to the machine architecture.
4. Constant folding.
5. Algebraic identities.
6. Operator strength reduction.
7. Common subexpression elimination.
8. Code motion.

This chapter discusses each of the last five methods. Methods 2 and 3 are discussed in the next chapter on code generation. The first method is the most fundamental. The best source of optimization is "thought." For example, replacing a bubble sort with a quicksort, using a hash table instead of linear search, and using LL(1) parsing rather than recursive descent parsing with backtracking, all have a far greater impact on overall performance than anything a compiler can do.

The payoff in execution time from the five principal optimization strategies discussed in this chapter can be dramatic, especially in languages such as Pascal, Ada, and PL/I which do not give the programmer as many opportunities for self-inflicted "trickery" as does C.

Example 11-1. Figure 11-1 contains a simple C program and its natural analog in Pascal. Both programs perform some silly arithmetic to compute 1, but the compilers that process them are not equally clever in spotting this nonsense. cc replaces the redundant arithmetic with the constant 1. The Pascal compiler, pc, actually executes each of the arithmetic operations indicated in the source code. The implications on

```
1    main ()    /* C program to do foolish arithmetic */
2    {
3        int i,j;
4
5        for (i=1; i<=100000; i++)
6            j = 1+1-1+1-1+1-1+1-1;
7    }
```

```
1    program sample (input, output);  { Pascal program doing likewise }
2    var
3        i,j: integer;
4    begin
5        for i:=1 to 100000 do
6            j := 1+1-1+1-1+1-1+1-1
7    end.
```

Figure 11-1. C and Pascal Programs Doing Needless Arithmetic.

performance are obvious, and from the study of data type implementation in the last chapter it should be clear that such arithmetic will come up more often than might otherwise be imagined in ways beyond the control of the programmer, such as in computing the offset to an array element. Furthermore, good programming style often leads to expressions involving symbolic constants such as "2*PI".

◆

Adding optimizations to a compiler is a little like eating chicken soup when you have a cold. Having a bowl full never hurts, even if you are not sure how useful it is. If the optimizations are structured modularly so that the addition of one does not substantially increase compiler complexity, the temptation to fold in another is hard to resist.

Language features and the target machine impact the choice of optimizations. A large complex language such as PL/I is very painful to compile correctly, much less optimize. The first PL/I compilers by IBM in the mid-1960s had numerous quality problems. Yet the very size and complexity of PL/I make it almost certain that without careful optimization the code generated will be awful. A PL/I programmer is very much at the mercy of the skill of the compiler writers.

C, on the other hand, was designed specifically to allow the programmer to hand optimize code. This is reflected in such features as the **register** storage attribute, ready access to the implementation of high-level data structures such as arrays, the *cpp* macro feature, and the "+=" and "++" instructions. The Portable C Compiler [Johnson 79], on which most commerical Unix compilers are based, has relatively few optimizations, yet the code it produces is good enough to yield acceptable performance of the Unix kernel which is written almost completely in C. This is due somewhat to the fact that experienced C programmers use a number of well-understood optimizing paradigms such as autoincrementing a pointer to step through an array rather than use subscript notation.

Example 11-2. The difference in performance by hand tuning C code is readily seen in Fig. 11-2. For one compiler on a Motorola 68000, the first program, using standard array subscript notation without a **register** variable for the loop index, took 5.0 seconds to run. The second program, with hand optimizations to use pointers and a **register** variable, ran in 2.3 seconds.

◆

The optimizations that will be studied in the rest of this section are demonstrated here on *basic blocks*, that is, on program segments each of which has a single entry point and a single exit point. Any program, no matter how complex, can be broken into a number of basic blocks using a simple algorithm presented in Section 11.3. It is fairly straightforward to apply these optimization strategies *within* individual basic blocks. The real trick in optimization is to apply them *across* basic blocks where flow of control becomes messy and side-effects from function calls must be considered. Most of the research in optimization has gone into developing more efficient algorithms to determine where in a program these basic techniques are applicable, taking into account more "global" information about the program.

```
1    int x[100000];
2
3    main ()
4    {
5        int i;
6
7        for (i=0; i<100000; i++)
8            x[i] = 1;
9    }
```

```
                    (a) Straightforward Coding
```

```
1    int x[100000];
2
3    main ()
4    {
5        register int *p;
6
7        for (p=(int *)x; p<(int *)x+100000;)
8            *p++ = 1;
9    }
```

```
                    (b) Hand Optimized Code
```

Figure 11-2. Hand Optimization of C Code.

11.1. SIMPLE OPTIMIZATIONS

Constant Folding

The first optimization looked at is *constant folding*. Arithmetic expressions can be evaluated at compile-time if the operands have values that are themselves known at compile-time. Whenever expressions such as "1+20*2" are encountered, the compiler can compute the result and emit code as if the input contained the result rather than the original expression.

Example 11-1 showed that not all compilers are equally smart in handling even this simple optimization, but to implement it is straightforward. For simplicity consider only integer operands. The action code in the SDT of the last chapter is altered so that it checks to see if the operands are integer literals or the result of a previous compile-time computation. If all operands have values known at the time three-address code is to be emitted, the SDT performs the arithmetic, emitting the result instead of code to compute that result. The resulting SDT is:

```
1    %token  ASSIGN  IDENT  INTEGER
2    %left '+'
3    %left '*'
4    %right '-'
5    %{
6        int i;
7    %}
8    %%
9
10   statement:
11       IDENT  ASSIGN  express
12           { ICemit (ASSIGN, $1, $3);};
13
14   express:
15       express '+' express
16           { if (const_value($1) && const_value($3)) {
17               i = value($1) + value($3);
18               $$ = newconst(i);
19           }
20           else
21               ICemit (ADD, $$=newtemp(), $1, $3);};
22
23   express:
24       express '*' express
25           { if (const_value($1) && const_value($3)) {
```

```
26                            i = value($1) * value($3);
27                            $$ = newconst(i);
28                       }
29                    else
30                       ICemit (MULT, $$=newtemp(), $1, $3);};
31
32    express:
33           '-' express
34                   { if (const_value($1)) {
35                       i = -value($1);
36                       $$ = newconst(i);
37                   }
38                    else
39                       ICemit (UMINUS, $$=newtemp(), $2);};
40
41    express:
42           '(' express ')'
43                   { $$ = $2; } ;
44
45    express:
46              IDENT
47                   { $$ = $1;}
48           ¦ INTEGER
49                   { $$ = $1;} ;
```

Function `const_value` indicates whether its argument has a known value. This information is in the symbol table. `newconst(i)` creates a new constant in the symbol table whose value is `i`. `newconst` returns the index of that new entry which is passed up the parse tree to the parent expression in lines 18, 27, and 36.

Performing arithmetic at compile-time could conceivably detect errors at this point which otherwise would not be found until run-time. If the operation leads to an error such as division by zero or an integer overflow, the compiler will detect it.

Example 11-3. The *C* program

```
1    main()
2    {
3         int x = 3/0;
4    }
```

provokes

```
"division.c", line 3: division by 0
```

from *cc*.

If the compiler is generating code for a machine other than the one on which the compilation is taking place, it must be careful to perform compile-time arithmetic consistent with architectural restrictions of the target machine. For example, if the host machine has 32-bit integers, but the target has only 16-bit integers, then constants in the source code larger than $2^{15}-1$ are illegal and can be trapped by the compiler.

Algebraic Identities

Code can be simplified further by taking advantage of a number of *algebraic identities*; for example,

```
1.    x + 0 = x
2.    0 + x = x
3.    x * 1 = x
4.    1 * x = x
5.    0 / x = 0
6.    x - 0 = x
```

The SDT can also look for these special cases when it is generating intermediate code.

Operator Strength Reduction

Related to algebraic identities is *operator strength reduction*, that is, replacing one operator by a "less expensive" one. Typical identities are

```
1.   i * 2 = 2 * i = i + i
2.   i / 2 = (int) (i *F 0.5)
3.   x *F 2.0 = 2.0 *F x = x +F x
4.   x /F 2.0 = x *F 0.5
```

where i is an integer and x is a real number. Normally addition is a faster operation than multiplication which in turn is faster than division. More sophisticated strength reduction occurs during loop analysis, which will be studied in Section 11.3 when *induction* variables are optimized.

During code generation, additional reductions in operator strength can normally be found by taking advantage of machine architecture; for example, in binary number representation a shift right by n is equivalent to division by 2^n. Shifting would be a big performance improvement over division. Some machines support an *immediate increment* operator which does the computation:

```
i = i + 5
```

as an atomic instruction

```
INCR  i  5
```

for small constants such as 5. This would normally be much faster than actually performing a general addition operation.

Example 11-4. Figure 11-3 shows two C programs and part of the object code produced on them by cc on a VAX. The autoincrement operator "+=" in the C source code provokes a more efficient instruction stream in the object code which directly adds the constant 5 to the value of i stored on the stack.
◆

11.2. COMMON SUBEXPRESSION ELIMINATION

Two operations are *common* if they produce the same result. In such a case, it is normally more efficient to compute the result once and just reference it the second time; for example, consider program *redundant* in Fig. 11-4. This could be translated into the three-address instructions in Fig. 11-5. This code can be optimized using the techniques described in the last section to eliminate the first addition, producing the code in Fig. 11-6. Second, note that both statements 4 and 8 perform x*x. If it could be shown that the value computed was the same in both places, then the second could be eliminated with

	Normal Addition	Autoincrement
C	```main()
{
int i = 5;
i = i + 5;
}```	```main()
{
int i = 5;
i += 5;
}```
VAX	```movl $5,-4(fp)
addl3 $5,-4(fp),r0
movl r0,-4(fp)```	```movl $5,-4(fp)
addl2 $5,-4(fp)```

Figure 11-3. Using Autoincrement Instruction.

```
1    main ()
2    {
3        int  x, y, z;
4        ...
5        x = (1+20)*-x;
6        y = x*x+(x/y);
7        y = z = (x/y)/(x*x);
8        ...
9    }
```

Figure 11-4. Sample Program *redundant*.

```
1    t1 := 1+20
2    t2 := -x
3    x  := t1*t2
4    t3 := x*x
5    t4 := x/y
6    y  := t3+t4
7    t5 := x/y
8    t6 := x*x
9    z  := t5/t6
10   y  := z
```

Figure 11-5. Straightforward Translation of *redundant*.

```
2    t2 := -x
3    x  := 21*t2
4    t3 := x*x
5    t4 := x/y
6    y  := t3+t4
7    t5 := x/y
8    t6 := x*x
9    z  := t5/t6
10   y  := z
```

Figure 11-6. Simple Optimization of *redundant*.

the resulting improvement both in execution time and storage space. A similar improvement might be possible for division x/y in statements 5 and 7.

The value of x does not change in lines 5–7. Therefore, the value of x in line 4 is the same as in line 8. These two computations are common and the second can be safely eliminated. On the other hand, the value of y changes in line 6. These two computations are not common—the computation in line 7 is not redundant. With these observations the code can be rewritten as shown in Fig. 11-7. Statement 8 has been eliminated and the reference to t6 in statement 9 has been replaced by one to t3.

```
1    for (i=1; i<=sizeof B; i++) {
2        for (each operand O in B[i])

2    t2 := -x
3    x  := 21*t2
4    t3 := x*x
5    t4 := x/y
6    y  := t3+t4
7    t5 := x/y
9    z  := t5/t3
10   y  := z
```

Figure 11-7. *redundant* After Common Subexpression Elimination.

Common subexpressions can be eliminated using the *value numbering scheme* of [Cocke and Schwartz 70]. The main data structure of this method is table *alivetab* of *alive expressions*. This table tracks where each computation of an expression is valid or *alive* within the basic block because the operands used to compute that expression have not yet changed value. An expression that is no longer *alive* is said to be *dead*.

Algorithm 11-1. Eliminate common subexpressions from block B.
Input: Block B in which B[i] is the i-th instruction.

```
3              if (O is marked in alivetab as being replaceable by R)
4                  replace reference to O by R in B[i];
5          if (operation in B[i] is in alivetab) {
6              mark in alivetab that future references to this
7                  tuple are to be subsumed by reference to
8                  previous one;
9              delete B[i];
10         }
11         else
12             enter tuple into alivetab;
13     }
```

Applying Algorithm 11-1 to the code in Fig. 11-6 produces the code in Fig. 11-7.

◆

Aliasing

Common subexpression elimination is compounded by the problem of *aliasing* which occurs when there are two or more names for the same storage location. Aliasing can happen in a variety of ways in actual programming languages. For example, the two FORTRAN statements

```
INTEGER X,Y
EQUIVALENCE X,Y
```

explicitly state that X and Y are to occupy the same physical location in memory. In code sequence:

```
1     A = X*3+Z
2     Y = (A/4)+Y*3
3     Z = X*3
```

expressions X*3 in line 1 and Y*3 in line 2 are common. Additionally, both of these computations are killed when statement 2 finishes execution because the assignment in line 2 changes the value of Y. This code offers both an opportunity to eliminate a common subexpression in line 2 if its presence can be recognized plus the possibility of botching code generation if the assignment to Y in line 2 is not recognized as killing X*3 from line 1. Aliasing reveals the perpetual struggle within optimization strategies. They should be aggressive enough to find as many optimization opportunities as possible, but conservative enough to guarantee that the generated code is correct.

To handle aliasing, the equivalence of X and Y must be noted in the symbol table during the semantic analysis phase. In line 3 of the algorithm to compute common subexpressions, the phrase "O is marked" must be replaced by "any alias of O is marked". Similarly, when determining in line 5 whether an operation is in alivetab, aliases of the operands must be checked as well. For simple variables, there usually are not many aliases.

Additional complexity arises when type constructors are allowed. In the worst case a variable may be an alias for every other variable in the block. This would happen if a language allowed unrestricted pointer variables which can literally point anywhere in storage.

Example 11-5. Consider the following *C*-like code:

```
1     pointer x;
2     int w, y, z;
3     ...
4     x = ...    /* x now points to some arbitrary point in storage */
5     ...
6     z = y*3;
7     *x = ...   /* storage pointed to by x changed */
8     w = y*3;
```

The assignment in line 7 could change the value of any variable in the program including y. The compiler must assume the worst case and kill off all expressions after line 7 is executed. The expression y*3 in line 6 is not common with the one in line 8.

◆

Clearly it does not take many statements such as those in line 7 of the last example to destroy any chance for reasonable optimization. Languages can help salvage the situation (as well as reduce programming errors) by restricting the values that pointer variables can assume. Pascal places two powerful restrictions on pointer variables which reduce considerably the number of expressions that must be killed when one is assigned a value. A pointer variable:

1. Is typed; that is, it only points to objects of a stated type.
2. May only point to objects created by calls to the function new.

The second restriction is very powerful because it means that no "ordinary" declared variable can ever be changed through a pointer variable.

Example 11-6. Example 11-5 is rewritten in Pascal:

```
1    x: ^integer;
2    w,y,z: integer;
3    ...
4    new (x);   { create new object of type ^integer }
5    ...
6    z := y*3;
7    x^ := ...    { x must point to object created by new() }
8    w := y*3;
```

Variables w, y, and z cannot be affected by the assignment in line 7. It is safe to consider y*3 in lines 6 and 8 to be common. The first restriction guarantees that even pointer variables can be partitioned into classes. An assignment to the storage pointed to by a variable of type ^integer can kill values involving other variables of type ^integer, but not those of other types such as ^real.
♦

Still further aliasing arises in arrays. Two subscripted array expressions are aliases if they overlap storage; for example, the two expressions B[i] and B[j] are aliases if i=j. It may be possible to tell whether i could ever equal j, but in general this cannot be determined. Pascal again offers some optimization opportunities lacking in most other languages through the use of scalar subranges in variable and type declarations.

Example 11-7. Consider Pascal code:

```
1    B: array[1..100] of integer;
2    i: 1..10;
3    j: 50..100;
4    ...
5    ... B[i]*3 ...
6    B[j] := ...
7    ... B[i]*3 ...
```

The fact that i and j cannot overlap implies that B[i] in lines 5 and 7 is never aliased to B[j] in line 6. The references in lines 5 and 7 are common.
♦

11.3. GLOBAL FLOW ANALYSIS

Although much is gained by optimizing each basic block in isolation, even better performance is possible by gathering and applying information on a *global* scale. For example, suppose expression A+C is computed in block B and it can be shown that:

1. Every path leading to B computes A+C in another block.
2. The values of A and C used in that computation do not change between the time A+C is computed in earlier blocks and it is computed in B.

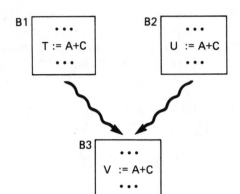

Figure 11-8. Redundant Computation of A+C.

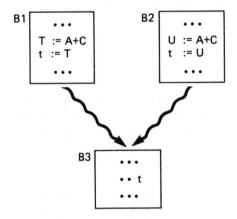

Figure 11-9. Removing Redundant Computation of A+C.

then the computation of A+C in B is redundant and can be safely removed. This is shown graphically in Figs. 11-8 and 11-9. V is shown as being subsequently used in B3. Imagine every path in Fig. 11-8 to B3 goes either through B1 or B2, and that nowhere on that path is either A or C redefined, nor is either redefined earlier in B3. Then expression A+C is said to be *available* at statement V:=A+C and its recomputation can be eliminated. The simpler code in Fig. 11-9 is equivalent. Temporary t saves the value of the computation in both cases so no matter which path is actually taken the value of A+C is available for use in B3. The reference to V in B3 is replaced by a reference to t.

Removal of redundant expressions in this manner requires first performing analysis on the flow of control and then determining the implications of that flow on data values. This section describes algorithms for performing several powerful optimization techniques based on global flow analysis.

Basic Blocks

Nearly all optimization strategies depend on first breaking a program into *basic blocks* and producing a graph showing flow of control. A basic block is a program segment that has only one entrance and one exit. Hence, a basic block contains only straight-line code. The Pascal program in Fig. 11-10 performs matrix multiplication on rectangular matrices left and right, placing the computed matrix in result. matrixMultiply uses the *conformant array* feature of Pascal which allows variable size arrays to be specified as the formal arguments of a procedure. The actual values of lrow, lcol, rrow, and rcol are bound at the time the call is made, allowing this one procedure to be used on any size arrays. matrixMultiply is translated into:

```
1    procedure matrixMultiply ( {using conformant arrays}
2            left: array [1..lrow] of array of [1..lcol] of integer;
3            right: array [1..rrow] of array of [1..rcol] of integer;
4            result: array[1..lrow] of array of [1..rcol] of integer);
5    var
6        integer i,j,k;
7    begin
8        for i := 1 to lrow do
9            for j := 1 to rcol do begin
10               result[i][j] := 0;
11               for k := 1 to lcol do
12                   result[i][j] := result[i][j] +
13                       left[i][k]*right[k][j]
14           end
15   end
```

Figure 11-10. *matrixMultiply.*

```
1            prolog                  // initialization
2            i := 1                  // for i := 1 to lrow
3            t1 := lrow
4    L0:                             // top of for loop
5            if i>t1 goto L1         // L1: is exit from loop
6            j := 1                  // for j := 1 to rcol
7            t2 := rcol
8    L2:                             // top of for loop
9            if j>t2 goto L3         // L3: is exit from loop
10           t3 := i * arg9          // address(result[i][j])
11           t4 := t3 + j
12           t5 := t4 * 4
13           t6 := arg6 + t5
14           result[t6] := 0         // result[i][j] := 0;
15           k := 1                  // for k := 1 to lcol
16           t7 := lcol
17   L4:                             // top of for loop
18           if k>t7 goto L5         // L5 is exit from loop
19           t8 := i * arg9          // address(result[i][j])
20           t9 := t8 + j
21           t10 := t9 * 4
22           t11 := arg6 + t10
23           t12 := i * arg9         // value(result[i][j])
24           t13 := t12 + j
25           t14 := arg6 + t13
26           t15 := result[t14]
27           t16 := i * arg7         //  value(left[i][k])
28           t17 := t16 + k
29           t18 := t17 * 4
30           t19 := arg4 + t18
31           t20 := left[t19]
32           t21 := k * arg8         // value(right[k][j])
33           t22 := t21 + j
34           t23 := t22 * 4
35           t24 := arg5 + t23
36           t25 := right[t24]
37           t26 := t20 * t25        // value(left[i][k]) * value(right[k][j])
38           t27 := t15 + t26        // value(result[i][j]) + ...
39           result[t11] := t27      // result[i][j] := ...
40           k := k + 1              // loop increment
41           goto L4
42   L5:                             // exit from for k := 1 to lcol do
43           j := j + 1              // loop increment
44           goto L2
45   L3:                             // exit from for j := 1 to rcol do
46           i := i + 1              // loop increment
47           goto L0
48   L1:                             // exit from for i := 1 to lrow do
49           epilog
```

where `prolog` represents the instructions executed at the beginning of a procedure call and `epilog` represents termination code. Recall that constants are normally precomputed to support array refer-

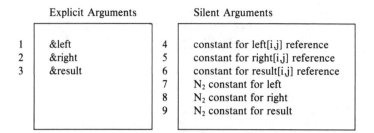

Figure 11-11. Arguments Passed to matrixMultiply.

ences as shown in Section 10.3. These would be computed by the calling program and passed to matrixMultiply as silent arguments as shown in Fig. 11-11. The i-th argument in the procedure is referenced under the name argi. This code never reuses a temporary variable to simplify the presentation even though there are several opportunities for reuse.

Algorithm 11-2. Compute basic blocks.

```
 1      compute_basic_block(stmt, program_size)
 2          tuple stmt; int program_size;
 3      {
 4          char entry_points[MAXPOINTS], remaining[MAXPOINTS];
 5          int  i, j;
 6
 7          entry_points[0] = '1';
 8          for (i=1; i<MAXPOINTS; i++)   /* initially no entry points */
 9              entry_points = '0';       /* except first statement */
10          i = 0;
11          while (i<program_size) {
12              if (stmt[i] is a branch to some stmt[j])
13                  entry_points[j] = '1';
14              i++;
15          }
16      }
```

◆

When Algorithm 11-2 completes, entry points[i] is '1' if statement i begins a basic block and is '0' otherwise. If entry_points[i] is '1' and entry_points[i+k] are '0' for 1≤k<n, and entry_points[i+n] is '1' then statements i through i+n−1 are in the same basic block. If the number of statements being processed is large, then a bitmap could be substituted for the **char** array to conserve storage. Figure 11-12 shows the basic blocks for the code together with the flow of control between them.

Applying common subexpression elimination to each of the blocks individually changes block 9, removing instructions 23, 24, and 25 which duplicate the computation necessary to compute the address of result[i][j]. The optimized code is shown in Fig. 11-13.

Computing Available Expressions

As mentioned earlier in this section, careful analysis across blocks can determine whether an expression is alive at the entry to a block. Such an expression is said to be *available* at that point. Once the set of available expressions is known, common subexpressions can be eliminated on a global basis.

Several relationships must be defined next. Each block is a node in the flow graph of the program. The *successor set*, succ(x) for node x is the set of all nodes that x directly flows into. The *predecessor set*, pred(x) is the set of nodes that flow directly into x.

Recall that an expression is *defined* at the point where it is assigned a value and *killed* when one of its operands is subsequently assigned a new value. An expression is *available* at some point p in a flow graph if every path leading to p contains a prior definition of that expression which is not subsequently killed.

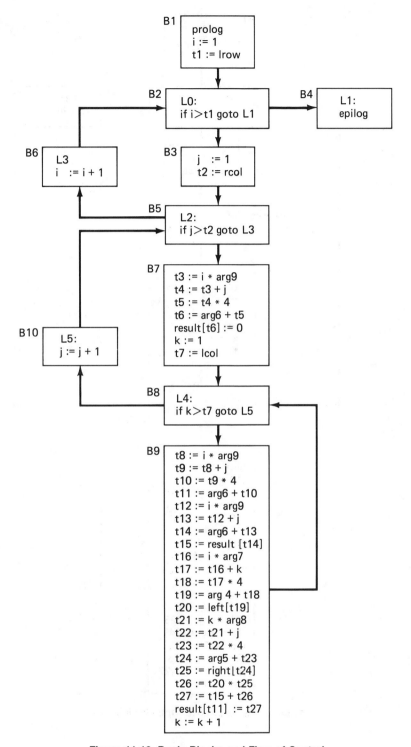

Figure 11-12. Basic Blocks and Flow of Control.

`avail[B]` is the set of expressions available on entry to block B from anywhere in the program, `exit[B]` is the set of expressions available on exit from B. Then

$$\texttt{avail[B]} = \bigcap_{x \,\in\, \texttt{pred[B]}} \texttt{exit[x]}$$

Similarly, let `killed[B]` be the set of expressions killed by B, and `defined[B]` be the set of expressions that are defined in B but not subsequently killed there. For each B

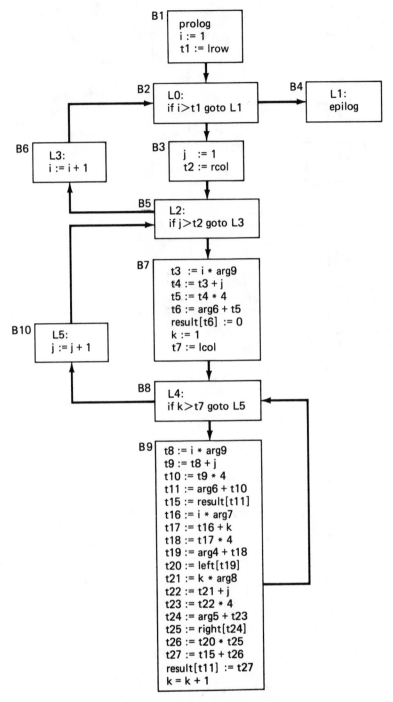

Figure 11-13. After Local Optimization.

$$exit[B] = avail[B] - killed[B] + defined[B]$$

Combining these two sets of equations produces the recurrence relation:

$$avail[B] = \bigcap_{x \in pred[B]} (avail[x] - killed[x] + defined[x])$$

By solving this set of equations for all blocks in a program, redundant available expressions can be eliminated.

A number of algorithms have been developed to efficiently solve these equations. In fact, the efficient solution of this and other similarly structured sets of equations is the heart of optimization techniques. In each case the developer of a solution must guarantee that the algorithm is conservative; that is, it may miss an optimization in order to guarantee correctness.

Algorithm 11-3. Compute availability.

```
1     for (i=1; i<num_blocks; i++) {
2          avail[B] = NULL;
3          exit[B] = defined[B];
4     }
5
6     do {   /* iteratively build other avail and exit sets */
7          changed = 0;
8          for (i=1; i<num_blocks; i++) {
9               avail[B] = exit[s] for some s in pred[B];
10              for (all x != s in pred[B])
11                   avail[B] = avail[B] ∩ exit[x];
12              oldexit = exit[B];
13              exit[B] = defined[B] + (avail[B]-killed[B]);
14              if (oldexit != exit[B])
15                   changed++;
16         }
17    } while (changed);
```

Algorithm 11-3 initially assumes that nothing is available and adds an expression only when it has been demonstrated to be available. Sets *defined* and *killed* are constant for each block and are computed prior to running this algorithm which iteratively approximates *avail* and *exit*.

This algorithm has much the same character as the one which eliminated left recursion from grammars in Chapter 5. It updates a block with information computed about its predecessors. After some number of iterations, information has been passed to every applicable node and no further changes occur.

Figures 11-14 and 11-15 show the application of this algorithm to `matrixMultiply`. `avail` and `exit` converge after one iteration through lines 6–17.

Global Common Subexpression Elimination

In the sample program statement `i*arg9` in `B9` always yields the same value as that computed in `B7`. In fact the computation in `B9` can be eliminated because it is common to the one in `B7`. Recognizing this fact requires first computing the set of available expressions using Algorithm 11-3.

Algorithm 11-4. Global common subexpression elimination.
Notation: Let ● stand for an arbitrary operation.

Block	avail	exit
B1	–	–
B2	–	–
B3	–	–
B4	–	–
B5	–	–
B6	–	–
B7	–	i*arg9 t3+j t4*4 arg6+t5
B8	–	–
B9	–	i*arg9 t8+j t9*4 arg6+t10 .. t15+t26
B10	–	–

Figure 11-14. After Lines 1–4 Executed.

Block	avail	exit
B1	–	–
B2	–	–
B3	–	–
B4	–	–
B5	–	–
B6	–	–
B7	–	i*arg9 t3+j t4*4 arg6+t5
B8	i*arg9	i*arg9
B9	i*arg9	i*arg9 t8+j t9*4 arg6+t10 .. t15+t26
B10	i*arg9	i*arg9

Figure 11–15. After One Iteration of Lines 6–17.

Steps:

1. Identify each statement s of the form $a:=b \bullet c$ in some block B such that $b \bullet c$ is available at the entry to B and neither b nor c is redefined in B prior to s.
2. Follow the flow of control backward in the graph passing back to but not through a block that defines $b \bullet c$. This restriction prevents cycling and identifies those blocks and those computations of $b \bullet c$ within those blocks which reach s. The last computation of $b \bullet c$ in such a block reaches s.
3. After each computation $d:=b \bullet c$ identified in step (2), add statement $t:=d$, where t is a new temporary.
4. Replace s by $a:=t$.
5. Make the obvious generalization of this method to statements of the form $a:=\bullet b$ and apply it to those expressions as well.

◆

Algorithm 11-4 was used in the example at the beginning of this section to illustrate one possible use of global flow analysis. Applying this algorithm to the graph in Fig. 11-13 produces the new graph in Fig. 11-16. The computation of i*arg9 in B9 has been eliminated because it is available at entry to that block. Instead a reference to t28 computed in B7 is used.

A number of potential optimizations have been missed by this algorithm. In B9 the assignment t8:=t28 effectively makes t9:=t8+j equivalent to t9:=t28+j. In B7 the assignment t28:=t3 makes the following statement t4:=t3+j equivalent to t4:=t28+j. If the compiler could recognize these equivalences, then a subsequent pass of Algorithm 11-4 would add t29:=t4 after t4:=t3+j and replace t9:=t8+j by t9:=t29. The equivalence of t9*4 to t4*4 and arg6+t10 to arg6+t5 would also be recognized, producing the code in Fig. 11-17 after four passes of Algorithm 11-4.

It is straightforward to extend the definition of *defined* in a block to cover the case of *computationally equivalent* expressions. Within block B suppose there is a statement s of the form b:=c. In all subsequent uses of c in B until either b or c is redefined, replacing c by b produces the same result. define[B] is extended to include all expressions actually in block B that are not subsequently killed plus expressions that are computationally equivalent to those actual expressions. With this change to define, and by likewise extending *avail* and *exit*, the optimization pictured in Fig. 11-17 can be performed. There are many more optimizations of this general type possible. For example, additional analysis can reveal which assignments of the form a:=b can be dropped from the code, substituting b for a in subsequent references. [Muchnick and Jones 81] is a good source of additional information on these optimizations.

Code Motion

Another powerful family of optimizations moves code across block boundaries from inside a loop to outside. Consider, for example, blocks B3, B5, B7, B8, B9, and B10 which implement the two innermost **for** loops of matrixMultiply. Statement t3:=i*arg9 from B7 is inside that loop.

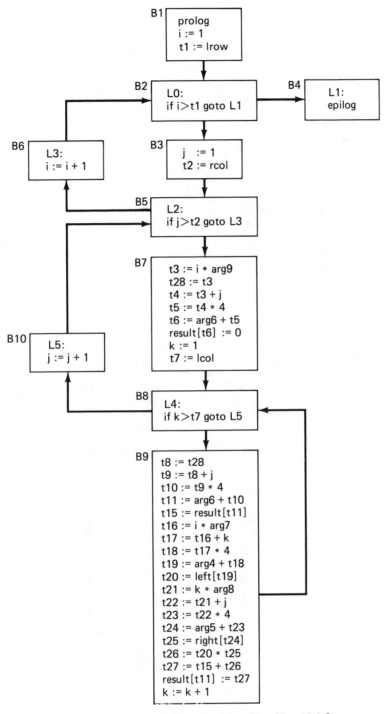

Figure 11-16. Flow Graph After Applying Algorithm 11-4 Once.

arg9 is a constant and i is a variable. However, i is only set in B1 and B6, which are outside the loop. t3:=i*arg9 could be safely moved outside the loop without affecting the overall computation, but with a reduction in execution time. It is moved to a new block created between B3 and B5 called a *pre-header*. A pre-header always sits ahead of the beginning of a loop. The definition of t3 still reaches B7. Placing t3:=i*arg9 in the pre-header moves it from the innermost loop of the program to the outermost. Note that this particular optimization is not available to the Pascal programmer who wishes to hand optimize code (although a C programmer, who has access to the representation of the array as a

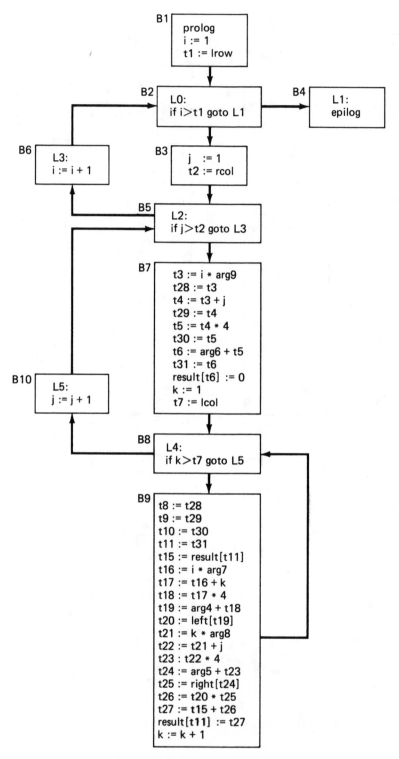

Figure 11-17. Flow Graph After Four Iterations of Algorithm 11-4.

contiguous block of storage could perform this optimization directly in the code at the expense of program clarity).

If `t3:=i*arg9` can be moved, so can `t28:=t3`. However, the subsequent `t4:=t3+j` cannot be moved because the value of `j` is set in `B10` which is inside the loop. Following this reasoning for the remaining statements in the graph produces Fig. 11-18. Three new blocks have been created, one for

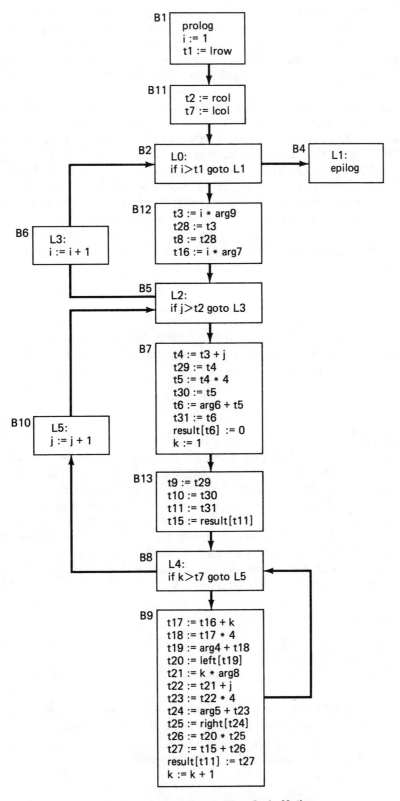

Figure 11-18. Flow Graph After Code Motion.

each loop. Computation, which is invariant with respect to all three loops has been moved to block B11. This includes the assignments to temporaries holding the index variable limits. Block B12 contains computations that are invariant with respect to the loops involving j and k—that part of the address computation for result[i,j] and left[i,k] which finds the offset into the storage block for row i. Finally, B13 includes the statements obtaining the value of result[i,j] since that is invariant with respect to k.

There is a danger in the optimization strategy just defined which turns out to be groundless in this particular example, but could prove disastrous under other circumstances. The definition of the **for** loop in Pascal allows for the possibility that the loop body will not be executed at all if the initial value is greater than the final value (in the **to** case). Moving computation from inside the loop to a pre-header guarantees that it will be executed at least once. If the program will behave differently because those computations are executed at least once, this optimization is unsafe. Note that only the computation of temporary quantities has been moved outside the loop. If the variables assigned values in the pre-header are not referenced outside the loop (except of course in the pre-header), the computation should not generally be harmful. This is the case in matrixMultiply. The one slight wrinkle on this assumption is in the possibility that executing the code in the pre-header could raise an exception; for example, if the code inside the loop were to contain the statement:

```
if x<>0 then
    z := y/x
```

and y/x were invariant within the loop, that computation might be moved to the pre-header with disastrous consequences. Even operations such as addition which intuitively seem less risky than division could cause a problem:

```
if x<>maxint then
    z := x+1;
```

although the likelihood of the latter code is very small.

As a result of these problems, it seems prudent for a compiler *not* to perform the code motion on matrixMultiply just shown. What are the conditions under which this type of code motion is safe? Intuitively, it is safe if analysis can guarantee that the code would eventually be executed anyhow if it were not moved, and that in both cases the operands would have the same values; hence, an exception for division by zero or integer overflow would have eventually been raised anyhow.

To perform the necessary analysis requires several preparatory definitions. A *loop* in a flow graph is a collection of nodes all of which are *strongly connected*, that is, there is a path between any two nodes; and the collection has a unique *entry* point, that is, any path that reaches a node inside the loop from outside the loop must go through the entry point.

Example 11-8. The loops in Fig. 11-17 are:

1. entry: B8   body: B8–B9
2. entry: B5   body: B5, B7–B10
3. entry: B2   body: B2–B3, B5–B10

B1 and B4 are not in a loop. Even though B5, B7, B8 and B10 are strongly connected, they do not form a loop by themselves because none of those three nodes is an entry point. B5 is not the entry point because B8 can be reached from B9 without going through B5. B7 is not the entry point for the same reason. B8 is not the entry point because B5 can be reached from B10.
◆

Node n *dominates* node m, written n DOM n, if all paths from the starting node to m must travel through n. Any node dominates itself.

Example 11-9. Figure 11-19 shows the node domination for the flow graph of Fig. 11-17.
◆

Node	Dominates
1	1 2 3 4 5 6 7 8 9 10
2	2 3 4 5 6 7 8 9 10
3	3 5 6 7 8 9 10
4	4
5	5 6 7 8 9 10
6	6
7	7 8 9 10
8	8 9 10
9	9
10	10

Figure 11-19. Dominators in Fig. 11-17.

With these two definitions, three conditions can be stated which if satisfied guarantee that for loop L moving invariant statement s in block B which defines variable v, to a loop pre-header is safe:

1. B dominates all exits from L.
2. No other statement assigns a value to v.
3. All uses of v inside L are from the definition in s.

The first condition guarantees that eventually s will be executed once the entry point of L is reached, so moving s to the pre-header simply forces the execution to occur earlier.

The second condition addresses the situation where because of multiple assignments in the unoptimized loop, v is first assigned the value x, then the value y, and finally the value x again during three iterations. If the assignment of x to v is moved outside the loop, then after v is assigned the value y, it cannot subsequently be reassigned the value x.

Finally, the third condition guarantees that if v already has a value z when the unoptimized loop is first entered, z is not used anywhere in L instead of the value assigned by s. This is necessary since moving s to the pre-header guarantees that the value of v reaching the entry point is the one defined in s.

Example 11-10. Suppose the definition of the `for` loop were changed so that the loop always executes at least once even if the initial condition is false. The flow graph now becomes that pictured in Fig. 11-20. To simplify the presentation, the original block names and labels have been retained, although this flow graph has three fewer blocks. The `if` statements terminating the loops have been changed slightly to reflect their new role and new labels have been added to be the targets of these revised statements. The loops in this new graph are:

1. entry: B9/8   body: B9/8
2. entry: B7   body: B7 B9/8 B10/5 B6/2
3. entry: B3   body: B3 B7 B9/8 B10/5 B6/2

The statements that were unsafely moved to the pre-header in Fig. 11-18 can now all be moved safely; for example, statement t3:=i*arg9 can be moved to a pre-header outside loop (2). This statement satisfies condition (1) because B7 dominates loop (2); it satisfies condition (2) because it is the only definition of t3 in the program; and it satisfies condition (3) because the only two uses of t3 are the two statements that immediately follow it.

One final definition is needed before presenting the algorithm for detecting loop invariant computation. For each use of a variable, a *use-definition chain*, or *ud-chain* for short, is a list of all definitions that reach it. Using Algorithm 11-3 as a starting point, it should be straightforward to construct an algorithm that computes ud-chains for each variable. This is left as an exercise as is the algorithm for detecting loops.

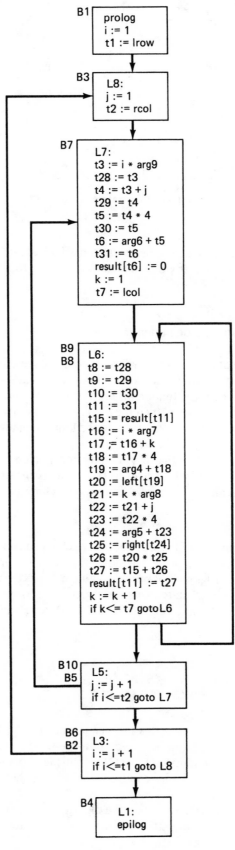

Figure 11-20. Flow Graph with Modified for Loop.

Algorithm 11-5. Detecting loop invariant computation.

Input: A loop L of basic blocks, together with ud-chain information on all variables in the loop. The i-th statement in L is L[i]. There are k total statements in L.

Output: Loop invariant statements.

Steps

```
1     for (i=1; i<=k; i++)
2         if (operands of B[i] are constant || operands
3             do not have a definition which reaches L)
4             L[i] is invariant;
5
6     do {
7         changed = 0;
6         for (i=1; i<=k; i++)
7             if (L[i] is not invariant && (its operands either
8                 are constant || its operands do not have a definition
9                 which reaches L || its operands have exactly one
10                definition reaching L which is invariant)) {
11                changed++;
12                L[i] is invariant;
13            }
14    } while (changed);
```

◆

Algorithm 11-6. Code motion for loop invariant computation.

Input: A loop *L* with ud-chaining and loop invariant statements marked.

Output: A revised loop which has had invariant code moved to a pre-header block.

Steps: For each invariant statement s that defines variable b, determine whether it meets all three conditions defined earlier. If s satisfies those conditions, move it to the pre-header block of the loop provided that if any of its operands are defined in L, those definitions have previously been moved to the pre-header.

◆

Induction Variables

An *induction variable* in a loop is one whose value in the ith iteration is a function of its value in the $(i - 1)$-th iteration. In many cases the induction relationship is very simple, allowing a standard set of optimizations to be applied.

In Pascal's **for** loop:

```
for v := initial [down]to final do statement
```

v is an induction variable which can be any scalar type. With each iteration its value varies by succ(v) if the loop goes up (to) and by pred(v) if the loop goes down (downto). In FORTRAN's DO loop

```
        DO label v = initial , final , increment
            ...
    label
```

v is integer valued, and the programmer is allowed to specify an arbitrary positive increment.

Such looping constructs not only improve programming style, but make it easier to optimize code because their very form tells the compiler that v is an induction variable. That fact does not have to be inferred from a detailed examination of the code. Both languages specifically forbid modification to the loop index variable inside the body of the loop, a restriction motivated as much by a desire to simplify code generation and optimization as to improve execution transparency to the reader.

Optimization and code generation schemes may rely on the fact that the index variable is not to be changed in the loop body of these two constructs. If a compiler does not actually check for a violation of this rule and the programmer either intentionally or accidentally does violate it, unpredictable behavior could result. Making such a check can require extensive analysis, especially if the loop body contains procedure and function calls that could have access to the index variable.

The similar *C* construct

```
for (initial; termination; increment) statement
```

is a more general flow control mechanism. The values of the three controlling expressions can perform arbitrary actions, and are evaluated each time through the loop. It is not safe for the compiler to assume that the seemingly simple

```
for (i=1; i<=MAX; i++) ...
```

actually increments i from 1 to MAX in steps of 1. The code in the loop body can legally alter the value of i or MAX in any iteration.

A *basic inductive variable* i is one whose only assignments within a loop have the form i:=i+c or i:=i−c, where c is a constant. This corresponds well to the standard looping constructs of most procedural languages. It then becomes trivial to identify the basic inductive variables. There are several standard operator strength reductions which can readily be implemented for inductive variable i. Two will be shown here.

Reduce *r * i*

Suppose a loop has the sequence

```
...
r = i * a
...
i = i + b
```

Each time through the loop r is increased by a*b. Hence, this code can be replaced by the pre-header and loop in Fig. 11-21. a*b is computed at compile-time.

Reduce *i * i*

Suppose a loop has the statement:

```
r = i * i
```

Each time through the loop r is increased by:

```
(i + b) * (i + b) - i*i = 2*b*i + b*b
```

b*b is a constant which can be computed at compile-time. 2*b*i has the form of the last reduction and can be reduced to addition. Replace the original code by the pre-header and loop statements in Fig. 11-22. There are many more such optimizations, some of which are left as exercises.

Pre-Header	Loop
t = i * a	... r = t ... i = i + b t = t + a*b

Figure 11-21. Replacing Multiplication by Addition.

Pre-Header	Loop

`t1 = i * i`
`t2 = 2*b * i`
`t2 = t2 + b*b`
	`r = t1`
	`...`
	`i = i + b`
	`t1 = t1 + t2`
	`t2 = t2 + 2*b*b`

Figure 11-22. Replacing Multiplication by Addition in `i*i`.

EXERCISES

1. The following Pascal program computes the minimum and maximum values of a list of number in a somewhat less than optimal fashion:

```
1    program minmax (input,output);
2    const
3        MAX = 100;
4    type
5        bounds = 1..MAX;
6    var
7        i: bounds;
8        min, max, first, second: integer;
9        numbers: array [bounds] of integer;
10   begin
11       for i := 1 to MAX do
12           readln (numbers[i]);
13       min := numbers[1];
14       max := min;
15       for i := 1+1*1 to MAX do begin
16           if numbers[i*1]>max then
17               max := numbers[i];
18           if numbers[i/1]*2<min*2 then
19               min := numbers[i];
20       end
21       writeln (min, max);
22   end.
```

   (a) Generate three-address code for this program.
   (b) Simplify the generated code using constant folding, algebraic identities, and operator strength reduction.
   (c) Draw the flow graph for this code.
   (d) Identify each loop.
   (e) Tell what nodes each node dominates.
   (f) Apply global common subexpression elimination.
   (g) Apply the code motion techniques shown in section 11.3.

2. For the following Pascal program:

```
1    program looped (input, output);
2    var
3        x: array [1..100] of integer;
4        i,j: integer;
5    begin
6        i := 1; j := 1;
7        repeat
8            j := j*i;
9            x[j] := i*i;
10           for k := 1 to j do
11               x[k] := j*k;
12           i := i + 2;
13       until i > 10;
14   end.
```

(a) Translate it into three-address code.
(b) Draw the flow graph.
(c) Identify each loop.
(d) Identify each induction variable.
(e) Reduce operations on induction variables using the two techniques shown in Section 11.3.

3. (a) Translate the following Pascal program into three-address code:

```
1    program common (input, output);
2    var
3        x,y: array [1..10] of integer;
4    begin
5        for i := 1 to 10 do begin
6            y[i] := i+1;
7            for j := 1 to 10 do
8                x[j] := y[j]/i;
9        end
10   end.
```

(b) Identify and remove all local common subexpressions from the code.
(c) Identify and remove all global common subexpressions.

4. Develop an algorithm that finds all of the loops in a flow graph.

5. Develop an algorithm that constructs use-definition chains.

6. Develop a reduction for the multiplication of two inductive loop variables by each other.

7. Division of an inductive variable by a constant $r:=i/c$ can be reduced to subtraction, addition, and branching within the loop. Develop an algorithm for performing this reduction.

8. Develop a reduction for exponentiation to an induction variable $r:=a^i$ to multiplication, which in turn can be reduced to addition.

Chapter 12
CODE GENERATION

12.1. FACETS OF CODE GENERATION

The final phase of a compiler maps optimized intermediate language (IL) into the assembly language (AL) of the target machine. Here the actual sequences necessary to call a subprogram, add two floating point numbers, and convert a value from integer to real are emitted. Quite often the overall code generation phase is broken into several minor phases such as *storage allocation*, *local code generation*, *register allocation*, and *peephole optimization*. The first three minor phases are usually performed concurrently or in the order shown. The peephole optimizer, which looks at a narrow code window for what are usually very machine specific optimizations is nearly always a separate subphase. It is a final code "proofreader" looking for last minute optimizations.

Of course the most important quality of a code generator is that it produce correct code, but that is relatively straightforward if little thought is given to optimization of the emitted code. The majority of the effort in writing commerical code generators goes into developing optimizations, many of them highly machine dependent (and usually the source of many subtle bugs). A poor code generator can effectively undo all the work of the earlier machine independent optimizing phase by ignoring the architecture of the target machine; for example, high-speed registers are a prized resource. Careful allocation of registers is well worth the effort. The recent trend in computer architectures is to reduce the size of the instruction set and the number of addressing modes, while increasing the number of registers. Such simplifications improve overall code performance in part by having less contention for registers [Patterson 85].

Instruction Cost

The *cost* of an instruction is its length in bytes or its execution time. To simplify the discussion, the execution time is reduced to integer values based on the number of references to main memory in an instruction. An instruction that only uses registers has zero cost because of its relative efficiency, while a memory to memory operation has cost two. Of course in any real machine more precise costing is appropriate, but the principles are well illustrated with this simple method.

Optimization strategies tend to focus directly on reducing execution cost since most users value speed more than space. In general this helps space optimization anyhow since speed is obtained by removing redundant instructions, and because instructions involving registers tend to occupy fewer bytes than those making memory accesses. A handful of speed optimizations will bloat code size.

Example 12-1. Consider the following three-address code which is the translation of the C statement z = (x+y)+x*(x+y):

```
1    t1 := x + y
2    t2 := x * t1
3    z  := t1 + t2
```

Common subexpression elimination has allowed t1 to be used in line 3 rather than recompute x+y. These three instructions can be translated into the two different IBM mainframe instructions sequences

	Instruction	Time	Length
1	L r,x	1	4
2	A r,y	1	4
3	ST r,t1	1	4
4	L r,x	1	4
5	M r,t1	1	4
6	ST r,t2	1	4
7	L r,t1	1	4
8	A r,t2	1	4
9	ST r,z	1	4
	Total	9	36

Instruction	Time	Length
L r,x	1	4
A r,y	1	4
L s,x	1	4
MR s,r	0	2
AR s,r	0	2
ST s,z	1	4
	4	20

(a) Clumsy   (b) Clever

Figure 12-1. Clumsy and Clever Code Generation for $z=(x+yp)+x*(x+y)$.

shown in Fig. 12-1. Solution (a) just uses one machine register pair, r and $r+1$, actually saving the results of each computation in main memory in order to free up the register for its next use (multiplication on an IBM mainframe is done in a register pair such as $r2-r3$ or $r8-r9$). Solution (b) uses three registers—r, s, and $s+1$. It saves the results of each computation in a register for later reference, being careful in lines 3 and 4 not to overwrite $x+y$ when computing $x*(x+y)$. The relative execution cost of each instruction as well as its length appear to the right. The second solution runs in 45% of the time of the first, and consumes 56% of the space.

◆

Apart from clever use of registers, there is usually a host of ways to perform even simple operations.

Example 12-2. The following four instruction sequences all clear m, a two-byte half-word of memory in an IBM mainframe:

1. SR   r,r   subtract register r from itself
    SH   r,m   store half of register r into m

      length = 6   time = 1

2. MVI   m,X'00'   move hex byte 00 into m
    MVI   m+1,X'00'   move hex byte 00 into $m+1$

      length = 8   time = 2

3. MVC   m(2),=H'00'   allocate and initialize two byte constant containing 0; move it to m

      length = 6   time = 2

4. LA   r,0   load address of location 0 into r
    SH   r,m   store half of register r into m

      length = 8   time = 2

◆

A code generator (or the code generator writer) should weigh the cost of these alternatives and select the cheapest instruction sequence. Clearly as the complexity of the machine increases so does the difficulty of making intelligent choices.

Instruction Ordering

Computations can be reordered to some degree without affecting the results of the computation. In some cases this can improve the code by reducing the number of stores of temporary quantities in registers. Unfortunately, the problem of determining the optimal ordering even for relatively simple situations is very hard computationally (said to be *NP-complete*) and is not practical. For now, code will be generated in the order in which it appears in the three-address statements. Later, some optimizations will be examined.

Minimizing Machine Dependence

Code generation is necessarily the most machine dependent phase, but like virtually all other areas of compiler writing, researchers have identified and isolated aspects of code generation which are common across compilers. Just as parser-writing systems separate the act of parsing and its attendent bookkeeping from the language being parsed, *code-generator generators* (CGG) separate actual code emission from the architecture of the target machine. CGGs are usually based on pattern matching, attribute grammars, and syntax-directed translation. Section 12.4 explores CGGs.

12.2. CODE GENERATION ALGORITHMS

The mapping from IL to AL can be done in a simple manner by emitting code in the order in which the three-address instructions appear. There is usually close to a one-to-one mapping from IL to AL because the intermediate language is intentionally crafted to be only slightly more abstract than assembly language. If they are too different, the translation is so radical that another major optimization phase is necessary. If they are relatively similar, then a modest peephole optimizer can be used to check for last minute optimizations.

A table lookup technique can be used to substitute one or more AL instructions for each IL instruction. When performing the substitution, the compiler must track the location of variables which can either be in a register or in main memory. The compiler must also take into account the run-time storage management scheme for the program; that is, will a variable be on the stack, in the heap, in global storage, and so on. The layout of variables into memory, *storage allocation*, must precede or take place concurrent with local code generation. By the time code generation begins, all relevant attributes of a variable such as whether it is static, automatic, local, external, or initialized are known. The storage allocator can simply step through the symbol table and position each variable relative to others. The following example illustrates how storage allocation affects local code generation.

Example 12-3. When a C program is compiled, it is normally broken into *text*, *data*, and *bss* segments. Actual program instructions go in the text segment, initialized global data in the data segment, and uninitialized global data in the bss segment. Local variables are housed on the stack. Each type of variable has different addressing needs as illustrated by the following trivial program:

```
1       int  b = 3, c[10]={0,1,2,3,4,5};  /* external data */
2       int  d, e[10];     /* external bss */
3
4       main ()
5       {
6           int  *p, q;        /* uninitialized local stack */
7           int  r=10, s=11;   /* initialized local stack */
8           static  t, u=12;   /* local data */
9
10          q = b+c[1]+d+e[2]+r+s;
11          p = (int *) malloc(q);
12          *p = q;
13          t = ++u;
14      }
```

Variables b and c go into the data segment since they are initialized global storage, d and e go into bss, and p, q, r, and s go on the stack. Additionally, p is assigned a pointer to storage from the heap in line

11 and both r and s are initialized on block entry even though they are automatic storage. t and u are local static variables. Using one Motorola 68000 C compiler, this becomes:

```
1                .data
2                .even
3                .globl    _b
4      _b:
5                .long     3
6                .even
7                .globl    _c
8      _c:
9                .long     0
10               .long     1
11               .long     2
12               .long     3
13               .long     4
14               .long     5
15               .space    16
16               .comm     _d,4
17               .comm     _e,40
18               .text
19               .globl    _main
20     _main:
21               link      a6,#-.F1
22               tstb      sp@(-.M1)
23               moveml    #.S1,a6@(-.F1)
24               movl      #0xa,a6@(0xfffffff4)
25               movl      #0xb,a6@(0xfffffff0)
26               .data
27               .even
28     .L17:
29               .space    4
30               .even
31     .L18:
32               .long     0xc
33               .text
34               movl      _b,d0
35               addl      _c+4,d0
36               addl      _d,d0
37               addl      _e+8,d0
38               addl      a6@(0xfffffff4),d0
39               addl      a6@(0xfffffff0),d0
40               movl      d0,a6@(0xfffffff8)
41               movl      a6@(0xfffffff8),sp@-
42               jsr       _malloc
43               addql     #4,sp
44               movl      d0,a6@(0xfffffffc)
45               movl      a6@(0xfffffffc),a0
46               movl      a6@(0xfffffff8),a0@
47               addql     #1,.L18
48               movl      .L18,.L17
49               bra       .L16
50     .L16:     moveml    a6@(-.F1),#0
51               unlk      a6
52               rts
53     .F1 = 16
54     .S1 = 0x0
55     .M1 = 136
56               .data
```

The code has been scrubbed for readability. Line 1 states that what follows goes into the data segment. Line 2 forces alignment on an even address boundary. Lines 3 and 7 state that b and c are external symbols. The assembler will force them to be so labeled in the object module it produces allowing *ld* to resolve references to those symbols in other separately compiled modules. Lines 4 and 5 actually declare symbol b's relative position and initialize it to 3. Lines 7–15 declare c and initialize its first six elements. Space is left for the rest in line 15. The .comm directives in lines 16 and 17 define d and e as external symbols that go into the bss segment. They also declare the length of these symbols. bss storage is reliably initialized to 0 by the Unix kernel when the *a.out* file is loaded into memory. Storage for these symbols is not actually allocated until then. Just symbolic names and offsets are used within the assembly code. There is no explicit declaration of p, q, r, or s since they are only offsets on the stack.

Within the instructions, local and global variables are referenced differently. bss and data variables are referenced by name and offset. Register a6 is the stack pointer. References to local variables are relative to it. Lines 21–23 are the prolog that ensures there is enough room on the stack for the four automatic variables in main plus any registers that need to be saved. Lines 24–25 initialize automatic variables r and s by moving the indicated hexadecimal constants onto the stack relative to a6. Lines 26–32 allocate room for static t and u in the data segment. t is at label .L17 and u is at .L18 which is also initialized to 12. In the subsequent lines, references to local variables are all relative to a6, while references to global variables are to their symbolic names possibly plus some offset. For example, line 35 references the location of c plus four bytes, which is the address of c[1]. Register d0 has been used to hold the value of b in line 34, and is successively updated with the value of c[1], d, e[2], r, and s in lines 35–39. The result is moved into q in line 40. malloc is called in lines 41–42. When it returns, register d0 holds the result, which is stored into p. References to t and u are through the labels .L17 and .L18 as illustrated in lines 47 and 48.

◆

Virtual Assembly Language

If the local code generation and register allocation phases are separated, the local code generator produces *virtual assembly language* (VAL), so called because it looks like assembly language in all respects except that it uses *virtual registers*. In practice machines have a limited number of registers forcing the code generator to be careful about which variables it assigns to them. A VAL machine is like the actual target machine except it has an unlimited number of registers allowing the local code generator to avoid having to make assignment decisions. The register allocator modifies the code as required to squeeze the numerous virtual registers down to whatever physical limitation the real hardware imposes.

12.3. REGISTER ALLOCATION

Effective register allocation is critical to good code generation. A register allocation scheme attempts to identify those operands that are most often referenced and place them into registers to minimize access time. Three factors make register allocation difficult:

1. Machines have a limited number of physical registers.
2. The set of most often referenced operands changes over time.
3. It is not possible to algorithmically decide in all cases which operands in fact will be most often used.

There is no optimal register management scheme for real programming languages; however, there are some rather good ones.

Virtually all computers have certain conventions for some subset of registers; for example, register a6 in a Motorola 68000 always points to the base of the stack frame. The Western Electric 32100 microprocessor has 16 general-purpose registers, but predefines uses for the last seven such as r9 for the stack frame pointer and r15 for the program counter. Additionally, many machines have special purpose registers; for example, the M68000 has separate data and address registers. A pointer variable is always loaded into an address register, others are assigned to data registers. Restrictions and subdivisions clearly inhibit effective register usage since it is possible for there to be a surplus of one type of register when there is a shortage of another.

When the set of *N* physical registers cannot be used interchangeably either because of convention or hardware restriction, they are said to be broken into *classes* or *pools*. Each pool serves a different purpose; for example, if register r15 is always the program counter, it is a pool consisting of one register. If register a6 is always a stack frame pointer, it is also in a pool by itself. If general registers r2–r8 can be used for any purpose the compiler writer wishes, they can all be placed into the same pool.

Sometimes it is useful for a register allocator to artificially divide a larger pool *P* of registers into two smaller ones, *P1* and *P2*. For example, *P1* might be set aside just to hold variables in loops in order to guarantee that there are enough registers for variables likely to be accessed frequently. *P2* would be used for other general purposes. There is no one right way to subdivide *P*. Each scheme approaches that problem differently.

The remainder of this section presents several allocation schemes. In all cases there is an implicit assumption that the register allocation scheme obeys whatever restrictions are imposed by the machine architecture and conventions.

The first scheme is a "seat of the pants" approach called *on the fly allocation* which aims more at ensuring correctness than being clever. Local code generation and register allocation are merged into simultaneous phases.

On The Fly Allocation

Function `getreg` is called whenever a register is needed. It maintains a list of *free* and *busy* registers. A register is busy if it has been assigned one or more symbols; otherwise, it is free. A single register can simultaneously hold the value of more than one symbol; for example, if y is assigned to register r, then the statement x:=y will cause x to also be assigned to r. In addition, the symbol table is augmented to indicate whether a symbol is held in a register. If there are no free registers, `getreg` calls `spill` to free up a register. The act of freeing an occupied register is called *spilling* because the contents of the register must be "spilt" or stored in main memory by emitting an appropriate store sequence. The cost of such a store will vary depending on the run-time management scheme and the type of variable (static, dynamic, local, . . .). If a subsequent reference to that value must be in a register, it must be reloaded from main memory.

The following version of `getreg` and `spill` is called *on the fly* register allocation because the decision as to which register to use and which register to spill is made only by looking at the current three-address instruction. The context of that instruction in an overall data flow analysis is ignored. This method is only good on straight-line code. The subsection on crossing blocks entends it to general flow graphs.

Algorithm 12-1. On the fly register allocation.

```
 1   int
 2   getreg (b, except) operand b; int except[];
 3   {
 4       if (there is no free register r)
 5           r = spill (except);
 6       update symbol table to show b is in r;
 7       assign b to r;
 8       emit code to load b into r;
 9       return r;
10   }
```

```
 1   int    /* spill any register but those in variable except */
 2   spill (except)  int except[];
 3   {
 4       if (there is no register r whose value is already
 5           in memory)
 6           emit code to save in main memory the value of register
 7               r needed furthest in code after s;
 8       deassign all symbols assigned to r;
 9       update symbol table to show symbols no longer assigned to r;
10       return r;
11   }
```

◆

Algorithm 12-2. On the fly code emission for a basic block.
Purpose: Code for statement s = x:=y●z is to be emitted, where ● is an arbitrary operation. y must be in a register in order to execute s. z is already where it needs to be—either in a register or main memory.

Steps

```
1    emitcode()
2    {
3        if (y is not assigned to some register r)
4            if (z is in register u)
5                getreg (y, list containing just u);
6            else
7                getreg (y, NULL);
8        emit code for s;
9
10       if (operation • has the side-effect of changing the value of
11           any registers)
12           unconditionally free those registers, deassigning all symbols
13               associated with them;
14       if (operation • causes the value of one or more operands
15           of s to be in a register it was not previously in)
16           assign those operands to the appropriate registers;
17   }
```

◆

Example 12-4. Consider the three-address code sequence

```
t1 := a + b
t2 := t1 + 5
t3 := c * t2
```

and suppose that when this point in code emission is reached, register r0 holds b, there is one free register r1, and r2 holds variables z and x. There are only three registers and all arithmetic operations require the first operand to be in a register. The code in Fig. 12-2 would be produced by calling emitcode for an imaginary machine with instructions as indicated in the comments.

◆

Algebraic Properties

The code generated in Fig. 12-2 is larger than necessary because emitcode does not take into account the commutativity of either addition or multiplication.

Example 12-5. Making emitcode a little smarter causes it to produce the code in Fig. 12-3.
◆

Code		Effect		r0	r1	r2
LD	r1,a	r1 := a		b	a	z x
AR	r1,r0	r1 := r1 + r0		b	t1	z x
AI	r1,5	r1 := r1 + 5		b	t2	z x
ST	r0,b	b := r0		evict b from r0		
LD	r0,c	r0 := c		c	t2	z x
MR	r0,r1	r0 := r0 * r1		t3	t2	z x

Figure 12-2. On the Fly Code Emission.

Code		Effect		r0	r1	r2
AR	r0,r1	r0 := r0 + r1		t1		z x
AI	r0,5	r0 := r0 + 5		t2		z x
M	r0,c	r0 := r0 * c		t3		z x

Figure 12-3. Using Commutativity to Simplify Code.

Assuming that algebraic optimization has previously been applied during the machine independent optimization phase, there should not be any three-address code sequences involving `x+0`, `x*1`, or other computations that can be simplified using standard algebraic identities.

Crossing Blocks

A variable is said to be *useless* after its last reference. Until then it is *useful*. Using data flow analysis techniques from the last chapter, it is straightforward to determine when a variable becomes useless. At the point where a variable assigned to a register becomes useless it can be flushed from that register. Its value does not have to be saved when the register is freed. When the end of a basic block is reached, the value of each useful variable must be preserved either in a register or in main memory.

The location of the current value of useful variable x must be consistent for all definitions which reach a block. If one block places x in main memory, then all blocks must do so. If one block places x in register r, then all blocks must place x in the same register r. Obviously it is much easier to simply store x into main memory at the end of each block than to try to guarantee that x leaves every block in r. x must then be reloaded into a register at block entry. This strategy has the advantage of simplicity but the weakness that potential optimizations are missed because it may be possible to keep a variable consistently in a register across blocks. On the fly allocation does not work across blocks without applying such a strategy since that allocation method does not account for flow control.

Usage Formulas

Usage formulas attempt to quantify the benefit of placing variable x in a register and keeping it there over some fixed code segment S such as a loop body. They take into account the number of times x will be referenced. `cost(x)` is computed for each variable in a flow graph. The variables in S with the greatest cost are permanently assigned to registers. The other variables compete for assignment in the remaining registers outside the pool and may exist in a register for only part (or possibly none) of the execution of that code segment.

Formulas for computing the cost depend somewhat on machine architecture and the difficulty of accessing a value. For example, if a variable is stored in a fixed address or in a known offset from an index register, the cost of obtaining that value from main memory is relatively cheap compared to having to chain through several levels of activation records for a nonlocal reference. In some machines such as the Intel 8086 the cost of accessing main memory "near" the point of reference is less than making distant accesses. Usage formulas can take such factors into account. [Chow and Hennessey 84] report excellent results applying such weighted usage counts in register allocation.

Suppose that the machine's architecture requires x to be in a register in order for its value to be changed. Assume the code generation method is smart enough to leave x in a register once it is already there until it must be spilt. One of the simplest usage models assumes that for each block B in S the cost of not placing x permanently in a register is 1 for each access to x until it is assigned a value. If x is modified within B and is useful on exit from B, that value must be stored, adding 1 to the cost. Hence, the total cost of not assigning x permanently to a register is

```
(# of references in B until first definition) + (x is useful at end of B ? 0 : 1)
```

The higher the cost, the more benefit to placing x in a register.

Applying usage analysis as a strategy for register allocation within loops normally offers substantial advantage. Those variables with the highest cost can be loaded into registers in the pre-header to the loop and stored at each exit point from the loop where they are still useful.

The compiler cannot, in general, tell how frequently any given leg within a loop will actually be executed, such frequencies varying with the input data driving the program in which the loop appears. It can be fooled into optimizing references to a little used variable. For example, the *error* leg of a loop may contain many references to an array containing the text of error messages, yet that leg will be executed only a tiny fraction of the time in normal usage. Optimizing for access to the array would not substantially improve execution time. Without a directive advising the compiler about which legs are most frequently executed, it cannot reasonably determine such behavior.

Usage formulas can be applied over large program segments up to the whole flow graph. Some number of registers can be set aside in a pool for the duration of a whole procedure or the entire program. In that case, the formula will probably want to bias references to variables within loops. [Wall 86] reports good results biasing references within loops by a constant factor of 10. Nested loops could be biased even more so that a loop with nesting level two would be biased a factor of 100, nesting level three a factor of 1000, and so on. Of course, such biasing could prove quite inaccurate for some programs, but overall seems to work well.

Graph Coloring

Register allocation can be reduced to a graph coloring problem. Given graph G, the *k-way graph coloring problem* attempts to find a way to label each node of the graph with one of k colors such that no two adjacent nodes have the same color. The smallest integer n for which a graph is colorable is said to be that graph's *chromatic number*.

Example 12-6. Figure 12-4 shows two colorings of the same graph with colors G (green), R (red), and B (blue). The first coloring is not correct because there are two adjacent nodes labeled by G; the second is correct. This graph's chromatic number is 3.

♦

In general the problem of deciding whether a graph has a k-way coloring and finding such a coloring if it exists is very hard computationally (*NP*-complete) and not practical. Fortunately, the special way in which coloring is used for register allocation leads to very fast algorithms that are essentially linear in the size of the graph. Heuristics are employed to guarantee good behavior even on pathological cases; that is, the algorithm does not necessarily construct a k-coloring, but will generate a reasonable approximation of one.

[Chaitin 82] described a graph technique he used in a compiler for a PL/I-like language for an experimental 32-bit minicomputer at the IBM Watson Research Center. The algorithm assumes a standard flow analysis has previously been performed so that at each point in the program it is known which variables are useful. It uses the observation that two variables x and y can share the same register r if they are not both useful at the same time. In that case x can occupy r for some period of time, then give up the register to y. Such situations are common in code with many legs since the code in alternative legs cannot both be executed unless it is part of a loop. Code that manipulates groups of variables in relatively isolated segments also displays this property. Within each group there are many variables that are simultaneously useful, but not many across the two groups. A single register might be shared by two variables in different groups.

Suppose local code generation is performed before register allocation producing VAL. There is likely to be many more virtual registers than physical registers available on the machine. Each virtual register must be mapped into a physical register in one of two pools, a primary pool P and a secondary pool S, for nonspilt and spilt virtual registers, respectively.

The first pass of the algorithm constructs a *register interference graph*. There is one node for each virtual register in the VAL. Two nodes are adjacent if they are ever useful simultaneously; that is, if one

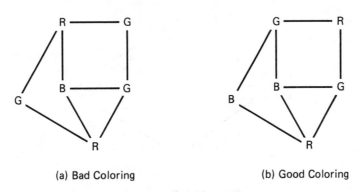

(a) Bad Coloring   (b) Good Coloring

Figure 12-4. Attempting to color a graph.

is useful at the definition point of the other. Suppose there are k registers in P. A k-coloring of the interference graph is a legal register allocation; that is, two virtual registers are assigned to the same physical register if their corresponding nodes have the same color. If the chromatic number of the graph is $n \le k$, then virtual registers can be assigned to just the registers in P; otherwise, the compiler must emit spill code to save the offending virtual register when it is defined and to reload it to a register in S when it is referenced.

Once graph G is built it is successively reduced to a smaller graph by removing any node that has fewer than k edges. Such a node and edges represent a register allocation which can be done without spilling. This reduction is performed repeatedly until either G becomes the null graph or it is blocked because all remaining nodes have more than k adjacent nodes. In the latter case a register must be spilt and the interference graph modified to reflect this.

A usage count formula can be used to decide which virtual register v to spill. Once that decision is made, `getreg` is called to obtain a physical register r from S. Suppose v is assigned to variable x. The VAL is modified to include a load of x into r prior to each use of v and a store into x after each definition. In fact, it is possible to be a bit more clever by not storing r back into x until r is forceably freed by subsequent use or the end of a block is reached. This minimizes loads and stores within a single basic block.

After the VAL has been modified, the node and adjacent edges for the spilt virtual register are removed from the graph. The algorithm continues by again trying to find a node with fewer than k adjacent edges, spilling more registers as required. Eventually the algorithm will spill enough registers to reduce G to the null graph.

The second pass reconstructs the graph, adding the nodes back in the reverse order they were removed. As each node that was not spilt is added, it is assigned an arbitrary register (color) from P that is different from all of its neighbors.

Example 12-7. Suppose there are three registers in P and the compiler is translating the code in the flow graph pictured in Fig. 12-5 into IBM assembly language. This leads to the VAL shown in Fig. 12-6. The pre-header shows the initial loading of variables into virtual registers. The associated interference graph is in Fig. 12-7. This graph indicates for instance that e and d could share the same register since they are never useful concurrently. Suppose there are two registers, p0 and p1 in P and only register s0 is available from S if needed. The reduction of the interference graph is shown in Fig. 12-8 assuming b and f are spilt. One legal coloring produces Fig. 12-9.

◆

Separate Compilation

Separate compilation presents new obstacles for effective global register allocation with standard compiler approaches. For example, static global variable x might be the most used variable in the overall program, but the compiler cannot ascertain that from each piecepart separately. If its flow analysis of

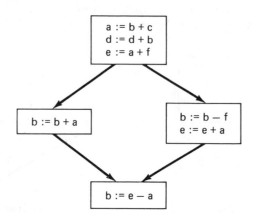

Figure 12-5. Flow graph.

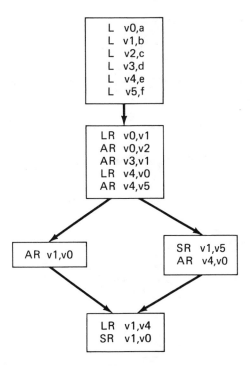

Figure 12-6. VAL code.

separately compiled module M indicates x should be permanently placed in a register, it cannot do so because there is no way to guarantee that x will be assigned to the same register when the other separate modules are compiled.

[Wall 86] has proposed a solution to this problem by delaying register allocation to link time when information about all modules is available. The compiler actually produces valid object modules together with additional information that can optionally be used by a link-time register allocator (LTRA). If invoked, the LTRA modifies the object modules to make more effective use of registers. Wall had two key design goals:

1. The compiler must produce valid code so that the LTRA truly is optional.
2. The compiler must perform enough analysis which it makes available to the LTRA so that the latter is relatively fast. It cannot redo the work of the compiler.

To achieve these two goals, the compiler annotates the code with information telling the LTRA what changes to make in the code if a variable currently in main memory is assigned to a register instead.

Example 12-8. The compiler might map the three-address instruction x:=y+z into the annotated assembly instructions shown in Fig. 12-10, where A3 is an assembly language instruction that adds the contents of r1 to the contents of r2, storing the result in r3. If neither x, y, nor z is allocated to a register by the LTRA, this code would be left alone. Three different modifications are possible depending on which variables are allocated by the LTRA as shown in Fig. 12-11. There are other annotations for more complex situations left as exercises.

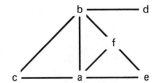

Figure 12-7. Interference graph.

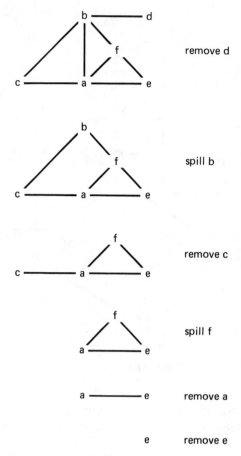

remove d

spill b

remove c

spill f

remove a

remove e

Figure 12-8. Reduction of interference graph.

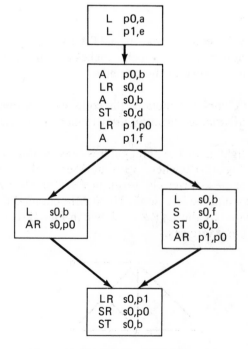

Figure 12-9. A legal register allocation.

instruction	actions
LD r1,y	REMOVE.y
LD r2,z	REMOVE.z
A3 r3,r1,r2	OP1.y OP2.y RESULT.x
ST r3,x	REMOVE.x

Figure 12-10. Annotated Assembly Code.

	y in r1	x in r1 y in r2	x in r1 y in r2 z in r3
placement			
code	LD r3,z A3 r3,r1,r2 ST r3,x	LD r3,z A3 r3,r1,r2	A3 r1,r2,r3

Figure 12-11. Modified Assembly Code.

LTRA uses basic flow information collected during compilation including usage estimates for each module the number of times each procedure is called and variable is referenced. It produces a global estimate by combining all of the information from each separate module from which it decides which variables to assign to registers. Wall reports between 10 and 20% speed improvement on a series of six benchmarks using this technique.

12.4. CODE-GENERATOR GENERATORS

Over the last decade many of the same techniques that have been used so successfully for earlier phases of compiling have been applied to code generation [Graham 80] [Ganapathi et al. 82]. *Code-generator generators* (CGGs) typically use syntax-directed methods to separate out the actual acts of code emission and pattern matching from the details of the target machine's architecture. Among the most successful are *Graham–Glanville* generators, named after the two researchers responsible for them [Graham and Glanville 78]. They have been used to develop a number of compilers including *C* and Pascal compilers for the VAX, M68000, and Berkeley's RISC-II machines.

The Graham–Glanville method assumes that the intermediate code is in polish prefix notation or possibly represented as trees. It further assumes that storage allocation has already been done; for a Unix *C* compiler this usually means that local variables have been assigned to their stack offsets, and global variables to their relative positions within bss and data. An SDT maps the intermediate code into assembly language invoking appropriate action routines during the parse. The SDT is usually LR based although [Christopher et al. 84] report excellent results using Earley's parsing algorithm [Earley 70].

Example 12-9. Consider an add immediate instruction ADDI that adds a constant to the value in a register. The production to represent this instruction is:

```
register: '+' register CONSTANT {emit ( ADDI, $2, $3); $$=$2;}
```

which says that the Polish prefix pattern of a '+' operator followed by a *register*, followed by a constant can be reduced to a *register*. When this pattern is seen, the ADDI instruction should be emitted. The attribute of a register or a CONSTANT is the name by which it can be referenced. Assignment $$=$2 states that the result of the ADDI operation is left in the same register that was used in the instruction.

◆

Such parsers tend to have many conflicts because there are usually numerous ways to generate equivalent code, requiring special resolution rules. The standard techniques for parsing programming languages are inadequate.

Example 12-10. The ADDI rule is a special case when the first operand is in a register and the second is a constant; however, there may also be a general rule governing addition:

```
1       register:  '+'  operand  operand
2                  { if ($2 in register)
3                        if ($3 in register)
4                            emit (ADDR, $2, $3); $$=$2;
5                        else  /* $3 in memory */
6                            emit (ADD, $2, $3); $$=$2;
7                     else  /* $2 in memory */
8                        if ($3 in register)
9                            emit (ADDR, $3, $2); $$=$3;
10                       else { /* $3 in memory */
11                           i=getreg();
12                           emit (LD, i, $2);
13                           emit (ADD, $2, $3);
14                           $$=$2;
15                       }
16                 }
```

where the call to emit(ADD,$2,$3) in line 6 produces

```
ADD   r  #c
```

if $3 is constant #c. Both rules could apply.

◆

Cost information is used to resolve reduce/reduce conflicts: choose the least expensive reduction. The fact that ADDI is cheaper than ADD would be given as part of the machine specification to the CGG. In the absence of cost data, choose the longest sequence. Shift/reduce conflicts are usually resolved in favor of shifting on the premise that one longer instruction is cheaper than two shorter ones. This is sometimes called the *maximal munch* method. Syntactic conflict resolution methods can be written so that it is never possible to *block*; that is, get into a situation where there is no legitimate way to continue the parse. In fact it is possible to algorithmically examine a grammar specification, determine whether blockage can occur, and eliminate it by modifying the grammar. This approach is reminiscent of the algorithm used to eliminate left recursion from context-free grammars to support recursive descent parsing.

A poor sequence of conflict resolution choices can cause the code generator to effectively paint itself into a semantic corner. *Semantic blocking* occurs when the action code includes tests for conditions that are not met.

Example 12-11. The VAX requires the address computed by displacement indexing to be 1, 2, 4, or 8. Production

```
dx:     '+'  '+'  CONST  register  '*'  CONST  register
        { if ($6 != 1 || $6 != 2 || $6 != 4 || $6 != 8)
             error - blocked;
          ...
        }
```

may be selected by the parser, but if $6 is not one of the four legitimate values, the action code cannot complete. In most cases semantic blocking can be prevented by converting the constraint into a syntactic one; for example, replace the token CONST with four alternative tokens ONE, TWO, FOUR, and EIGHT. Unfortunately, this bloats the grammar.

◆

The parser can be extended to allow action code to not only determine code emission, but to also guide parsing by helping to resolve conflicts (a concept that has broad applicability outside code generation). Such an extension is called a *semantic-syntax-directed translator* (SSDT) in which the action code is viewed as the semantics. This is reminiscent of *lex*'s REJECT operation which causes *lex* to reject an otherwise good pattern match and look for another. In the example above, when the action failed, a SSDT would pretend that rule were never selected and try another choice. Of course, backtracking can become very expensive if allowed to retreat arbitrarily far back; in this case, however, it is restricted to just the current rule.

Actual machine architectures are usually rather messy to specify, having many special cases and quirks. The complexity of the formal description of a programming language is usually a significant consideration in its design. That can be said less often about actual machines. The restriction on the value of constants allowed in a VAX address illustrates this. Consequently, writing specifications for real machines is rather challenging and error prone. An intimate understanding of the quirks of the machine is necessary, but this is largely true when writing a code generator using any technology.

The Graham–Glanville approach has the advantage of being very fast. LR parsing and SDT (and SSDT) are well understood and there are many existing systems available to support it. The major difficulty with this method is that it forces the intermediate language to be semantically very low level and cannot be invoked until storage allocation is completed. Moreover, it tends to operate on very isolated segments of the intermediate code, overlooking many machine-dependent optimizations. A strong peephole optimizer can compensate for this.

Graham and several of her colleagues conducted an experiment where they replaced the back-end of the Portable *C* compiler with a code generator of their own called *codegen* [Aigrain et al. 84]. *pcc* is a two-pass compiler in which the first pass produces intermediate code which is mapped into assembly language by the second pass. The intermediate code representation was left unchanged in this experiment, that is, they just replaced the standard *pcc* code generator. Since Berkeley's FORTRAN *f77* and Pascal *pc* compilers use the same code generator as does *pcc*, they generated compilers for those two languages as a by-product of their effort. Code generators for the VAX, M68000, and RISC-II machines were developed.

Compilers with the two types of code generations performed almost equally indicating that this technique can be successfully applied to compiler generation. One of the goals of their experiment was to discover how much of the code generator could be shared across the three different machines. The VAX code generator was written first, then the other two. Seventy-nine percent of the source code and data is shared among the three code generators indicating the degree to which machine-independent code generation is possible.

12.5. PEEPHOLE OPTIMIZATION

Peephole optimization is the last phase of code generation where the assembly code is scanned through a narrow window for instruction sequences that can be replaced by more efficient ones. A savings of between 2 and 7% in both time and space can normally be gained through by such an optimizer. Because of all the code movement and modification that takes place during optimization and register allocation, it is not unusual to generate sequences such as

```
load    r,x      // load x into register r
store   r,x      // store register r into x
```

If the two instructions are part of the same basic block, the store is surely redundant and can be eliminated.

Another optimization replaces the assembler equivalent of

```
        if (expression) goto L1
        goto L2
L1:
```

by

```
        if (!expression) goto L2
    L1:
```

These instruction sequences are contiguous, making them particularly easy to find. If a peephole optimizer is a little smarter, it can find non-contiguous sequences of cascading goto's:

```
        goto L1
        ...
    L1: goto L2
        ...
    L2: goto L3
        ...
    L3: not a goto
```

is replaced by

```
        goto L3
```

If L1 is only reachable through the single goto L1 statement, then L1: goto L2 can also be eliminated, saving space but not execution time.

Machine specific optimizations look for instruction patterns that can be replaced by more efficient ones; for example, the VAX supports a three-address addition instruction ADDL3. The VAX VMS C compiler occassionally produces the sequence

```
    ADDL3   x,y,t       // t := x+y
    MOVL    t,z         // z := t
```

where all operands may be either registers or in main memory. t is a temporary. If t is not useful after this segment, the peephole optimizer replaces it with the shorter

```
    ADDL3   x,y,z       // z := x+y
```

This peephole optimizer also performs some operator strength reduction. If t is not useful after the sequence

```
    ADDL3   x,y,t       // t := x+y
    MULL3   z,t,w       // w := z*t
```

it is replaced by

```
    ADDL3   x,y,w       // w := x+y
    MULL2   z,w         // w := w*z
```

MULL3 needs three operands, while MULL2 uses two, making it smaller and faster.

Example 12-12. The peephole optimizer /lib/c2 for the Berkeley cc looks for possible loop optimizations. Given source program:

```
1   int x[100000];
2
3   main ()
4   {
5       int i;
6
7       for (i=0; i<100000; i++)
8           x[i] = 1;
9   }
```

invoking cc without the peephole optimization phase produces

```
1   LL0:
2           .data
3           .comm   _x,400000
```

```
4               .text
5               .align
6               .globl  _main
7       _main:
8               .word   L13
9               jbr     L15
10      L16:
11              clrl    -4(fp)
12      L19:
13              cmpl    -4(fp),$100000
14              jgeq    L18
15              movl    -4(fp),r0
16              movl    $1,_x[r0]
17      L17:
18              incl    -4(fp)
19              jbr     L19
20      L18:
21              ret
22              .set    L13,0x0
23      L15:
24              subl2   $4,sp
25              jbr     L16
26              .data
```

The **for** loop is implemented by an explicit comparison in line 13 of **i**, stored on the stack at location -4(fp), with 100,000. If they are equal, a condition code is set causing the branch to be taken to L18 in line 14. The value of **i** is explicitly incremented in line 18.

The VAX supports special instructions for loops which */lib/c2* detects. Invoking it on this code with the *-n* option so it also displays statistics about its operation produces:

```
1       .data
2       .comm   _x,400000
3       .text
4       LL0:.align      1
5       .globl  _main
6       .set    L13,0x0
7       .data
8       .text
9       _main:.word     L13
10      subl2   $4,sp
11      clrl    -4(fp)
12      L2000001:movl   -4(fp),r0
13      movl    $1,_x[r0]
14      aoblss  $100000,-4(fp),L2000001
15      ret
16      4 iterations
17      0 jumps to jumps
18      0 inst. after jumps
19      2 jumps to .+1
20      5 redundant labels
21      0 cross-jumps
22      1 code motions
23      0 branches reversed
24      0 redundant moves
25      0 simplified addresses
26      1 loops inverted
27      1 redundant jumps
28      0 common seqs before jmp's
29      0 skips over jumps
30      1 sob's added
31      0 redundant tst's
32      0 jump on bit
33      0 field operations
34      51K core
```

The loop has been replaced with the much more efficient

```
aoblss  limit, index, address
```

instruction which increments the index by 1 and branches to the address as long as the index stays less than the limit. The convoluted branching in the original code has also been removed. Note that the optimizer also announces it took four iterations to complete its work. Because one optimization can cause another to be found, *lib/c2* iterates until no further changes are found.

◆

EXERCISES

1. Generate code for the following *C* assignment statements assuming that x is a static integer and a, b, and c are automatic integers. c is also an array of four elements. Use any assembly language you are familiar with. Assume two registers are available for general use and there is one special stack pointer register sp.

   (a) x = 3
   (b) x = a
   (c) x = a + 3
   (d) b = (a+c[a])/2
   (e) c[b+1] = c[b+1]*(a-2.0)

2. Generate code for the following Pascal program:

```
program  arrays (input, output);
type
     s = array  [5..10] of integer;
var
     i: integer;
     t: s;
begin
   i := 0;
   while i<5 do begin
       if i>0 then
           t[i+5] := i*t[i+4]
       else
           t[5] := 2;
       i = i+1
   end
end.
```

3. Prove that the chromatic number of the graph in Fig. 12-4 is 3.

4. Construct the interference graph and bind the virtual assembly code in Fig. 12-6 assuming that three registers are available in *P* rather than the two shown in the example.

5. Extend the LTRA of Section 12.3 to handle:

   (a) The "++" operator of *C*; that is, describe an annotation that handles the statement

   x = y++ + z;

   in which y is first used and then modified.
   (b) The multiple "=" operator, which handles the statement

   x = y = a+b;

6. Explain all of the peephole optimizations performed on the code in Example 12-12.

7. The peephole optimization for the **for** loop illustrated in Example 12-12 works even if the loop variable is modified in the body of the loop. Why?

BIBLIOGRAPHY

The bibliography has been chosen to provide a mix of historical as well as current readings. It is more than a list of references. Starred (**) references have particular historical interest.

**ACM [1978] *Proc. of the ACM History of Programming Languages Conf.* Los Angeles, June 1–3, 1978. A delightful collection of papers by the principals of most of the influential languages of the 1960s and 1970s.

ANSI [1966] *American National Standard FORTRAN.* (ANS X3.9-1966) ANSI, New York, NY.

ANSI [1977] *American National Standard FORTRAN.* (ANS X3.9-1977) ANSI, New York, NY.

ANSI [1978] *American National Standard BASIC.* (ANS X3.60-1978) ANSI, New York, NY.

ANSI [1983] *Military Standard Ada Programming Language.* (ANSI/MIL-STD-1815A-1983), ANSI, New York, NY.

ANSI [1985] *American National Standard COBOL.* (ANS X3.23-1985) ANSI, New York, NY.

Abel, N.E. and J.R. Bell [1972] "Global optimization in compilers." *Proceedings First USA-Japan Computer Conference,* AFIPS Press, Montvale, NJ.

Aho, A.V., J.E. Hopcroft, and J.D. Ullman [1974] *The Design and Analysis of Computer Algorithms.* Addison-Wesley, Reading, MA.

Aho, A.V., J.E. Hopcroft, and J.D. Ullman [1983] *Data Structures and Algorithms,* Addison-Wesley, Reading, MA.

Aho, A.V. and S.C. Johnson [1974] "LR parsing." *Computing Surveys* 6:2, 99–124.

Aho, A.V. and S.C. Johnson [1976] "Optimal code generation for expression trees." *JACM* 23:3, 488–501.

Aho, A.V., S.C. Johnson, and J.D. Ullman [1977] "Code generation for expressions with common subexpressions." *JACM* 24:1, 146–160.

Aho, A.V., B.W. Kernighan, and P.J. Weinberger [1979] "Awk-a pattern scanning and processing language." *Software-Practice and Experience* 9:4, 267–280.

Aho, A.V. and J.D. Ullman [1972a] "Optimization of LR(k) parsers." *JCSS* 6:6, 573–602.

Aho, A.V. and J.D. Ullman [1972b] *The Theory of Parsing, Translation and Compiling.* Vol. I, *Parsing,* Prentice-Hall, Englewood Cliffs, NJ.

Aho, A.V. and J.D. Ullman [1972c] *The Theory of Parsing, Translation and Compiling.* Vol. II, *Compiling,* Prentice-Hall, Englewood Cliffs, NJ.

Aho, A.V. and J.D. Ullman [1973] "A technique for speeding up LR(k) parsers." *SIAM J. Computing* 2:2, 106–127.

Aho, A.V. and J.D. Ullman [1977] *Principles of Compiler Design.* Addison-Wesley, Reading, MA.

Aho, A.V. and J.D. Ullman [1986] *Compilers: Principles, Techniques, and Tools.* Addison-Wesley, Reading, MA.

Aigrain, P., S.L. Graham, R.R. Henry, M.K. McKusick, and E. Pelegri-Llopar [1984] "Experience with a Graham-Glanville style code generator." *SIGPLAN Notices* 19:6, June 1984, 13–24.

**Allen, F.E. [1969] "Program optimization." *Annual Review of Automatic Programming* 5, 239–307. One of the earliest papers on compiler optimization.

Allen, F.E. [1970] "Control flow analysis." *SIGPLAN Notices* 5:7, 1–19.

Allen, F.E. [1975] "Bibliography on program optimization." *RC-5767,* IBM T.J. Watson Research Center, Yorktown Heights, NY.

Allen, F.E., J.L. Carter, J. Fabri, J. Ferrante, W.H. Harrison, P.G. Loewner, and L.H. Trevillyan [1980] "The experimental compiling system." *IBM J. Research and Development* 24:6, 695–715.

Ammann, U. [1977] "On code generation in a Pascal compiler." *Software-Practice and Experience* **7**:3, 391–423.

Anderson, P. and G. Anderson [1986] *The Unix C Shell Field Guide*. Prentice-Hall, Englewood Cliffs, NJ.

Anklam, P., D. Cutler, R. Heinen, and M.D. MacLaren [1982] *Engineering a Compiler*, Digital Press, Bedford, MA.

Bach, M.J. [1986] *The Design of the Unix Operating System*. Prentice-Hall, Englewood Cliffs, NJ.

Backhouse, R.C. [1979] *Syntax of Programming Languages*. Prentice-Hall, Englewood Cliffs, NJ.

Backhouse, R.C. [1984] "Global data flow analysis problems arising in locally least-cost error recovery." *TOPLAS* **6**:2, 192–214.

**Backus, J.W., R.J. Beeber, S. Best, R. Goldberg, L.M. Haibt, H.L. Herrick, R.A. Nelson, D. Sayre, P.B. Sheridan, H. Stern, I. Ziller, R.A. Hughes, and R. Nutt [1957]. "The FORTRAN automatic coding system." *Western Joint Computer Conference*, 188–198. The original FORTRAN paper.

**Backus, J.W. [1959] "The syntax and semantics of the proposed international algebraic language of the Zurich ACM-GAMM conference." *Proc. Intl. Conf. on Information Processing*, UNESCO, 125–132. The first widely published account of a context-free grammar to represent a programming language. This became "Backus Normal Form" or "BNF".

Bauer, F.L. and J. Eickel [1976] *Compiler Construction: An Advanced Course*, 2nd ed., Lecture Notes in Computer Science 21, Springer-Verlag, New York, NY.

Bell Labs [1983] "Unix Programmers Manual." 2, Revised and Expanded Version, Bell Laboratories, Murray Hill, NJ.

Brooker, R.A. and D. Morris [1962] "A general translation program for phrase structure languages." *JACM* **9:1, 1–10. The compiler-compiler defined.

Cattell, R.G.G. [1980] "Automatic derivation of code generators from machine descriptions." *TOPLAS* **2**:2, 173–190. One of the earliest papers on practical code generator generators.

Chaitin, G.J. [1982] "Register allocation and spilling via graph coloring." *SIGPLAN Notices*, **17**:6, June, 1982, 98–105.

Cheatham, T.E., Jr. [1967] *The Theory and Construction of Compilers*. Computer Associates, Wakefield, MA.

Chomsky, N. [1956] "Three models for the description of language." *IRE Trans. on Information Theory* **2:3, 113–124. Chomsky invented the fundamental notions of regular, context-free, and context-sensitive grammars for the study of natural languages.

Chomsky, N. [1957] *Syntactic Structures*. Mouton, The Hague.

Chomsky, N. [1959] "On certain formal properties of grammar." *Information and Control* **2**:2, 137–167.

Chow, F. and J. Hennessey [1984] "Register allocation by priority-based coloring." *SIGPLAN Notices* **19**:6, June 1984, 222–232.

Christopher, T.W., P.J. Hatcher, and R. Kukuk [1984] "Using dynamic programming to generate optimized code in a Graham-Glanville style code generator." *SIGPLAN Notices* **19**:6, June 1984, 25–36.

Cleaveland, J.C. and R.C. Uzgalis [1977] *Grammars for Programming Languages*. American Elsevier, New York, NY.

Clocksin, W. and C. Mellish [1981] *Programming in Prolog*. Springer-Verlag, New York, NY.

Cocke, J. [1970] "Global common subexpression elimination." *SIGPLAN Notices* **5**:7, 20–24.

Cocke, J. and J.T. Schwartz [1970] *Programming Languages and Their Compilers, Preliminary Notes*. 2nd revised edition, Courant Institute of Mathematical Sciences, New York, NY.

Davidson, J.W. and C.W. Fraser [1984] "Automatic generation of peephole optimizations." *TOPLAS* **6**:4, 505–526.

**DeRemer, F.L. [1969] *Practical Translators for LR(k) Languages*. Ph.D dissertation, MIT, Cambridge, MA. SLR and LALR parsers defined, making LR parsing practical.

DeRemer, F.L. [1971] "Simple LR(k) parsing." *CACM* **14**:7, 453–460.

DeRemer, F.L. and T. Pennello [1982] "Efficient computation of LALR(1) look-ahead sets." *ACM Transactions on Programming Languages and Systems* **4**:4, October 1982, 615–649.

Dwyer, B. [1985] "Improving Gough's LL(1) lookahead generator." *SIGPLAN Notices* **20**:11, 27–29.

Earley, J. [1970] "An efficient context-free parsing algorithm." *CACM* **13**:2, 94–102.

Earnest, C. [1974] "Some topics in code optimization." *JACM* **21**:1, 76–102.

Elson, M. [1973] *Concepts of Programming Languages*. SRA, Palo Alto, CA.

Farrow, R. [1984] "Generating a production compiler from an attribute grammar." *IEEE Software* **1**, 77–93.

Feldman, S.I. [1979a] "Make-a program for maintaining computer programs." *Software-Practice and Experience* **9**:4, 255–265.

Feldman, S.I. [1979b] "Implementation of a portable Fortran 77 compiler using modern tools." *ACM SIGPLAN Notices* **14**:8, 98–106.

Floyd, R.W. [1961] "An algorithm for coding efficient arithmetic expressions." *CACM* **4:1, 42–51. One of the earliest published parsing algorithms.

Floyd, R.W. [1963] "Syntactic analysis and operator precedence." *JACM* **10**:3, 316–333.

Floyd, R.W. [1964] "Bounded context syntactic analysis." *CACM* **7**:2, 62–67.

Fraser, C.W. [1977] *Automatic Generation of Code Generators*. Ph.D Thesis, Yale Univ., New Haven, CT.

Fraser, C.W. and D.R. Hanson [1982] "A machine-independent linker." *Software-Practice and Experience,* 351–366.

Galler, B.A. and A.J. Perlis [1970] *A View of Programming Languages*. Addison-Wesley, Reading, MA.

Ganapathi, M. C.N. Fischer, and J.L. Hennessy [1982] "Retargetable compiler code generation." *Computing Surveys* **14**:4, 573–592.

Ginsburg, S. [1966] *The Mathematical Theory of Context-Free Languages*. McGraw-Hill, New York.

Glanville, R.S. and S.L. Graham [1978] "A new method for compiler code generation." *Fifth ACM Symp. on Principles of Programming Languages,* 231–240.

Goldberg, A. and D. Robson [1980] *Smalltalk-80: The Language and Its Implementation*. Addison-Wesley, Reading, MA.

Gough, K.J. [1985] "A new method of generating LL(1) lookahead sets." *SIGPLAN Notices* **20**:6, 16–19.

Graham, S.L. [1980] "Table-driven code generation." *Computer* **13**:8, 25–34.

**Gries, D. [1971] *Compiler Construction for Digital Computers*. Wiley and Sons, New York, NY. The first widely used text on compilers.

Griswold, R.E. and M. Griswold [1973] *A SNOBOL4 Primer*. Prentice-Hall, Englewood Cliffs, NJ.

Hoare, C.A.R. and N. Wirth [1973] "An axiomatic definition of the programming language PASCAL." *Acta Informatica* **2:4, 335–356. An early seminal discussion of formal programming language semantics.

**Hopcroft, J.E. and J.D. Ullman [1969] *Formal Languages and Their Relation to Automata*. Addison-Wesley, Reading, MA. The first widely used text to explain formal languages and automata theory.

Hopgood, F.R.A. [1969] *Compiling Techniques*. American Elsevier, New York, NY.

ISO [1982] *Specification for Computer Programming Language Pascal*. ISO 7185-1982, International Organization for Standardization. See [Jensen and Wirth 85] for a more lucid discussion of standard Pascal.

Intermetrics [1976] *HAL/S Programmer's Guide*. Intermetrics, Cambridge, MA.

Irons, E.T. [1961] "A syntax-directed compiler for Algol 60." *CACM* **4:1, 51–55. Syntax-directed translation defined.

Jensen, K. and N. Wirth [1985] revised by A.B. Mickel and J.F. Miner. *Pascal User Manual and Report*. 3rd ed., ISO Pascal Standard, Springer-Verlag, New York, NY.

Johnson, S.C. [1975] *Yacc-Yet Another Compiler Compiler*. CSTR 32, Bell Laboratories, Murray Hill, NJ, also in [Bell Labs 83].

Johnson, S.C. [1979] *A Tour through The Portable C Compiler*. Bell Laboratories, Murray Hill, NJ, also in [Bell Labs 83].

Johnson, S.C. and M.E. Lesk [1978] "Language development tools." *Bell System Tech. J.* **57**:6, 2155–2175.

Kernighan, B.W. and R. Pike [1984] *The Unix Programming Environment*, Prentice-Hall, Englewood Cliffs, NJ.

**Kernighan, B.W. and D.M. Ritchie [1978] *The C Programming Language*. Prentice-Hall, Englewood Cliffs, NJ. No one can touch their writing style. Still the best primer on *C* even if a little dated.

Knuth, D.E. [1965] "On the translation of languages from left to right." *Information and Control*, **8:6, 607–639. LR(k) parsing defined.

Knuth, D.E. [1968] "Semantics of programming languages." *Math Systems Theory* **2:2, 127–145. Here Knuth defines attribute grammars, the basis for so much subsequent work in compilers.

Knuth, D.E. [1971] "Examples of formal semantics." *Lecture Notes in Mathematics*. Engler (ed.), No 188, Springer-Verlag, Berlin.

**Knuth, D.E. and L.T. Pardo [1977] "Early development of programming languages." In *Encyclopedia of Computer Science and Technology* 7, Marcel Dekker, New York, NY. 419–493. One of the best written expositions on the early history of language as only Knuth can do.

Korenjak, A.J. [1969] "A practical method for constructing LR(k) processors." *CACM* **12**:11, 613–623.

Lauer, P.E. [1968] *Formal definition of ALGOL 60*. TR25.088, IBM Laboratory, Vienna. One of the first major published works on the *Vienna Definition Language*, a major semantic modeling tool of the late 1960s and early 1970s. See also [Lucas 68].

Lee, J.A.N. [1974] *Anatomy of a Compiler*. Van Nostrand Reinhold, New York, NY.

Lesk, M.E. and E. Schmidt [1983] *LEX-a lexical analyzer generator*, in [Bell Labs 1983].

Leverett, B.W., R.G.G. Cattell, S.O. Hobbs, J.M. Newcomer, A.H. Reiner, B.R. Schatz, and W.A. Wulf [1980] "An overview of the production-quality compiler-compiler project." *Computer* **13**:8, 38–40.

Lewis, P.M. II, D. Rosenkrantz, and R. Stearns [1976] *Compiler Design Theory*. Addison-Wesley, Reading, MA.

Lewis, P.M. II and R. Stearns [1968] "Syntax-directed transductions." *JACM* **15:3, 465–488. LL parsing defined.

Lohro, B. [1984] *Methods and Tools for Compiler Construction*. Cambridge Univ. Press, New York, NY.

Lowry, E. and C.W. Medlock [1969] "Object code optimization." *CACM* **12**:1, 13–22.

Lucas, P., et al. 1968. *Method and Notation for The Formal Definition of Programming Languages*. TR25.087, IBM Laboratory, Vienna.

Lucas, P. and K. Walk [1969] "On the formal description of PL/I." *Ann Rev Auto Prog* **6**:3, 105–182.

McKeeman, W.M. [1965] "Peephole optimization." *CACM* **8**:7, 443–444.

McKeeman, W.M., J.J. Horning, and D.B. Wortman [1970] *A Compiler Generator*. Prentice-Hall, Englewood Cliffs, NJ.

Muchnick, S.S. and N.D. Jones [1981] *Program Flow Analysis: Theory and Applications*. Prentice-Hall, Englewood Cliffs, NJ.

Nauer, P. [1963] "Revised report on the algorithmic language ALGOL 60." *CACM* **6:1, 1–17. The definition of the first formally specified programming language and with the exception of FORTRAN, the most influential. The report is still marvelous for its crispness. Compare it to ANSI Ada [ANSI 83].

OOPSLA [1986]. *Proceedings of the Object-Oriented Programming Systems, Languages and Applications Conference, SIGPLAN Notices* **21**:11, November 1986.

Patterson, D.A. [1985] "Reduced instruction set computers." *Communications of the ACM* **28**:1, January 1985, 8–21.

Pennello, T.J. [1986] "Very fast LR parsing." *Proceedings of the SIGPLAN '86 Symposium on Compiler Construction* in *SIGPLAN Notices* **21**:7, July 1986, 145–151.

Pollack, B.W., ed. [1972] *Compiler Techniques*. Auerbach, Philadelphia, PA.

Pratt, T. [1984] *Programming Languages: Design and Implementation*, 2nd ed. Prentice-Hall, Englewood Cliffs, NJ.

Pyster, A. [1980] *Compiler Design and Construction*, Van Nostrand Reinhold, New York, NY.

Pyster, A. [1981] *Zuse User's Manual*, TRCS81-04 revised, Department of Computer Science, University of California, Santa Barbara.

Pyster, A. and A. Dutta [1978] "Error checking compilers and portability." *Software-Practice and Experience* **8**:1, Jan–Feb.

Ritchie, D.M. [1979] *A Tour Through the Unix C Compiler*, in [Bell Labs 83].

**Rosen, S., ed. [1967] *Programming Systems and Languages*. McGraw-Hill, New York, NY. One of the earliest books on operating systems and language implementations.

Rustin, R. [1972]. *Design and Optimization of Compilers*. Prentice-Hall, Englewood Cliffs, NJ.

**Sammet, J.E. [1969] *Programming Languages: History and Fundamentals*. Prentice-Hall, Englewood Cliffs, NJ. An excellent accounting of the first decade of higher-level languages by one of the best computer historians.

Sammet, J.E. [1972] "Programming languages: history and future." *CACM* **15**:7, 601–610.

Schaefer, M. [1973] *A Mathematical Theory of Global Program Optimization*. Prentice-Hall, Englewood Cliffs, NJ.

Schreiner, A.T. and H.G. Friedman Jr [1985] *Introduction to Compiler Construction with Unix*. Prentice-Hall, Englewood Cliffs, NJ.

Sethi, R. [1975] "Complete register allocation problems." *SIAM J. Computing* **4**:3, 226–248.

Softool [1977] *A Comparative Analysis of the Diagnostic Power of Commercial FORTRAN Compilers*, Report #F001-10-77, Softool Corporation, Goleta CA.

Stearns, R.E. [1971] "Deterministic top-down parsing." *Proc. 5th Ann. Princeton Conf. on Information Sciences and Systems*, 182–188.

Stoy, J.E. [1977] *The Scott-Strachey Approach to Programming Language Theory*, MIT Press, Cambridge, MA.

Stroustrup, B. [1986] *The C++ Programming Language*. Addison Wesley, Reading, MA.

Tennent, R.D. [1976] "The denotational semantics of programming languages." *Comm ACM* **19,** 437–456.

Tennent, R.D. [1981] *Principles of Programming Languages.* Prentice-Hall, Englewood Cliffs, NJ.

Van Wijngaarden, A., B.J. Mailloux, J.E.L. Peck, and C.H.A. Koster [1969] "Report on the algorithmic language ALGOL 68." *Numerische Mathematik,* **14, 79–218. The first major paper on ALGOL 68 and on the Van Wijngaarden method for semantic modeling.

Waite, W.M. [1974] "Optimization." In [Bauer and Eickel 74].

Wall, D.W. [1986] "Global register allocation at link time." *SIGPLAN Notices* **21:**7, July 1986, 264–275.

Wirth, N. [1971s] "The programming language Pascal." *Acta Informatica* **1:1, 35–63. After FORTRAN and ALGOL 60, the most influential programming language ever defined.

Wirth, N. [1971b] "The design of a Pascal compiler." *Software-Practice and Experience* **1:**4, 309–333.

Wulf, W., R.K. Johnsson, C.B. Weinstock, S.O. Hobbs, and C.M. Geschke [1975] *The Design of an Optimizing Compiler.* American Elsevier, New York, NY.

INDEX

INDEX

263